SEX LIV
GREAT ARTISTS

SEX LIVES
OF THE
GREAT ARTISTS

Nigel Cawthorne

PRION

First published in Great Britain in 1998
This edition published 2004 by

Prion
an imprint of the
Carlton Publishing Group
20 Mortimer Street
London W1T 3JW

A catalogue record for this book is available from the British Library

ISBN 1 85375 544 3

Printed in Great Britain
by Mackays

CONTENTS

SEX LIVES OF THE GREAT ARTISTS

INTRODUCTION

I know nothing about art, but I know what I like, at least that was what I thought when I started this book. And what I like has nothing to do with art:

Then I discovered that art was principally about sex.

The nude has been the staple diet of artists since classical times. Rediscovered in the Renaissance, artists depicted biblical, mythological and epic scenes and packed them with nudes – male or female, according to taste.

More often than not, the female models were hookers for whom posing nude was a lucrative sideline. Naturally they would be available after modelling to smooth overheated artists by reverting to their principal calling.

Until the nineteenth century, nudes were coy. Then Rodin persuaded his models to open their legs. Picasso delved deeper into the centre of women's sex. After all, as the crucible of life, this is the centre of the human universe. If we really want to know what life is all about, that is where we should start looking.

Gauguin and Modigliani both felt they had to get right inside the model. They believed they could not paint a naked woman unless they had sex with her.

SEX LIVES OF THE GREAT ARTISTS

Other painters have explored the byways of human experience, but overwhelmingly sex has been their theme. They struggled to find new ways to express their own sexuality on the canvas.

Living in London, along with the natives of all great cities, I rarely bothered to visit the great art galleries that the tourists go traipsing around. Now, on a Sunday, when the British Library where I research and write my *Sex Lives...* books is closed, I go to the galleries because I now understand the relationship between the artist and their models. That makes the whole thing come alive. And art galleries are great places to meet women.

I should also like to make a special dedication to the staff of the British Library who have been especially helpful to me during the move of the library into its new building. The British Library remains one of the greatest pulling palaces in London and I should like to apologize to other readers if they find my antics distracting.

Even so, after writing *Sex Lives of the Great Artists*, I feel I have missed my real vocation. I should have been a painter or sculptor. Then, instead of running through the usual line of feeble patter, I could simply have said, like the denizens of this book: "Take your clothes off, baby, I'm an artist."

Works every time, it seems.

Nigel Cawthorne, 1998

1

Lobe Story

Vincent van Gogh is the quintessential artist – tormented, deranged, starving in a garret for his art. And everybody knows that he lopped off his ear to give it to his lover. Actually he only cut off the lobe and he gave it to a prostitute. I am sure she would have preferred cash.

This act of masochistic self-mutilation speaks eloquently of his tortured attitude to sex. He expressed it best himself in a poem he wrote in 1885 when he was thirty-two:

All evil had come from women – Obscured reason, appetite for
    lucre, treachery…
Golden cups in which the wine is mixed with lees,
Every crime, every happy lie, every folly
Comes from her. Yet adore her, as the gods
Made her… and it is still the best thing they did.

His mixed feelings towards women began, naturally enough, with his mother. Though it was not exactly her fault. On 30 March 1852, she gave birth to a baby boy, whom she called Vincent van Gogh. But he died soon after. Exactly a year later, on 30 March 1853, she gave birth to another boy. He too was named Vincent and he lived. Until he was sent to boarding school at the age of eleven, van Gogh saw the grave of his dead brother at least once a week when he went to the Dutch Reformed Church in Zundert where his father was minister. The gravestone bore his own name, Vincent van Gogh. It had to have an effect on the boy.

Van Gogh's mother took no joy in Vincent's birth. She was still grieving for her first-born.

"My childhood was gloomy and cold and sterile," van Gogh wrote.

In fact, Mrs van Gogh was little better with her other children. Vincent's brother Theo suffered attacks of anxiety and depression. Sister Wil, to whom Vincent was particularly close, was a schizophrenic who was confined to a mental hospital until she died in 1941. Cor, their youngest brother, committed suicide in South Africa at the age of thirty-three.

After van Gogh had finished boarding school, he found lodgings in The Hague rather than return home. There he turned in on himself. With women he would sometimes lose the power of speech, convinced of his own ugliness and worthlessness.

He got a job with the art dealer Goupil, who sent him to work in their branch in England. In London, he found lodgings in Kennington and promptly fell in love with his landlady's nineteen-year-old daughter, Eugenia Loyer. She was small-boned, slender with large eyes and a piquant smile, and Vincent savoured her dulcet voice as she softly called him down to breakfast each morning. But it was the relationship between Eugenia and her mother that particularly attracted him.

"I never saw or dreamt of anything like the love between her and her mother," he wrote. By comparison, he said, his own parents' attitude towards him was as if he were a dog dirtying a room.

Nursing his secret love, he immersed himself in books like Jules Michelet's *L'Amour*, a book about love, and copied out large passages. He also tried his hand at drawing, but his inability to handle perspective made him depressed.

Van Gogh was then twenty. He would dash home every night, eager to be with Eugenia. He said nothing of his feelings but he was convinced that she loved him too. For a whole year he remained silent – and would have continued to do so had not his brother Theo written to tell that a friend had just got engaged. Marriage was now on his mind.

In the glorious summer of 1874, he found himself alone in the garden with Eugenia. He seized the opportunity and declared himself. In that moment, all his dreams were dashed. Eugenia was shocked, horrified, contemptuous. She did not, could not, love him, and told him she was secretly engaged to the man who had occupied his room previously.

Why had he not been told, he demanded. Where was this man? Why had he not come to see her in the past year? Van Gogh simply would not accept that Eugenia did not love him. His intensity scared the poor girl. He tried everything to make her break off her engagement, but she would not.

Van Gogh may have consoled himself with one of the army of prostitutes that inhabited London at the time. Tolstoy, visiting London ten years before, had put their number at around eighty thousand. Visiting prostitutes was certainly a habit van Gogh took up in later life.

Eugenia's rejection of him lost him not just the love of one woman, but of two. Denied the love of a potential bride, he had also lost the love of a putative mother-in-law. Eugenia's mother, he was convinced, could have loved him much better than his own mother had. He returned to Holland briefly in 1875. When he got back to London, he found his room was taken over again by Eugenia's fiancé and his humiliation was complete.

He took a room far away from the Loyers in Kensington. There he withdrew into himself again and began pondering on the relationship between men and women.

"A man and wife can be one," he wrote, "that is to say one whole and not two halves."

But he did not really believe that. Women, he knew, were completely different from men and somehow unknowable. He took consolation in the Bible.

He was transferred to Goupil's in Paris, where he shared a room in Montmartre with eighteen-year-old Harry Gladwell. Van Gogh spent much of his time there praying. He advised Gladwell to steer well clear of Jules Michelet's *L'Amour* and read only the Bible. He himself read George Eliot's *Scenes from Clerical Life* and was particularly struck by the story "Janet's

Repentance", where a woman, a reformed drunk, nurses a poverty-stricken clergyman through a long illness. Van Gogh longed to be that clergyman.

He quit Goupil's and went back to England just to be near Eugenia. In Isleworth, west London, he was taken on as a curate. It became obvious that winning Eugenia was a lost cause. He returned to Holland, where he worked in a bookstore and spent most of his free time at church services – Dutch Reformed, Lutheran and Catholic.

One Sunday in Amsterdam, his uncle, a pastor, invited him to dinner, where he met his cousin Kee Vos. She was tall and slender with blonde hair with reddish tints and eyes as blue as his mother's. When they kissed, her cheeks flushed. But then, to his surprise her husband Christoffel turned up.

The Voses invited him to visit. He did and was deeply impressed by their relationship.

"They love each other truly," he wrote. "When one sees them sitting side by side in the evening, in the kindly lamplight of the living room, quite close to the bedroom of their boy, who wakes up every now and then and asks his mother for something, it is an idyll."

But van Gogh wanted to be a part of the idyll, not just an outside observer. He became obsessed with Kee and suicidally depressed.

Then Christoffel died suddenly of a lung disease. In mourning, Kee took her young son Johannes to stay at van Gogh's parents' parsonage. Flat broke after a period as a missionary in the coalfields of Belgium, van Gogh had returned there too. At the sight of Kee, he could not contain himself. Despite her recent loss, he poured out his feelings and begged her to marry him.

"No, never," she said. It was as brutal as Eugenia's rejection seven years before.

Again van Gogh would not accept that no meant no. His reaction was so violent that Kee fled back to Amsterdam. Vincent rowed with his parents when they refused to give him the money to go after her. After a month, he persuaded his brother, Theo, who was then in Paris enjoying the absinthe and "an hour of flesh", to send him the fare.

Arriving in Amsterdam, van Gogh rushed directly to his uncle's house. Kee was there, but the pastor refused to let him see her. Vincent thrust his hand out over the candle and said: "Let me see her for as long as I can keep my hand in the flame."

The pastor simply pursed his lips and blew the candle out. Singed and humiliated, van Gogh left the house. In a dangerous state of mind, he returned to The Hague, where he went to look for a prostitute.

"I didn't have to look far," he wrote to Theo. "I found a woman, not young, not beautiful, nothing out of the ordinary, if you like, but maybe you are curious. She was tall and well built; she did not have ladies' hands like Kee, but the hands of one who works a lot. But she was not coarse or common, and had nothing very womanly about her."

She reminded him of a figure by Chardin or Frère. He felt sorry for her because her life had been hard and she had many cares.

"Oh, she was not distinguished, nothing extraordinary, nothing unusual," he said. "But that woman was very good to me, very good, very kind, in a way that I shall not have to tell my brother Theo about because I suspect my brother Theo has had some experience. So much the better for him."

He did not spend much money on her; he did not have much. "I wish I could have spent more, for she was worth it."

They got drunk and talked a lot. "We talked about everything, about her life, about her cares, about her health, and with her I had more interesting conversations than, for instance, with my very learned, professional cousin." And, what the hell? Kee had some sexual experience, hadn't she? If Kee now wanted to starve herself of sex because her husband was dead, in the ground, let her. From then on prostitutes were to be van Gogh's most frequent – and often only – female companions.

If van Gogh had stayed away from the ladies of the street in London, he would have been twenty-nine when he popped his cherry. He realized at last that he was "a man, a man of passion". And his urges were urgent.

"I must go with a woman, otherwise I shall freeze or turn to stone," he recorded.

Sex became for him a quasi-religious act.

"Every woman, at every age, if she loves and is a good woman, gives a man, not the infinity of a moment, but a moment of infinity."

He sang the praises of prostitutes and he did not consider the pleasure he derived from them a sin.

"Sin, bah!" he wrote. "Is it a sin to love, to need love, not to be able to live without love? I think a life *without* love a sinful and immoral condition."

Vincent's whoring humanized him. One morning he found himself in the bed of a part-time whore, who was a washerwoman by day, and sang the praises of waking in the morning to find "a fellow creature in bed beside you; it makes the world look so much more friendly". For once, he was happy. And around this time, van Gogh began painting.

He joined the Pulchri Arts Club, where he could draw the models for free. What little money he had went on prostitutes.

"I tell you frankly that in my opinion one must not hesitate to go to a prostitute occasionally if there is one you can trust and feel something for," he advised Theo. "For one who has a strenuous life it is necessary, absolutely necessary in order to keep sane and well."

He became so enamoured of prostitutes, he moved in with one. Her name was Christine Clasina Maria Hoornik, but he called her Sien. She was three years older than him, but her hard life made her look a lot older. She had a five-year-old daughter and was pregnant again. The father had run off. She was a drunkard and, like her mother before her, put herself on the streets to make ends meet.

With almost masochistic glee, Vincent tidied up after her, fed her and looked after her daughter. He used Sien as his model and tried to reform her. He failed. But he did succeed in getting her cleaned up a bit by taking her to the public baths.

As he could not get Sien to change, he tried to elevate her

and all prostitutes. Although some thought they were bad, he did not have the slightest scruple in associating with them.

"If our society were pure and well regulated, they would be seducers," he said. "But now, in my opinion, one may consider them sisters of charity."

And he claimed that Jesus had said that harlots would go to heaven before respectable citizens. But the drawings he made of Sien naked did not elevate her at all. They show her scrawny and misshapen with a scraggy neck and drooping breasts. She looked sad, pathetic and old before her time. Van Gogh used her ugliness to mock his mother. One picture of gnarled and bedraggled Sien is entitled *The Great Lady*.

When van Gogh announced he was going to marry Sien, his parents threatened to put him in a lunatic asylum. But he would not give her up.

"She and I are two unhappy people who keep together and carry our burdens together," he wrote. "In this way unhappiness is turned into joy, and the unbearable becomes bearable."

To further outrage his father, he claimed that Sien was "pure".

"It is wonderful how pure she is," he told him, "notwithstanding her depravity." She was Mary Magdalene. What was more she helped him in his vocation.

"I think I shall become a better artist with her, than if I had married Kee," he said.

In June 1882, van Gogh was admitted to hospital with a fever. He also had gonorrhoea. Though he told Theo that it was only a "mild dose" he had to insert a catheter into his penis to pee.

While he was in hospital, Sien was admitted too, to give birth. Vincent suffered his bladder plains stoically, saying that they were nothing compared with the pains of childbirth Sien suffered.

Van Gogh found a bigger flat that would double as a studio. There he painted the foul-mouthed Sien and her jaundiced baby as Madonna and child. In fact, Sien was anything but a good mother, drinking, smoking and neglecting the children.

If Sien herself was not bad enough, he also had her family

to contend with. Her brother, who had put his own wife on the streets, then divorced her, wanted to pimp for Sien. For a cut of the takings, Sien's mother backed him.

The family began to play tricks on van Gogh to get rid of him. He became depressed and lonely, and only found peace and consolation out at the city's public ash dump.

Theo came to visit him. He too had rescued a fallen woman. But she was a different kettle of fish from Sien. An educated woman, she had been forced on to the streets by misfortune and, when Theo found her, she was on the verge of suicide. Vincent thought this was wonderful news. Now his brother could truly understand him. Theo said drily that they were just a couple of idealistic fools.

But Van Gogh's domestic situation was becoming desperate. He told Sien that he had to get out into the countryside to paint. He tried to get her a job before he left. But, instead of turning up at the job interviews he had set up for her, she went to the wine shop and got drunk.

When Sien came with her daughter and baby to see him off at the station, he was overcome with emotion. After that, he said he could never see a mother and child without wanting to cry.

When he returned from his painting trip, he found that Sien had gone back to whoring. He thought marriage might save her, but nothing came of it. Sien drowned herself in 1904.

Van Gogh's mother was ill and he dutifully went to visit her. The matronly Margot Begemann who lived next door was nursing her. Margot was a spinster in her forties. She was soft-hearted and would go for long walks with Vincent. Like him, she was a tortured soul who had been damaged by life and often talked of killing herself. Together, they had a masochistic orgy of sadness and self-pity.

She told him of her unhappy childhood. Growing up had been miserable for him too, he said, but he had fought back. Soon she saw him as an ally and possible husband. Her family saw things differently though. To them, Margot was a valuable worker and they were not about to let her walk off with some artistic misfit.

LOBE STORY

Van Gogh indicated to brother Theo that he had had sex with Margot. They planned to marry, but van Gogh became increasingly alarmed by *her* disturbed state. He told her brother that he wanted to delay their marriage for at least two years. The brother said that he had better marry her straight away or not at all.

One day, when they were out in the fields together, Margot collapsed in convulsions. She had taken strychnine. He put his fingers down her throat and got her to throw up. She was rushed to hospital in Utrecht. He visited her there and when he asked her why she had done it, she said: "I too have loved at last."

Van Gogh was too touched and too ashamed to speak. Love had turned to disaster once more. He retreated to the countryside again to paint. But whoring in The Hague had left him with an appetite for nude models and hookers that he could not slake in the country.

He headed for Antwerp where there were women of all types who would sit for him. One prostitute particularly took his fancy. She was a mysterious Chinese girl with an oval face and jet black eyes – "small, bedbug-like in character and was quiet like a mouse". He economized on food to pay for models. His taste now ran to slimmer, prettier girls, but he sometimes got robust Flemish women to strip off too. All were rendered with unflinching realism and his nudes are some of the ugliest and unappealing in the history of art.

Soon he was back at the doctors. This time he had syphilis.

When he ran short of money for models, he enrolled at the Antwerp Academy where he had heard nude models were available in the evenings. But they turned out to be male wrestlers. It was a bitter disappointment. So he joined two private sketching clubs and attended their night sessions to get access to female nudes. Women were central to art, in van Gogh's view. And although he still preferred the company of whores to "respectable pious ladies", he still had a hankering to get married.

Van Gogh went to stay with Theo in Paris. Deprived of nude models, he began painting flowers as if they were women. Despite his terrible appearance – he was dressed in rags and most of his teeth had fallen out – he managed to attract the

9

attention of the Comtesse de la Boisière who was rather taken with him.

Even when he could afford nude models, they would often refuse to sit for him, such was his reputation as a crazy man. So he made friends with other artists and sat in on their modelling sessions. Some ateliers were virtually open to anyone who turned up and a horde of rowdy young men would crowd around the nude model. Van Gogh favoured the atelier of Ferdinand Cormon. Cormon's students reckoned he had three mistresses on the go at the same time. It was there that Vincent met Henri de Toulouse-Lautrec, who introduced him to Edgar Degas.

Lautrec painted van Gogh in Le Tamborin on the Boulevard de Clichy, where Vincent would drink absinthe. It was owned by Agostina Segatori who had come to Paris from Naples years before to pose for the great artists of the time. She had made a lot of money out of it, but now her looks had faded. Nevertheless she generously consented to model nude for van Gogh in provocative poses. She also gave him food and drink in exchange for paintings – but only those of flowers that she thought she might be able to sell.

Van Gogh put on an exhibition of Japanese prints at Le Tamborin. They fascinated him, particularly as they depicted the courtesans and geishas of the "floating world" – the red light district of Japanese cities.

But it was in the Restaurant de Chalet that he met Paul Gauguin who was five years his senior. Gauguin had just returned from Panama and Martinique. Normally robust, he was suffering the after-effects of anaemia, malaria, hepatitis and dysentery. In his weakened state, he looked remarkably like the hunched and emaciated van Gogh.

In Martinique, Gauguin had found his own geishas in the form of the hugely available island women. Immediately the two of them hit it off. Van Gogh loved Gauguin's colourful canvases and his tales of bare-breasted beauties who would offer themselves to anyone who came along.

Theo and his mistress grew tired of Vincent and wanted him

to leave. He did nothing around the apartment and they were constantly picking up after him. He became even more irascible when the doctor told him, that because of his syphilitic condition, he should give up women.

Lautrec suggested that van Gogh should go to Arles where life would be cheaper and, in February 1888, he left Paris, a city he had once said was as welcoming as a woman.

Arles was described by Gauguin as "the dirtiest hole in the south". However, the women of the town were famed for their beauty. The local prostitutes were busy catering to the notorious Zouaves, a French infantry regiment normally stationed in Algeria. Shortly to be posted back to North Africa, the men were allowed to indulge themselves with the local "Grecian beauties" in the *Maisons de Tolérance* established just inside the city walls.

Van Gogh witnessed a brawl outside one of the brothels. Two Zouaves were killed by a couple of Italians. A lynch mob gathered, but in the confusion, the two Italians got clean away. Vincent seized the opportunity to slip into the brothel.

"I saw a brothel here last Sunday," he wrote to Theo. "It had a large room. The walls were covered with blue whitewash, like a village school. There were fifty or more military men in red and civilians in black, their faces a magnificent yellow or orange (what colours there are in faces here). The women were in sky blue, vermilion, as unsubtle and garish as possible. The whole thing was bathed in a yellow light. It was a good deal less lugubrious than such places in Paris."

After much shopping around, Van Gogh became a regular at *Maison de Tolérance* No 1, run by Madame Virginie. He went there whenever he could afford it to indulge in what he now called "hygienic practices". His particular favourite was a shy, withdrawn, young girl named Rachel.

He had interests outside the brothel too. He saw a young girl on the outskirts of Arles who had coffee-colour skin, ash blonde hair, grey eyes and a rose print bodice "under which you could see the breasts, shapely, firm and small". Later he used even younger models.

Van Gogh maintained a correspondence with the painter Emile Bernard. Degas was something of a voyeur and his paintings should be more "spermatic", he told Bernard.

"He watches while human animals, stronger than himself, get excited and fuck," wrote van Gogh. "He paints them well, precisely because he does not get excited himself."

Rubens, on the other hand, was "a handsome man and a good fucker. Courbet, too. Their health permitted them to drink, eat and fuck."

And his own condition? He was cursed by belonging to the white Christian race.

"The horrible white man with his bottle of booze, his money, and his syphilis," he lamented. "When shall we see the end of him?"

Van Gogh wrote to other painters, inviting them to establish an artists' colony at Arles which he called the "Studio of the South". He rented and made ready the Yellow House, so called because of this yellow wash. But the only one who turned up was Paul Gauguin.

When he arrived, he found van Gogh in a bad state. The syphilis was taking its toll. He was drinking heavily, particularly absinthe and he was suffering bouts of impotence.

Gauguin was a great womanizer – "a virgin creature with savage instincts; with Gauguin blood and sex prevail over emotion," van Gogh said. In the brothels, while van Gogh often only talked to the girls, Gauguin had sex with them. His visitor's unbridled virility upset Vincent. It made him feel inadequate, threatened. What is more Gauguin was popular with the locals – van Gogh was not – and, as well as visiting the brothels regularly, Gauguin would take "nocturnal promenades for reasons of hygiene".

Their rivalry in art and women made it impossible for them to live together. The situation grew worse when Vincent heard Theo was about to marry.

On the evening of 23 December 1888, Gauguin went out on one of his nocturnal promenades. Van Gogh followed him, keeping to the shadows. Perhaps he wanted to witness Gauguin picking up a woman, allowing him further masochistic pleasure in humiliation.

Gauguin heard footsteps behind him. He turned to confront his pursuer, to find van Gogh razor in hand.

"My look at that moment must have had great power in it," said Gauguin, "for he stopped and, lowering his head, set off running towards home."

Back at the Yellow House, van Gogh used the razor to cut off the lobe of his left ear. He wrapped it in newspaper and took it to *Maison de Tolérance* No 1, perhaps expecting Gauguin to be there. He asked for Rachel, handed her the package and told her: "Guard this object carefully".

When she opened the parcel, Rachel screamed and passed out. A Gendarme on his beat outside heard the scream and rushed into the *Maison de Tolérance* and found the ear lobe surrounded by bloody newspaper on the floor.

No one is very sure why van Gogh cut off his ear lobe. He had been drinking and had only the haziest recollection of the whole business. Dutch psychologist A.J. Westerman Holstijn has noted the Dutch word for ear – "*lel*" – sounds like the Dutch slang word for penis – "*lul*". He believes that it has something to do with unresolved homosexual feelings towards Gauguin.

"Van Gogh lived under the constant overpowering threat and masochistic homosexual unconscious wish for castration," Westerman Holstijn says. "Finally, when he slices off his ear and gives it to the prostitute who accepted Gauguin, he brings it about rather than face the threat any longer."

Van Gogh, an avid reader of the newspapers, may have read about Jack the Ripper who liked to slice off his victims' ears, among other things.

Gauguin headed back to Paris and, although the incident at *Maison de Tolérance* No 1 had been reported in the papers, van Gogh was still at large and painting better than ever. He even went back to the brothel. Rachel had recovered from the shock and was back at work. And the girls told him not to worry, a lot of people were sick in the head.

Two days after that visit to the brothel, Van Gogh had a

breakdown and was taken to hospital. Five days later, he discharged himself. But when the gendarmes came for him, he put up no resistance.

In the asylum at Saint-Rémy-de-Provence, he continued painting. Some of his most famous paintings were created there. His only frustration was the lack of suitable models. After a year, he was released. Six months later, in Auvers, van Gogh shot himself and died.

2

Sex in the South Seas

While van Gogh's life was a living hell, his friend Paul Gauguin gave us a vision of paradise. He is best known for his paintings of naked, inviting brown-skinned girls, bathed in the brilliant sunlight of the South Pacific. Of course, Tahiti, by the time he reached it, was nothing like that. The Pacific islands were already riddled with the diseases, particularly syphilis, brought by Europeans, including Gauguin himself. They were far from the paradise he portrayed. But the women were still willing and what more could you want if you were a man with Gauguin's prodigious sexual stamina.

When in 1873 the young Danish woman Mette Gad married a stockbroker's junior, Paul Gauguin, she knew nothing of his artistic ambitions. As far as she was concerned, after five years in the merchant navy, he was launched on a prosperous career in finance.

However, her twenty-five-year-old husband had already lived an exotic life. Born in France, he had been brought up in Peru. His father, a republican journalist, had been forced into political exile there by Napoleon III, but died on board ship on the way. As a young man, Gauguin returned to France, then went to sea and, by the time he was married, he had already visited many of the exotic locations that he would depict in his paintings.

He "first sinned" at seventeen in the French port of Le Havre, a sensible precaution before taking off on his first voyage which would take four months. On board, he was regaled by the older men's recollections of sexual adventures around the four corners of the Earth. One story made a great impression on him. One night, on watch, a lieutenant told him that when he was a cabin boy he had fallen overboard and been picked up by a passing ship that dropped him off on a Polynesian island. There he lost his virginity and spent two years in sexual rapture until another passing ship took him back to France.

In Rio, the young Gauguin gained more experience in the hands of Madame Aimée, the leading singer in Offenbach's operas that were then being performed there. She was the mistress of the son of the Tsar of Russia, but she still had time for a short seaman who, by his own admission, looked about fifteen.

"Aimée threw my virtue overboard," Gauguin said. "The soil was prepared, I suppose, for I soon became a great rascal."

He began to be bad on board as well as ashore. He had sex in the sail store with a passenger, a Prussian woman, on the voyage home to France. She wanted to see more of him, but he gave her a false address. It was wrong of him, he admitted, but "I could hardly have sent her round to my mother's home". Quite.

The letters home were full of sexual adventures, but otherwise life at sea did not suit him. But it earned him enough to acquire a camera. He knew that Delacroix was already collecting nude photographs for his figure studies and planned a little study himself.

Back in Paris, Gauguin was spending his spare time doing a little amateur sketching when he met Mette. He was immediately smitten by the "beauty with the heart of stone". But she soon allowed herself to be won over. During their year-long courtship, they learnt little about each other, although they spent a great deal of time together. Behind her back, he managed to visit prostitutes and go and see the erotic sensation of the age, Manet's *Olympia*. While controversy raged over whether the reclining nude was a courtesan awaiting her next client, or innocent young bride awaiting her bridal bouquet, Gauguin took more of an interest in Olympia's black maidservant. Manet's Afro-Caribbean model Laure reminded Gauguin of the girls he had known while he was growing up in Lima.

Both of his parents were dead by the time Gauguin married, but he gave their names to his children – Aline, born in 1877, and Clovis, his second son, born in 1879.

When Gauguin's mother had died in 1867, Gustave Arosa, a prominent stockbroker, was named as his guardian. With Arosa's help, Gauguin's career in stockbroking blossomed and he led a comfortable bourgeois life in Paris from 1873 to 1883 when there was a stockmarket crash.

While other middle-class husbands would spend their spare time gambling or womanizing, Gauguin indulged his passion for painting, especially at the live classes at the Académie Colarossi. In 1881, his *Etude de nu*, showing a naked woman sitting on a bed sewing, drew particular praise.

The crash of the Union Fédérale bank and the financial crisis of 1882 hit Gauguin's stockmarket earnings. It was then that he decided to become a full-time painter, convinced he could make more money that way.

He could not have been more wrong. The financial crisis had hit everybody, including art buyers. Mette did not cope very well with poverty. So after a year, she with their four children and a fifth on the way went back to her native Copenhagen. Gauguin followed. But artistic talent could not thrive under the shackles of normal married life. He had to leave her, he said. His genius demanded it.

Mette was not unappreciative of her husband's talent. She was amazed by the quality of work he sent from Tahiti later. And, judging by their correspondence, they remained friends until 1894 when she broke off communication during a row over money. But she just could not understand the impulse that drove her husband to wreck her life and those of their children.

Gauguin returned to Paris but could not get on with Impressionism which was then in vogue. He went off to Pont-Aven in Brittany where he established an artists' colony.

Getting the local Breton girls to pose was a good deal cheaper than paying the professional models in Paris.

Short of money, Gauguin jumped on board ship with his friend, the artist Charles Laval. They headed for Taboga, an island off the coast of Panama where Laval had family. But Laval's relatives refused to put the two artists up and Gauguin was forced to work on the Panama Canal, then under construction, to pay for his passage home. On the way, he stopped off in Martinique.

He was particularly impressed by the women there. He wrote to his wife: "I can tell you that here a white person has great difficulty in keeping his virtue in tact, for the wives of Potiphar are everywhere."

Potiphar was the Egyptian captain in the book of Genesis whose wife tried to seduced Joseph. In desperation, she tore his clothes off and afterwards she claimed that he raped her, offering his clothes as proof. As a result, Joseph was imprisoned. In other words, Martinique was full of jailbait.

The women of Martinique ranged in colour from ebony black to white with a slight hint of colour. They had spells to seduce you, Gauguin explained to his wife, involving fruit.

"The day before yesterday, a young negress of sixteen – and my word she was pretty – offered me a guava, which had been split and squeezed at one end. I was about to eat it when a yellow-skinned notary grabbed the fruit from me and threw it to the ground."

The mulatto was an educated man, who knew the ways of the local women.

"You are a European and you don't know the ways of this country," he said. "You must never eat fruit without knowing where it comes from. This fruit possesses a charm; the black girl has rubbed it on her sexual parts, and after you have eaten it you will be hers to command."

Now that he had been warned, Gauguin promised his wife, he would be on his guard.

"I shall not succumb," he said. "You can rest assured about my virtue."

However, in his wood carving entitled simply *Martinique*, he depicts a naked Martiniquan Eve picking the forbidden fruit. But instead of a serpent, there are a goat and a monkey, two potent symbols of sexual licentiousness, urging her on. From the size and firmness of her breasts, the girl was young, perhaps the sixteen-year-old he mentioned in his letter.

From his paintings of Martiniquan women, it is clear to see that they awaken in him a sexual desire that had long been repressed. He would have stayed longer on his paradise island, but fell ill and had to return home to France.

The Parisian fashion was enamoured of everything exotic at the time. Gauguin went to an exhibition where he was much taken by the pretty little Javanese and Khmer dancers. He met a beautiful mulatta who became his mistress and the model for the nude sculpture *La Femme Noire*.

Gauguin returned to Pont-Aven where he was now much more susceptible to the promiscuous affairs that ripped through the artists' colony. He fell in love with the artist Emile Bernard's sister Madeleine, but he had a funny way of showing it. He painted her clothed and told her to consider herself "an androgyne, without sex".

"The soul, the heart, everything which is ultimately divine, should not be a slave to matter, that is to say the body," he said.

These are hardly the sentiments of a red hot lover.

He wintered in Brittany, staying at the auberge of Marie Henry, who refused to extend her favours to him on the grounds that he was married while others much more ugly than him were given *accès*. The great artist found himself in the humiliating position of having to creep downstairs at night to amuse himself with the serving maid who slept behind the bar.

Gauguin went to visit van Gogh in Arles, where they visited the brothels together. Van Gogh liked to sit and talk to Rachel, while Gauguin preferred to more robust activities. Just to pique his moody chum, he may well have had sex with Rachel too. Which would have explained a lot.

The night van Gogh cut off his ear lobe, Gauguin did not return home to the Yellow House. Fearing for his safety, he found a hotel. Before he reached home, he was stopped by the police superintendent who asked him: "What have you done to your comrade, Monsieur?"

At the Yellow House there was a trail of blood leading up the stairs. At the top, they found van Gogh curled up on his bed. Fearing the worst, Gauguin touched him and, to his relief, found that he was alive.

"Wake this man with great care," he told the superintendent. "If he asks for me, tell him I have left for Paris. The sight of me might prove fatal."

By then, Gauguin was forty and grew eager to go to Polynesia where he was sure that he could find a paradise even more liberating that Martinique. He put all his efforts into making money and persuaded his latest mistress, twenty-year-old seamstress Juliette Huet, to strip off for his version of *Olympia*. Gauguin tactlessly called his nude study of Juliette *The Loss of Virginity*. She holds a white flower flecked with blood in her hand.

In fact, Juliette's loss of virginity must have taken place some time before. She was two months pregnant when he painted her. But in his rendering, Gauguin managed to preserve her slender pubescent figure. After a brief showing, the canvas was bought by the homosexual Comte Antoine de la Rochefoucauld for his private collection. Juliette was ruthlessly discarded when Gauguin got his papers to go to Tahiti as an official government artist.

Before he went, Gauguin paid a quick visit to Copenhagen to see his wife and children. Mette was now wearing her hair close cropped, the badge of the Danish feminist movement. Gauguin found it hard to renew any sexual relationship with this harsh masculine figure. But his thirteen-year-old daughter Aline was a comfort, telling him that she would marry him when she grew up.

Gauguin was forty-three when he first set foot on Tahiti. Captain Cook had called the island paradise when he first saw it in 1769 and the first French visitor Antoine de Bougainville called it New Cytheria, after the Goddess of Love. Even

SEX IN THE SOUTH SEAS

Captain Bligh of the HMS *Bounty* had had fun there. But that was a century before. Now the capital Papeete was a run down shanty town built in timber and corrugated iron with a population of some three thousand. The only brick building was the garrison.

On the voyage, Gauguin had grown his hair long. The locals had never seen such a thing before. The women jeered at him and called him *taata vahine* – or man-woman. But Gauguin was on a *mission officielle* and had to be greeted by the local big-wigs who took an instant dislike to him. Which was okay, as he took an instant dislike to them too.

Gauguin moved into a native hut and set about learning the language and the customs. He steered clear of the French inhabitants who seemed, largely, bored with the place. But he did attend the dances that they put on in the park on a Saturday night because of the girls that it attracted.

He was pleased to discover that a century of missionaries had done little to change the Tahitians free-and-easy attitude towards sex. In Papeete, this amounted to more or less casual prostitution. However girls who came in from the surrounding area to see the sights were happy to accommodate visitors free of charge, just as their ancestors had. Not that Gauguin minded paying. The girls were hardly charging European prices and they offered both youth and beauty.

While Gauguin avoided the Europeans, they shunned him. Having a discreet Tahitian mistress was one thing, picking up *vahines* in the market square was quite another. The only white friend he made was the photographer Charles Spitz, who made a good living out of selling photographs of topless native girls.

Not all Gauguin's women were quite so casual. One beautiful girl of mixed English–Tahitian blood became a regular girlfriend. Her name was Tehura – though he called her Titi for obvious reasons. Of Titi he said: "The amorous passion of a Maori courtesan is something quite different from the passivity of the Parisian coquette. There is fire in her blood, which calls forth love as its essential nourishment; which it exhales like a fatal perfume. These eyes and this mouth cannot lie. Whether calculating or not, it is always love that speaks from them."

21

Gauguin was running out of money fast. As well as paying for girls, he had to pay rent and he decided to moved out of Papeete to some more remote – and cheaper – spot.

Twenty-five kilometres out of Papeete, he stopped at a place called Paea. Rural Tahitians were renowned for their hospitality and a family took him in. But still he had not found his paradise. It was still too close to the capital. The girls would drift off to sell themselves in the capital, while the men had turned to drink.

He went back to Papeete, packed up his things and, with Titi in tow, set off in a carriage he had borrowed from a friend in the police. A European orange grower offered Gauguin the colonial mansion he had almost completed, but Gauguin insisted on living instead in the bamboo hut the planter had occupied during its construction.

Titi was less than pleased with his decision and Gauguin sent her back to Papeete, figuring that he would do all right with the local girls.

It was not all plain sailing. The food that grew wild was not readily to hand and he had to buy import supplies from a local Chinese shop at exorbitant prices. The missionaries took against him and the local gendarme threatened to arrest him for bathing naked in a stream.

Although Titi had been a good model, he wanted to paint a pure Tahitian and invited a local woman back to his hut. He showed her a reproduction of Manet's *Olympia* and asked her if she would like to be painted like that. She jumped to the conclusion that Olympia was Gauguin's wife and refused to pose naked like for him. She did let him paint her though, but not even topless as she would go about her everyday business. She posed fully covered with a flower behind her ear.

It took quite some time to persuade the local girls to pose nude for him, and even longer to get them to entertain him in bed. In desperation, he sent to Papeete for Titi. But she chattered incessantly and he kicked her out.

Most of the ripest young *vahines* went to the mission school. In an attempt to get closer to them, he began sketching their teacher a nun called Sister Louise. To further this trust-building exercise, he painted a number of Christian themes in Tahitian settings.

Then Gauguin fell ill. He was covered in sores and started vomiting blood. Back in Papeete he was admitted to the military hospital where he was treated for heart disease – though, given the symptoms, that was probably not the whole of the story. He may have been suffering from yaws contracted on Martinique or Panama. More likely he was suffering from the secondary stage of syphilis. He would not have caught this from the girls he had slept with on Tahiti. The disease was too well advanced. It would have had to have come from his earliest sexual encounters in Le Havre or Rio.

He could not afford the twelve francs a day it cost to stay in hospital, so he discharged himself before the doctors had a chance to get to the bottom of his problem. Soon he ran out of money completely and survived on small handouts from a few close friends who found him an amusing diversion in this far-flung corner of the French empire.

His landlord insisted that he move out of his hut and into the now-completed colonial house as it was now the rainy season. There he painted on the glass doors. One surviving painting showed one of his earliest Tahitian nudes, *Eve proffering an apple*. In 1917, the writer Somerset Maugham was in Tahiti researching his book *The Moon and Sixpence*, a fictionalized account of Gauguin's life. He came across the door, still in place, with the naked Eve on it and bought it for two hundred francs. In 1962, he sold it for seventeen thousand dollars.

Gauguin began studying Tahitian religion. The sexual element in it particularly appealed to him. Tahitian gods and goddesses have frequent couplings, obliging their followers to do likewise. According to Tahitian legend, mankind was created when their god Oro left his wife and descended to earth to make love with the beautiful Vairaumati.

Gauguin was particularly fond of a religious sect called the Areois who preached free love and proselytized wherever they went. Members were forbidden to marry. They practised infanticide to deter permanent relationships and, with missionary zeal, put on displays of erotic dancing and sexual demonstrations.

Captain Cook witnessed one of these shows.

"A young man, nearly six feet tall, performed the rites of Venus with a little girl about eleven or twelve years of age, before several of our people and a great number of natives, without the least sense of its being indecent or improper, but, as it appeared, in perfect conformity to the custom of the place," he wrote. "Among the spectators were several women of superior rank, who may properly be said to have assisted in the ceremony; for they gave instructions to the girl how to perform her part, which, young as she was, she did not seem much to stand in need of."

The popularity of these displays held back the spread of the Christian religion, but by the time Gauguin arrived they were rare.

The more Gauguin got to know of Tahitian culture, the more he admired it. He enjoyed the casual nudity and the relaxed behaviour between the sexes. He even began to find the lithe young men as attractive as the women, though he was horrified at the way they circumcized themselves.

When a young man came of age, he would hold his foreskin closed while urinating, so that it ballooned out away from the glands. When this was done repeatedly, the end of the foreskin would simply rip free.

There is a strong homosexual element in Tahitian culture. In island mythology both gods and men make love to each other. Some men were exclusively homosexual, but most practised some degree of bisexuality. The hula-hula was originally a homoerotic dance, with the dancers bumping and grinding against one another. Gauguin joined in the hula-hula – though, according to his own account, he preferred doing it with nubile young girls.

He was nearly overwhelmed by his homosexual feelings for a boy named Jotefa with whom he went for a walk naked in the forest. The contours of young man's body appeared to him so graceful that he could almost have been an hermaphrodite. His beauty and fragrance set Gauguin's temples throbbing, and he had to cool off by jumping in a cold mountain stream. He later expunged his feeling towards Jotefa and other young men from his memoirs.

Although he depicted some Tahitian men in his paintings, it is naked young Tahitian girls who appear most often. His most famous, *Manao tupapau*, shows a young girl naked on a bed, with her pert buttocks turned invitingly towards the artist and viewer. When Gauguin's wife Mette saw it, she said that it was going to take a lot of work to convince the public that this was not indecent.

When Mette put his nudes on show in Copenhagen, the critics were outraged, but the paintings soon began selling. It must have been difficult for Mette to act as agent for these paintings of nudes as her husband had plainly been sleeping with the girls he painted. He made no secret of that, saying that his nudes were "preparing themselves for love". But perhaps, in her new cropped-haired feminist role, Mette was getting a buzz off the nude girls herself.

The children enjoyed the notoriety. Gauguin's ten-year-old son Pola became the most popular boy in his school, using his free pass to take his mates to see the nudes. Aline especially enjoyed the controversy surrounding *Manao tupapau*, as her father had painted her on a bed at around the same age as his Tahitian model, though she, of course, was clothed. She had said, three years before, that she had wanted to be his wife. Now, in a kind of a way, she felt she was.

Taking a break from work, Gauguin made a trip down to the western end of the island. Stopping to share a meal with a local family, the mother of the clan, a handsome woman of about forty, asked him the purpose of his journey.

"I am looking for a wife," he said.

"Look no further," she said. She had a daughter.

Gauguin asked her three questions: "Is she young? Is she pretty? Is she healthy?"

The answer to all three was yes.

"Okay," said Gauguin. "Go and get her for me."

The woman disappeared, while Gauguin ate a meal of wild bananas and crayfish. Half-an-hour later, the woman returned. She brought with her a tall young girl, wearing a transparent dress of pink muslin. Through it, Gauguin said, he could see her golden skin and her nipples standing out hard from her firm, young breasts. Her face was beautiful, different from the others he noted. He found out later she was Tongan.

The beautiful young girl sat down beside him and he asked three more questions

"Aren't you afraid of me?"

"No," she said softly.

"Have you ever been ill?"

"No."

"Would you like to come and live in my hut?"

"Yes."

It was as simple as that.

Her name was Teha'amana, which means the Giver of Strength. They lived openly together. Disapproving, the wife of the local gendarme called her a trollop. But Gauguin was deeply in love with her. He painted her voluptuously nude over and over again, and the titles of his nude studies of her speak openly of erotic delights and sexual satisfaction. On the bottom of a canvas showing her naked with another nude Tahitian woman lovingly rendered, he wrote: "What, are you jealous?"

At last, Gauguin had found his earthly paradise. Soon Teha'amana was pregnant.

"I am soon to be a father again in Oceania," he wrote. "In Tahiti a child is the most beautiful present you can give."

Despite, his impending fatherhood, Gauguin began making plans to return to Europe and applied to the French authorities to be repatriated. In one of his paintings, he shows Teha'amana dressed in white, the traditional colour of mourning in Tahiti. She may have lost the child, as there is no further mention of it in Gauguin's letters. Or she may have been in mourning because he was going away.

His imminent departure took the bloom off their relationship. She may even have left him for a while because he began to use other nude models. And his painting again talk of sexual ambivalence.

If Teha'amana did leave him, she returned. He painted her nude one more time before he left. This painting was known in France as *Les Adieux de Tehamana*, so he was saying goodbye. But it also has a Tahitian name which means alternatively "Teha'amana has many ancestors" – meaning that she belongs with her ancestors in Tahiti – or "Teha'amana had many parents". The practice of communal parenting was common in Tahiti, so he may have been saying that there would be plenty of people to look after her when he had gone. And she appeared bare-breasted one final time in the painting *Where are you going?*

On the first leg of his journey, he went back to Papeete, where he stayed with a Madame Charbonnier. Although she was draped in a widow's black respectability, as a young girl she had been a whore in Paris and had been deported, along with other surplus prostitutes, to the French penal colony of New Caledonia. From there, they spread out across the South Seas. Madame Charbonnier enjoyed having Gauguin to stay and liked to spy on him when he brought models home.

From Papeete, Gauguin took the boat home. He was given a terrific send off. He had been in Tahiti for just two years but he said he felt twenty years younger.

The exhibition of his Tahitian paintings opened in Paris to mixed reviews, but soon it proved itself to be popular and influential. Gauguin published his Tahitian diaries, judiciously edited to emphasize his sexual adventures and boasting of his thirteen-year-old child-bride, who taught him all he needed to know about Tahitian culture in bed.

Gauguin's early work soon began fetching good prices and the artist moved into a studio and, again, painted the glass doors with erotic scenes. Judith, the thirteen-year-old daughter of the Swedish sculptress Ida Ericson-Mollard, visited him there. Her father was the alcoholic opera singer Fritz Alberg, who had abandoned her mother when she became pregnant. Her mother married the composer William Mollard, who was much younger than her. The three of them lived together in the one-room studio below Gauguin's, with Judith sleeping next to the marital bed behind a screen. Her breasts had just developed to the point where they were beginning to attract Mollard's attention and there were jealous scenes.

Naturally Judith fell head over heels in love with great artist. She reminded him of his daughter Aline, who was thirteen when he had last seen her. And he could not keep his hands off her tits.

"Without the slightest surprise, I let his beautiful plump hands caress the recent roundness as if they were caressing a clay pot or a wooden sculpture," she recalled. In ecstasy, she said nothing.

On other occasions too, he "cupped his hands like a shell around my budding breasts".

"These, these are mine," he said.

Judith did not mind him molesting her one bit. She was so much in love with him that she did not mind him seeing other women. Juliette Huet, his first Olympia and the abandoned mother of his child, regularly dropped by. It was only when Judith's mother came upstairs to find her pubescent daughter posing nude for the old goat that the tender little affair came to an end.

Gauguin soon found a new model. She was known as Annah the Javanese. The opera singer Nina Pack had let it slip to a banker with contacts in the Far East that she rather fancied having a black serving maid. A month or so later, a gendarme turned up on her doorstep with a young brown-skinned woman. She had been found at the Gare de Lyon with a label around her neck which read:"*Madame Nina Pack, rue de la Rochefoucauld, à Paris. Envoi de Java.*"

Annah was half-Indian and half-Malayan, and she had a mind of her own. She soon fell out with her mistress. To help Nina out, Gauguin's dealer Ambroise Vollard offered the house-maid as a model to Gauguin. He accepted with alacrity and the girl was soon stripped off. Gauguin claimed she was thirteen.

But his nude portrait of her shows her full breasted and with an extensive pubic bush.

The innocent thirteen-year-old Judith refused to believe that Annah was Gauguin's mistress and, finding her in his bed during the day, concluded that she was ill. To add insult to injury, Annah's nude portrait, according to experts, was painted over the half-finished nude study of Judith, some details of which can still be seen in the finished work.

Annah the Javanese was another version of Manet's *Olympia*. And it carried the idea of the unabashed female nude through to the new generation of young artists who thronged around Gauguin. Among their number was the young Pablo Picasso.

Another of Gauguin's disciples was the poet Julien Leclercq. He tried to seduce Judith. When she refused him, he told her that he had wept all night over her.

"Weep on," she told him. "You'll have to piss less."

For Judith, it was Gauguin or no one.

Gauguin also managed to contrive to have Juliette round when Annah was out. But one day he screwed it up. Juliette and Annah came face to face. Juliette let fly with a string of coruscating insults in French, assuming the black woman would not understand. But when she paused for breath, Annah said: *"Alors, Madame a fini?"*

Juliette withdrew, humiliated.

In Paris and Pont-Aven, Gauguin continued to rework ideas he had brought back with him from the South Seas. He missed Tahiti and longed to be back there. His mind was made up to return after a fight in Brittany. While Gauguin recuperated, Annah went back to Paris, cleared his studio of everything except the canvases and disappeared.

Even though Gauguin was now a famous artist, fêted by the likes of the composer Frederick Delius and the playwright August Strindberg, at the age of forty-seven, he cut loose once more. This time, he did not even bother to go to Copenhagen to see his wife and children.

He sailed from Marseilles on board the steamer

L'Australien. In Port Said, he took the precaution of laying in a stock of pornographic postcards.

When Gauguin arrived back in Tahiti, he realized that he now had to find somewhere more remote to live. In the two years that he had been away, Papeete had been transformed from the rundown shanty town into something resembling a Paris suburb. Fortunately, the governor was going on a tour of the outlying islands and Gauguin was invited to come along. The visit to Bora-Bora was particularly not to be missed. To mark her submission to French rule, the queen there had temporarily annulled all marriages so that the visiting dignitaries could be greeted in traditional style.

Gauguin's syphilis obliged him to return to Tahiti though, where he temporarily set up residence. Teha'amana was pleased to see him back.

"The woman I used to live with got married while I was away," he wrote home. "I have been obliged to make a cuckold of her husband, but she can't live with me again, although she has run away from him for a week."

Not that he really needed her. He now had something of a reputation on the island.

"Every night frenzied young girls invade my bed," he reported. "Last night I had three of them to keep me company."

But all this fun was distracting him from his art. He resolved to "stop this wild behaviour and install a responsible woman in the house and work like mad".

Good as his word he got the delightful young Pau'ura to move in. He claimed she was thirteen but, according to her birth certificate, she was fourteen and a half. Despite the huge differences in their ages, they slept together and Pau'ura remembered him in her later years as a "rascal".

She was pretty enough to be his model and became his new Eve and Olympia. Soused on imported claret, which he bought by the two-hundred-litre barrel, he too was naked while he painted her.

Soon Gauguin was broke again. In Paris, he had been attacked as a plagiarist. No one would buy his pictures. The local Chinese store keeper Ah-Kong only took his work in exchange for food out of pity and he used Gauguin's drawings as wrapping paper.

He tried to get commissions to paint portraits, but his reputation was so bad that no self-respecting man would let him near their wives or daughters. Except for one, the wealthy lawyer and businessman Auguste Goupil. Rather than let Gauguin bankrupt the Chinese store keeper, Goupil let Gauguin paint his ten-year-old daughter Jeanne, who was known in Tahitian as *Vaïte*.

The little girl was terrified of Gauguin and Goupil hated the results. Nevertheless, he kept Gauguin on as art teacher for his children. But after two months, Gauguin's increasingly eccentric behaviour became too much for him and he sacked the great artist.

Gauguin took his revenge on the entire white community by erecting a crude statue of a naked woman outside his hut. The local priest said that if Gauguin did not at least cover the statue's naked loins he would tear it down with his own hands. Gauguin called his bluff. He went to the gendarmes, who had to warn the turbulent priest that if he touched the statue, offensive though it was, he would be prosecuted for trespass.

Pau'ura fell pregnant. Gauguin kept on painting her as her belly swelled. He even recorded her melancholy when the baby was born dead in his painting *Nevermore*.

In 1897, in Copenhagen, Gauguin's daughter Aline died of pneumonia. She was nineteen. The owner of the land where Gauguin had built his hut had also died and he was forced to move on to a new shack at Punaauia. He fell into despair. While the whole of Europe imagined him in a sunny paradise surrounded by compliant native women, Gauguin knew the truth. He was fifty, with three dead children, an incurable disease and crippling debts. Lethargy overwhelmed him. By the end of that year, he mustered all his strength for one last canvas. It was to be huge and sum up all he knew about existence. The name of this pictorial valedictory was to be *Where do we come from? What are we? Where are we going?*

SEX LIVES OF THE GREAT ARTISTS

When it was finished, he went up into the hills, lay down and swallowed a phile of arsenic. His plan was that the ants there would devour his body. That way he would be remembered only for his last great work.

But it was not to be. He took too much of the poison. Unconscious, he vomited it up. And after an unpleasant night on the hilltop he returned home.

After that he quit painting and took a government job at six francs a day. It meant he had to wear trousers and a jacket, and move back into Papeete. Pau'ura hated city life and left him, taking with her everything she could carry.

When Gauguin's latest batch of paintings got back to Paris, he was hailed a genius. *Where do we come from? What are we? Where are we going?* was seen as a masterpiece. The money raised was sent to Gauguin. He was urged to spend it on a ticket home so that he could cash in on his new fame.

Instead, he quit his job and moved back to Punaauia. His shack was in a sorry state. Insects were eating his unfinished work, even though Pau'ura was there. But he did not have the heart to be angry with her. She was five months pregnant and he was going to be a father again.

In spite of being freed from regular work and back in the paradise of his outlying shack, Gauguin could not bring himself to paint again. He felt he had nothing else to say.

This time Pau'ura gave birth to a healthy boy, whom Gauguin named Emile after the first son he had had with Mette. He went to Papeete to try and have the child legitimized. But as he was still married to Mette, there was no way he could do that under French law. The child he had with his mistress would have to remain a bastard. That did not mean Gauguin loved him any the less. The new child inspired him and Gauguin made of a series of paintings showing Pau'ura nursing the child.

His syphilis was now entering its third stage and he began to get paranoid and unstable. Tahiti was turning into everything he hated. It was becoming built up. Even the interior was being cultivated and the locals diluted by the influx of Chinese labourers.

SEX IN THE SOUTH SEAS

Gauguin sold his house, paid off his loans, packed up everything he owned – including his pornographic postcards – and headed for the Marquesas, leaving Pau'ura behind. Years later, she was asked what it was like to live with Gauguin. She said, despite their ups and downs, at least life with him was never boring.

On the Marquesas, Gauguin was greeted as hero who might defend the interests of the settlers against officials in Paris. One of the leading citizens was Nguyen Van Cam, known locally as Ky Dong. He was a Vietnamese nationalist who had been arrested by the French authorities and sentenced to life on Devil's Island. On the way, the boat had stopped off at Tahiti. The governor there had taken an interest in the case, had him released and exiled him to the Marquesas where he settled. Ky Dong persuaded Gauguin to stay on the main island of Nukuhiva, rather than travel on to the outlying Hivaoa as he had planned. Another factor, no doubt, was the astonishingly good-looking women there.

Ky Dong wrote a play about Gauguin called *The Loves of the Old Painter on the Marquesas*, in which the protagonist quickly beds three Marquesan beauties and, by mistake, a hunchback. The mistake occurred because great artist's eyesight was failing and he was too vain to wear his glasses when chatting up the local girls.

Gauguin built himself a home. To the outrage of the local missionary, it had two huge carved wooden female nudes either side of the door. On the right-hand side of the door, there was panel, saying: "Love and you will be happy." On the left-hand side was a panel saying: "Be mysterious and you will be happy." And above the door there was a panel which read: "*Maison du Jouir*" – The House of Orgasm.

Inside, the walls were decorated with the pornographic postcards he had bought in Port Said. The house drew quite a crowd. When local women studied the carvings or the pornographic postcards, Gauguin would run his hands under their wraps to get a feel for his subject and say, in Marquesan: "I would like to paint you."

They often complied. He photographed them nude too, adding the pictures to his walls. He also had sex with his models. Gauguin considered this was not just one of the perks of the job, it was essential.

"I was aware that my skill as a painter depended on the physical and moral possession of the model," he said. He had to get inside his subject.

He also drank a good deal of absinthe.

Across the square from Gauguin's house was a Catholic boarding school for girls. His window overlooked it. The girls who studied there were supposed to be off limits. But Gauguin realized French law required that only girls who lived within four kilometres had to go to the school. The local missionaries had told the natives that girls further afield must attend too, as a way of separating them from their easy-going parents.

Gauguin informed the chief of a tribe who lived ten kilometres away of this. He had a fourteen-year-old daughter called Vaeoho. And in exchange for a few clothes and ribbons bought from the local store, Gauguin took Vaeoho as his wife. Soon he felt able to paint again.

He did not use Vaeoho as his model though. Instead, he used his mistress Tohotaua, who was from Tahuata, home of a unique strain of Polynesians who have red hair. She was married, but that did not mean much to Polynesians. While the missionaries were trying to get the native women to cover up, Gauguin insisted on showing Tohotaua naked or at least bare breasted.

Gauguin began painting men again at this time, but they are usually very feminine and sexually ambiguous. And he kept them wrapped while surrounding them with naked women.

In his later work, Gauguin signed himself Pego – nautical slang for penis. And he carved the handle of his walking stick into the shape of an erect penis.

Although the syphilis was getting worse, plainly Gauguin could still enjoy sex. In 1902, Vaeoho became pregnant. With her husband too sick to look after her, she went back to her family to have the baby.

Gauguin began casting a lecherous eye in the direction of

the girls' school again. They were warned about the artist from the pulpit by the local bishop. This only incited some of the more adventurous girls to come round under cover of darkness. Gauguin delighted in showing them his collection of pornography just to get them in the mood.

He also related a tale of how an old blind woman had slipped her hand under the wrap he wore and felt his penis.

"Popa'a," she muttered – "European" – and wandered off. But for most of the local girls, it made no difference.

The bishop's condemnation of the great artist began a feud. Gauguin told more outlying families that they need not send their daughters to school. Attendances dropped by half.

Then he erected two statues outside his home, in full view of the church. One showed the devil with the face of the local bishop. The inscription on its base read *Père Paillard* – Father Lechery. The other showed a naked woman, bearing the legend *Thérèse* – the name of the bishop's maid in whom, it was rumoured, he took a more than pastoral interest.

The bishop complained to the authorities, who sent a gendarme around to enforce an unpaid tax bill. When Gauguin refused to pay, the gendarme seized the statues. But under French law he had to return them to Gauguin's home and auction them there to recover the money owing in tax. When he did so, he found Gauguin holding a party and the liquor flowing freely. In this raucous atmosphere, the gendarme tried to auction the statues. The reserve price the authorities had set was sixty-five francs. Gauguin offered that. There were no other bids. Gauguin refused even to get up from his drink at the table to pay the gendarme and got his cook to do it instead.

For the rest of his life, he battled with the authorities, often taking the side of the natives against what he increasingly saw as colonial oppression. As the syphilis gnawed away at his body, he became a morphine addict. He died in bed on the morning of 8 May 1903. Whether he went to heaven or hell it is hard to say. But if he did go to heaven, it could not be a patch on the paradise that he painted and experienced on this good earth.

3

The Agony, the Ecstasy and the Anally

Nowadays, Michelangelo is best known for his David. But during his lifetime, he was just as well known for his Tommaso, Gherardo and Febo. Even the time he spent flat on his back painting the ceiling of the Sistine Chapel was done for the syphilitic Pope Julius II, followed by the flamboyantly homosexual Pope Leo X, whose family had been Michelangelo's patron in Florence.

Michelangelo was the greatest artist of the human body. Throughout his life he was surrounded by nude models. Michelangelo thought that nothing was more beautiful than a young man naked and his sculpture and painting gave him a unique opportunity to indulge his passion. No other artist, gay or straight, male or female, concentrated so much on the male nude. Following the convention of the time, their genitals are undeveloped, boyish, but he imbued a sensual, loving quality to their pert buttocks.

Although his work also featured female nudes, they were never rendered with quite the same ardour. Despite his incomparable draughtsmanship, he was never good at breasts. He never had a female model. He could not bear to look at a woman naked. That's why all his female nudes look like men with some bits added and others taken away.

Attitudes to homosexuality in the Renaissance were complex. Michelangelo and the other artists of the age struggled to re-establish the Platonic ideals of ancient Greece when the Greeks actively embraced homosexuality. However, in Florence, where Michelangelo was brought up, it was frowned on. In 1502, when Michelangelo was twenty-seven, it was outlawed. Four years later, the laws were strengthened to the point where the penalty for procuring was the amputation of a hand. Fathers who allowed their sons to engage in homosexual practices were punished and houses where homosexual acts took place were to be burnt down.

In 1524, when a young boy complained that he had been sodomised by four men, his father complained to the magistrates. One of the perpetrators was seized, tried, condemned and beheaded.

Unlike Leonardo da Vinci and Sandro Botticelli, Michelangelo was never charged with sodomy. From a study of his work, many experts have deduced that he sublimated his homosexual impulses into art. It regularly depicts masturbation, sometimes mutual male masturbation. Psychoanalysts say that Michelangelo's work reveals an urge to be sodomized, that he felt that sex with a woman will be punished by castration, and that being sodomized by a young male god was the route to immortality. However, psychoanalysts read that sort of thing in everyone's tea leaves.

His homosexual impulses came out in his life as well as his art. That is why he spent most of his life in Rome where attitudes to homosexuality were much looser. Things there were so lax that Roman artist Giovanni Antonio de' Bazzi, who regularly slept with his apprentices, was known to one and all as "Sodoma". Not only was homosexuality widespread, under Pope Leo X is was practically compulsory. Michelangelo certainly indulged himself. In 1546, he was even blackmailed because of it by the satirist and "Scourge of Princes" Pietro Aretino. Michelangelo bought his silence with a few of his drawings.

However, Michelangelo seems to have controlled himself until quite late on in life. In his Neoplatonic way, he saw human beauty as a chaste ideal. It was only in the face of the decay of that beauty with age that he realized sex was the appropriate response.

In 1520, when Michelangelo was forty-five, he became attached to Gherardo Perini. He wrote to him often and gave him drawings. In February 1522, Michelangelo wrote to Perini asking him to come over, so that he would not have to spend another night alone drawing. What would happen if Perini did not show up was made clear. The letter is decorated with a picture of a small boy with his penis in his hand, an image that he later used in the work *Children's Bacchanal* which Michelangelo gave to another lover.

In the autumn of 1522, sixteen-year-old Antonio Mini moved into Michelangelo's house. They lived together for nine years until, in 1531, Mini left for France. As a parting gift, Michelangelo gave him the painting *Leda and the Swan*, which shows a naked Leda kissing a swan that lies between her legs. The swan's neck is extremely phallic and Leda is plainly in sexual ecstasy. This is easily the most erotic image Michelangelo ever created.

There had been other apprentices who enjoyed Michelangelo's special favours. Piero d'Argento left him in 1509, but remained in regular communication. Silvio Falcone was dismissed in 1517, but fifteen years later he was still writing to Michelangelo asking to be allowed to repay "the love you bore me when I was in your service". But neither of these boys was allowed to share in Michelangelo's personal art collection, the way Mini did.

While Mini was still in residence, Michelangelo met Andrea Quaratesi, the teenage offspring of a Florentine banking family. The only surviving portrait that Michelangelo completed is of Quaratesi. In a scribbled note Michelangelo asks Quaratesi to "love me" and calls him his "great consolation".

Quaratesi is also depicted on an exercise sheet. From his figure is it estimated that he is about fourteen. Next to him Michelangelo drew a screaming satyr and a man defecating. The shrinks say this shows that Michelangelo associated the pubescent Quaratesi with unrestrained sexual desire – the screaming satyr – and anal functions – the man defecating. What do you think? Casual mentions of Quaratesi appear in Michelangelo's correspondence for the next twenty years.

In the great artist Benvenuto Cellini's autobiography, he mentions that Michelangelo was infatuated with the poet Luigi Pulci, because of his great beauty. Pulci was later beheaded for having sex with his daughters.

Now it could have been that all these friendships were entirely innocent. But in 1533, Michelangelo had a relationship with a young Florentine Febo di Poggio, which was definitely not so. It forced him to leave Florence for good. He wrote de Poggio letters assuring him of his love and love poems that positively reeked of sex:

> I truly should, so happy was my lot.
> While Phoebus was inflaming all the hill
> Have risen from the earth while I was able,
> With his feathers, and made my dying sweet.

Phoebus was, of course, Febo and "*Poggio*" in Italian means hill, though there are other hills around the body that can be inflamed. The feathers are important too. *Leda and the Swan* is not the only place that Michelangelo depicts sex with birds. It is a motif that appears throughout his work. *In The Rape of Ganymede*, he shows the full-frontal youth being sexually assaulted by Zeus in the form of an eagle. Ganymede, who becomes Zeus's catamite, is shown in ecstasy while the eagle's clawed feet spread his legs. The eagle is plainly taking him from behind and its penis emerges through what appears to be a vaginal cleft in the boys' scrotum. And in the *Punishment of Tityus*, a naked man is overpowered by a big bird. In Michelangelo's day, the word "bird" – *uccello* – was slang for the male genitals, as it is today in the United States. A "bird" or "young thrush", in Florentine slang, was also a boy who might be bagged and plucked.

Michelangelo had to get out of Florence because di Poggio was blackmailing him. He wrote demanding money. When he went round to Michelangelo's house to collect, he found the great artist had vanished. So he sent a letter to him in Rome, telling him to send a money order to Florence by messenger.

"Do not fail to answer," he threatened. "I will not write more... praying God to keep you from harm."

In Rome, Michelangelo already had another boyfriend. He was a handsome young aristocrat named Tommaso de' Cavalieri, aged twenty-three to Michelangelo's fifty-seven.

They had met a few months before and Michelangelo had been plying him with love letters and poetry, and drawings, including the *Children's Bacchanal, The Rape of Ganymede* and the *Punishment of Tityus*.

At first, Michelangelo said his love for Tommaso was "chaste". But Tommaso, he raved, had "not only incomparable physical beauty, but so much elegance in manners, such excellent intelligence, and such graceful behaviour, that he well deserved, and still deserves, to win more love the better he is known". Soon, Michelangelo's poems to Tommaso were full of phrases like "burning" and the "fire that consumes me".

> If the hope you have given me is true,
> And true the good desire that's granted me,
> Let the wall set between us fall away,
> And there is double power in secret woe.

This can mean only one thing and Michelangelo gave himself eagerly to his lover.

> If capture and defeat must be my joy,
> It is no wonder that, alone and naked,
> I remain prisoner of a knight-at-arms.

A knight-at-arms in late medieval Italian is *un Cavalier armato*, a pun on Tommaso de' Cavalieri's name. This poem was written while Michelangelo was still seeing Febo, so perhaps the Florentine started blackmailing the great artist because he was annoyed that he was two-timing him.

Fleeing to Rome, Michelangelo moved in with Tommaso

and for about six months nothing is known about his activities. He fell silent as if the two of them were enjoying a homosexual honeymoon.

Then Michelangelo came out. He spoke openly of his love in his letters. It was an enduring love too. Ten years later, he wrote to Tommaso:

> The love for what I speak of reaches higher;
> Woman's too much unlike, no heart by rights
> Ought to grow hot for her, if wise and male.
>
> One draws to Heaven and to earth the other,
> One in the soul, one living in the sense
> Drawing its bow on what is base and vile.

The poem goes on and is, again, full of images of birds descending to pluck up mortal men, hearts melting and things being pierced.

Michelangelo continued his close relationship with Tommaso, even after Tommaso was married. But Michelangelo had a new love interest too. His name was Cecchino de' Bracci and he was the nephew and "adopted son" of Michelangelo's close friend and advisor in Rome, Luigi del Riccio. He died at the age of fifteen in 1544, when Michelangelo was sixty-nine. Michelangelo wrote forty-eight epitaphs, a sonnet and a madrigal, raving about the beautiful youth. These writings show that, if they did not have a physical relationship, Michelangelo certainly wanted one.

His love for the dead boy also found expression in his drawing *The Dreamer* which shows a winged boy blowing a horn into the ear of a naked man. The man is surrounded by representations of six of the seven deadly sins. Lust is portrayed by four details – a man with an erection climbing on to a reclining naked woman, a clothed woman kissing a naked man, a free floating set of male genitals which are out of scale with the rest of the drawing, and hand holding an erect penis. From the grip, it can be deduced that the hand and the penis do not belong to the same man.

SEX LIVES OF THE GREAT ARTISTS

Michelangelo had a real problem with women. He called them "pigs and prostitutes". Most of his women have very masculine features. This is not surprising. Michelangelo did not use female models. Men were used as models for his female nudes, even though women who would take their clothes off for a few lire must have been readily available.

He wrote poems vilifying women on the backs of letters and sketches. In one, he talks of an ugly, tormenting old woman, with teeth like turnips, hair like leeks, a mouth that resembles a bog filled with beans and breasts like two water melons in a bag, who, he says, he would chase after if he were young.

From the positioning of female figures in relationship to men, it is clear that the only sort of sex he could imagine between a man and a woman was fellatio. Even on the ceiling of the Sistine Chapel, in the temptation scene in the Garden of Eden, Adam's penis is suspiciously near the mouth of the kneeling Eve.

Psychoanalysts put this, and Michelangelo's homosexuality, down to the fact that his mother did not breast feed him, but put him out to be suckled by a wet-nurse. The wet-nurse was the daughter of one stone mason and the wife of another one. Michelangelo, it was said, imbibed his sculptor's art with her milk. So he had no excuse for getting the tits wrong.

4

Who Made the Mona Lisa Smile?

In 1476, Leonardo da Vinci appeared in court in Florence, charged with sodomy. His paintings are full of pretty young men. And no less an authority that Sigmund Freud said that it is "doubtful whether he ever embraced a woman with love". In that case, who put the smile on the face of the Mona Lisa?

The sodomy charge against the twenty-four-year-old Leonardo is presented as damning evidence that he was gay. But the accusation was made anonymously. At that time, around Florence, there were a number of the special cylindrical letter boxes called *tamburi*, or drums. To denounce a fellow citizen, all you had to do was drop an accusation, unsigned, into one of these drums.

In Leonardo's case, the anonymous accuser said that the young artist and three other friends had sodomized a seventeen-year-old male prostitute named Jacopo Saltarelli. Sodomy was a serious charge, punishable by burning at the stake. However civilized societies have long since abandoned the practice of allowing charges to be drawn on the basis of anonymous accusations.

Like all other unattributed accusations dropped in the *tamburi*, the complaint against Leonardo and his chums was registered with the appropriate authorities and an inquiry was set up. The first hearing was held on 9 April 1476. But for the trial to proceed evidence was required and signed statements from witnesses. The prosecution had none.

The proceedings were postponed until 7 June. Again the prosecution turned up empty-handed. The judge dismissed the case and the charges were dropped for good.

So the case for Leonardo being gay was not proven. But, you may say, there is no smoke without fire. Why would anyone accuse an unknown young painter of so heinous a crime as sodomy if there was nothing to it?

It so happened, that one of Leonardo's co-defendants was a member of the powerful Medici family who then governed Florence, so the accusation was probably a malicious falsehood aimed at besmirching the Medici name for political reasons.

And justice is an imperfect thing. Benvenuto Cellini, no shrinking violet when it came to women, was twice convicted of sodomy. The rapacious Pietro Aretino was also accused. So was Botticelli, with more reason. His name alone invited suspicion.

Naturally Leonardo surrounded himself with pretty boys. The male nude was in vogue at the time. But his paintings of women betray such tenderness it is impossible to believe that he had never been in love with a woman.

Another bit of circumstantial evidence used against Leonardo was that one of his pupils was the notorious Sodoma. But Raphael studied with Sodoma and he was definitely not gay. Raphael simply adored women. But, like many men, he was torn between two types, the virgin and the whore. He was betrothed to Maria Bibbiena, the niece of Cardinal Santa Maria in Portico who died just a few days before him at the age of eighteen. But he was also in love with his more amenable model, the passionate La Fornarina, whom he often depicted in a state of undress. La Fornarina's real named was Margherita Luiti, the young daughter of a baker from Siena. She serviced many of the young bucks of the Trastevere. Prey to jealousy, Raphael would often break off his work on the fresco in the Farnesina palace to rush down to her house. This happened so often that Raphael's patron Agostino Chigi persuaded La

WHO MADE THE MONA LISA SMILE?

Fornarina to come and live in the palace so that the great artist could get on with his work. This may have had its downside. When Raphael died in 1520 at the age of thirty-seven, his first biographer Giorgio Vasari ascribed his death to the fact that he "continued with his amorous pleasures to an inordinate degree". La Fornarina was certainly at his bedside during his last illness. If Raphael died with a smile on his face, he tried to put one on La Fornarina's too. Altering his will on his deathbed, "he sent his beloved out of the house giving her the means to live as an honest woman," according to Vasari. Raphael then had himself buried beside his virginal Maria, but not before La Fornarina had broken through the crowd at the funeral procession and thrown herself on the coffin. She only allowed herself to be removed when she was told that the Pope was thinking of beatifying Raphael. Rather than spend the rest of her days as an "honest woman" she became a nun and spent her remaining years in austere contemplation.

In his anatomical studies, Leonardo often drew women, even making detailed drawings of their sexual organs. In one, he shows the vagina open and inviting as if the woman had just had sex, or was just about to. He also depicted men and women fornicating with none of the squeamishness you would expect if he did not like that sort of thing. He even described how to go about it: "A man wishes to learn whether the woman will consent to the demands of his lust, and as he learns that this is the case and she desires him, he requests her participation and does what he intended to do. And he cannot discover this unless he confesses, and as he confesses he fornicates."

Leonardo saw sex as a religious thing, with the man and the woman "confessing" to one another. It is true, men and women often confess that they love one another while they are making love.

Da Vinci was very interested in how a man got an erection. At that time, it was thought the penis was inflated by the retention of wind. Leonardo demonstrated that an erection was caused by the organ being "suffused by a large quantity of blood". He did this by dissecting criminals who had been hanged and had died with a hard-on. But he could not bring himself to measure and dissect the organ itself.

He wrote a famous essay called *Della Vergha* – "Concerning the Rod" – detailing what a troublesome thing a penis is.

Concerning the Rod

It holds conference with the human intelligence and sometimes has intelligence itself. When the human will desires to stimulate it, it remains obstinate and follows its own way, sometimes moving by itself without the permission of the man or any mental impetus. Whether he is awake or asleep, it does as it desires. Often the man is asleep and it is awake, and often the man is awake while it sleeps, and often when the man wishes to use it, it desires otherwise, and often it wishes to be used and the man forbids it.

Therefore it appears that this creature possesses a life and intelligence alien from the man, and it seems that men are wrong to be ashamed of giving it a name or of showing it, always covering and concealing what deserves to be adorned and displayed with ceremony as a ministrant.

True. The penis does have a life of its own.

Castration interested Leonardo too. He had noticed that the testicles – "the witnesses to coition" – also seem to be the source of animosity and ferociousness. Bulls, boars, rams and cocks all became craven cowards once they were removed.

Leonardo is usually pictured as an old man with a long beard. In fact, he depicted himself on numerous occasions clean shaven. Most men in the Renaissance shaved and, it is thought that, like other men, Leonardo regularly shaved off his beard to please women.

The classic Leonardo drawing showing a clean-shaven male nude in a circle and a square with four arms and four legs showing their movement is thought to be Leonardo himself. He is certainly much better endowed than Michelangelo's models.

And while Michelangelo's women look like men, Leonardo's men often have a very womanly look to them.

The gay lobby point to the fact that Leonardo lived with three young boys in the Vatican. Well, he needed models and pupils to assist him. And this was in the Vatican, where men living together should have passed without comment. The Renaissance papacy was lax to the point of licentiousness and there would have been plenty of women around if he needed one.

In the Renaissance, as in Ancient Greece, the idea was abroad that homosexual love was more spiritual than base heterosexual love. It was said that Leonardo's affection for the beautiful young Giovanni Francesco, when the artist was fifty-six, was homosexual in nature. But it could also have been an expression of an unmarried old man's longing for a son. Leonardo may have taken Francesco under his wing because the boy showed some talent as a painter. He adopted Francesco and made him his heir, but the boy's father was a nobleman and is hardly likely to have given the boy up to a painter, no matter how illustrious, simply to share his bed. But then, people were bound to gossip.

Although Leonardo never married that was not uncommon for artists at the time. He certainly used prostitutes.

Alessandro Vezzoisi, the director of the Leonardo da Vinci museum in Vinci, unearthed evidence that Leonardo frequented a brothel in Milan in 1490, when he was thirty-eight. He was particularly fond of one of the girls there. And it was not just in Milan. Leonardo confessed as much in his writing. In one passage complaining about the toll you had to pay to enter the city of Modesta, Leonardo consoled himself with the fact that it cost less to enter Modesta with your whole body, than for just your prick to enter a prostitute in Florence.

Leonardo was still at it when he was in his sixties. According to Professor Carlo Pedretti, director of the Hammer Center for Leonardo Studies at the University of California, there was one prostitute in particular called *la Cremona* with whom Leonardo had an "intense relationship" in his later years.

In his portrait of Cecilia Gallerani, Leonardo depicts what is supposed to be a symbol of purity. Yet her large brown eyes are inviting and her décolletage so daring that it looks as if the dress could slip from her shoulders at any moment. It is possible that

Leonardo was even in love with her. He wrote in his notebook: "*Madonna Cecilia – Amanisssima mia Diva – Lecta le tua soavissima*" – "My Lady Cecilia – my most beloved goddess – having read your sweetest letter." So something was going on.

So who made the Mona Lisa smile?

There is a mystery surrounding who the Mona Lisa is. By convention, she is thought to be the second wife of Francesco del Giocondo, a wealthy silk trader from Tuscany. In Italy, the Mona Lisa is called *La Gioconda*.

Freud, of course, says that it is Leonardo's mother. That is why Leonardo was a homosexual. Thank you, Sigmund.

Other authorities believe that she was the mistress of Leonardo's patron Giuliano de' Medici. Others still say mischievously that she is both the second wife of Francesco del Giocondo and the mistress of Giuliano de' Medici.

In either case, why did Leonardo not hand it over to the man who commissioned it and get paid? Instead, he took it to France with him, which is why it ended up in the Louvre.

The truth could be that Leonardo was a little more intimate with the sitter than he should have been. The clue comes from the fact that there was once a nude Mona Lisa. Although it has been lost, there are copies of it and many references to the fact that a nude portrait of the woman in question did exist.

In the clothed Mona Lisa that hangs in the Louvre, Leonardo paints just a hint of cleavage. The hands are lovingly rendered, as are lips and eyes. In fact, there is a hint of a glint in those eyes and her scarcely suppressed smile is world famous. But there is nothing puzzling about her expression, if you think about it. Every heterosexual man knows that look. It is the look of a woman who has just been made love to and is about to be made love to again, just as soon as her lover puts his brushes down.

5

Caravaggio's Bardassa

Caravaggio's canon was high camp – naked prepubescent boys, dreamy youths in girls' clothing, floggings and plenty of crucifixions. Not a single female nude survives. So Caravaggio was co-opted into the queer nation by Derek Jarman's film of the same name. But again there is evidence that he might have been a closet heterosexual.

Certainly Caravaggio's first patron Cardinal Del Monte was gay, and Caravaggio obliged the priest with a number of paintings of a homoerotic nature. Caravaggio also left Messina in rather a hurry in 1609. It is said this was because he was taking too much of an interest in schoolboys at play. But this conjecture seems to date from 1724 and its author, the priest and artist Susinno, says that Caravaggio simply wanted the boys to model for him.

However, in 1603, the painter Tommaso Salini testified in court that a certain *bardassa* Giovanni Battista was shared by Caravaggio and his friend Onorio Longhi. A *bardassa* was a man who adopts a female role in sex and society or, as an English visitor to Italy in the seventeenth century neatly put it, "a buggered boy".

The court case was a libel suit brought by the painter Baglione who had been satirized as a bad artist in a poem written, Salini maintained, by Caravaggio and Longhi. Salini said that he knew that they had written the verse because their *bardassa* Giovanni Battista had told him so.

When called to the witness stand, Caravaggio denied knowing any Giovanni Battista. Battista himself could not be found. Other witnesses said that Salini was lying and Caravaggio was found not guilty.

Caravaggio was also supposed to have lived with Minnitti, the model for the lutist in the *Concert*, before Minnitti went off to get married. Caravaggio's co-defendant Onorio Longhi also married and Caravaggio painted portraits of both him and his wife.

The cheeky young boy who posed nude for *Cupid Victorious* was also said to have been Caravaggio's "owne boy or servant that laid with him". However, at the same time, a rumour circulated that Caravaggio had deflowered the virgin who modelled for *The Death of a Virgin*. After 1599, he dropped the gay themes of his paintings for Del Monte and began to paint women who were attractive. At least one female nude is thought to have been lost.

Certainly, after 1600, his behaviour became much more aggressive and macho. In July 1605, he wounded a notary called Pasaqualone with a blow from a sword to the side of the head because he said he had been with a woman prostitute in the Piazza Navonne whom Caravaggio liked. Her name was Maddalena and she modelled for his *Madonna with St. Anne* and *Seven Works of Mercy*. Everybody said that she was Caravaggio's woman.

So the jury is still out on Caravaggio's sexual orientation. But he may yet prove to be a candidate for outing – as a heterosexual.

6

Well Come Benvenuto

Benvenuto Cellini wanted to leave no questions about his sexuality. After being condemned to four years imprisonment for sodomy in 1557, later commuted to confinement to his own house, the fifty-six-year-old artist dictated his autobiography to an ailing fourteen-year-old boy. Cellini's *Life* has become probably the most widely read book written in Italy during the Renaissance. It is full of prostitutes, criminals, murders, battles and daring escapes. Some of it is made up. For example, Cellini claimed that his family was one of the oldest families in Florence and that the city had been named after one of his ancestors. This is nonsense. But when it comes to sex, he is shockingly frank.

Cellini was first charged with sodomy in 1523. The maximum fine was then thirty gold florins, but Cellini had to pay just twelve measures of flour. He certainly did nothing to hide his admiration for male beauty. He called his fourteen-year-old assistant Paolino "the most honest and best-looking boy I ever saw in my whole life".

"His modest behaviour, together with his extraordinary beauty and his affection for me, bred in me as great a love for him as a man's breast can hold," Cellini wrote. "This passionate love led me often to play to him, so that I could watch his marvellous face, which was usually serious and melancholy, relax. When I took up my cornet, he broke into a smile so honest and sweet that I do not marvel at the fables which the Greeks have written about about the deities."

So Cellini was gay then? No. The following year, he wrote: "As was natural at the age of twenty-nine I had taken on a girl of exceptional beauty and grace, whom I used to draw. I still enjoyed carnal pleasure in my youth... I used frequently to spend the night with her and though I sleep as light as ever did a man upon this earth, after indulging in sexual pleasure, my slumber is sometimes very deep and heavy."

In Naples, he fell for a prostitute named Angelica and he would have taken her back with him to Rome had her mother dropped the price a bit.

He does not seem to have been a jealous lover. Once he gave one of his mistresses called Pantesilea to the painter Bacchiacca, whom he described as "my dearest friend". There may have been more to this than meets the eye as Cellini frequently suffered from venereal diseases, so he may have been trying to nobble a rival.

In 1548, a prostitute named Gambetta accused Cellini of seducing her son Cencio, who was one of the great artist's assistants. This seems to have been a crude blackmail attempt. When Cellini confronted the boy and asked whether he had sinned against him, the boy burst into tears and said no.

It was the young girls he used as nude models that he could not resist. In France, he had a long affair with Caterina, the model for his *Nymph of Fontainebleau*. He was fiercely jealous of her. He even wrote to a friend and fellow Florentine named Pagolo Micceri, asking him to keep an eye on her.

"You know that poor young girl Caterina," Cellini said. "I keep her principally for my art's sake, as I cannot do without a model. But being a man too, I have used her for my pleasures, and it is possible that she may bear me a child. Now I do not want to maintain another man's bastards, nor will I sit down under such an insult. Were I to become aware of it, I believe that I would kill both her and him. So, dear brother, I entreat you to be my helper. Should you see anything, tell me at once, for I am sure to send her, her mother and her lover to their graves."

Micceri swore that he would be vigilant. But, of course, Cellini returned unexpectedly a couple of days later to catch Micceri and Caterina *in flagrante*.

"No sooner had I reached that place than her mother, that French bawd, cried out: 'Pagolo! Caterina! Here is the master!' When I saw the pair, their clothes in disorder, not knowing what they were doing or saying, like people in a trance, it was not difficult to guess what they had been about. The sight drowned reason in rage. I drew my sword and resolved to kill them both."

Caterina fell to her knees and begged for mercy. Micceri made a dash for it. Cellini chased after him but could not catch him.

His anger cooled slightly and he thought it was best to boot Caterina and her mother out, rather than kill them. But they went to see a lawyer. He told them to accuse Cellini of having "used her in the Italian fashion" – that is, sodomized her. At the very least, the lawyer said, Cellini would shell out several hundred ducats to keep them quiet.

But Cellini would not pay up and the matter went to court. Caterina repeated her accusations there. Cellini denied it and told the judge: "If I have consorted with her after the Italian fashion, I have only done the same as you folk of other nations do."

The judge explained: "She means you have improperly abused her."

Cellini said that this, far from being the Italian fashion, must be the French fashion as Caterina plainly knew all about it and he did not. Then he asked Caterina to spell out exactly what he was supposed to go have done with her. She did, in great detail. Cellini asked her to go through the whole thing several times. Then he told the judge: "I know that by the laws of his Most Christian Majesty such crimes are punished by burning at the stake. The woman confesses her guilt, while I admit nothing."

He also demanded that her mother, as go-between or rather, procurer, should be burnt as well.

Cellini threatened that if Caterina and her mother were not punished he would go to the King – who was Cellini's patron at the time – and complain.

"The little hussy and her mother fell to weeping, while I shouted at the judge: 'Fire, fire! To the stake with them!'" Cellini reported.

Case dismissed.

Cellini still needed Caterina as his model. He took his revenge in posing her naked and "keeping her for hours in one position, greatly to her discomfort. This gave her as much annoyance as it gave me pleasure, for she was beautifully made and brought me great credit as a model."

He took on another model, a poor girl of about fifteen who was, again, "beautifully made and of a brunette complexion".

"Now this girl was a clean maid and I got her with child," he said. "She gave birth to a daughter on 7 June, at thirteen hours of the day, in 1544, when I had exactly reached the age of forty-four... This is the first child I ever had, as far as I remember. I settled enough money on the girl for a dowry to satisfy an aunt of hers, under whose tutelage I placed her, and from that time onwards I had nothing more to do with the girl.

He had a son by a model named Dorotea. They stayed together for some time and he had the child legitimized. However, it was his second sodomy charge that hit the headlines. In February 1557, it was alleged that "for about five years he had kept as his apprentice a youth named Fernando di Giovanni da Montepulciano, with whom he had carnal intercourse very many times and committed the crime of sodomy, sleeping in the same bed with him as his wife".

The boy had indeed been in his employ for five years. In 1555, Cellini even drew up a will, leaving him thirty gold florins and thirty *staia* of grain. But the following year, he dismissed the lad and cancelled the bequest. This precipitated the accusations, which came from the boy's family.

Cellini got wind of the accusations and tried to make a run for it. But at Scarperia he was caught and arrested. At his trial, he pleaded guilty. A not-guilty plea inevitably resulted in torture. He was fined fifty *scudi*, permanently deprived of his civil rights and jailed. But the Bishop of Pavia, a friend, lodged an appeal on his behalf.

After fifty-seven days in a filthy prison known as *La Stinche*, he was released and sent home, where he began his *Life*. However, the book is curiously silent on the subject of Fernando di Giovanni da Montepulciano and his time in jail.

7

Worshipping Venus

Titian was the master of the female nude and he was something of a ladies' man, professionally at least. His friend, the bawdy writer Pietro Aretino, wrote of Titian: "What makes me really marvel at him is that, whenever he sees lovely ladies, no matter where he is, he fondles them, makes a to-do of kissing them, and entertains them with a thousand juvenile pranks, but goes no futher."

This is not entirely true. Aretino was not around a lot of the time. By his own admission, he spent so much time in the brothel that it almost killed him. Titian's Venuses were prostitutes, but the great artist took time out to celebrate their naked beauty in his art, as well as using them for their professional pleasures.

As a teenager, Titian was sent from the small town of Cadore in the Piave valley to Venice to study under the Bellini brothers. The city and its women fascinated him. Then the Venetian prostitutes paraded on high platform shoes, so they could be seen above the crowds. Young men slept with nuns. As the fashion of the time was for men to wear women's clothing, the laws of the Serenissima encouraged women, even nuns, to bare their breasts to cut down on gender confusion. Rich men kept concubines. Poorer men, artists included, kept *mamole*. A *mamola* was a housekeeper who fulfilled the conjugal duties of a wife without being bound by a marriage vow.

WORSHIPPING VENUS

The Bellinis dominated painting in Venice at the end of the fifteenth century. Giovanni Bellini was the better painter of the two, but his work was mainly religious or portraiture. But Gentile Bellini had spent time in a Turkish harem when he had been commissioned by the Sultan Mahomet II to paint nudes and erotic scenes for him.

Titian was taught the ways of love by Giorgio da Castelfranco, another student of the Bellinis. Giorgione, as he was known, was just one year older than Titian, but he knew the amorous ways of the city and initiated the small-town boy.

While Titian was away in Padua, Venice was hit by the bubonic plague. Giorgione was found dead in bed with his mistress, the beautiful Cecilia. The rumpled sheets showed that they had been making love in the dying minutes of their lives.

Titian was commissioned to complete the Sleeping Venus, which Giorgione had left unfinished at his death. Titian used it as the prototype for a Venus of his own, the *Venus of Urbino*, which you will see on the jacket of this book. Both show the fingers curled suggestively around the crotch, drawing attention to it and, possibly, pleasuring themselves. But Giorgione's Venus was asleep, while Titian's *Venus*, like all his nudes, was wide awake.

Titian's model for the *Venus of Urbino* was one Violante. She became his mistress. She was also his model in *Sacred and Profane Love*, which shows two women, one clothed, the other naked. Both were Violante.

Titian also had a Cecilia of his own. She had been a servant at his parents' house in Cadore. Titian had persuaded her to model for him. Soon she became pregnant. Titian gave her money. After she had had the child, she became his model for the *Madonna*. He painted her with their second son Orazio suckling at her breast. But her naked figure he kept for his private delectation.

His Venuses and other nudes he found elsewhere. One of his plump and voluptuous nudes was Laura Dianti, mistress of his patron Alfonso d'Este. His sensual *Danaë* was certainly a prostitute. He depicts her lying languorously naked on a rumpled bed with a shower of golden coins descending from the sky.

Titian set up home with Cecilia and, eventually, married her. They had five children. Another model gave him an illegitimate daughter called Emilia. Titian gave her the same dowry, 700 ducats, that he gave his legitimate daughter Lavinia.

In 1527, Aretino settled in Venice and he and Titian became inseparable friends. When Aretino was not in the brothel, he would spend his time lounging around his house naked, surrounded by girls. Once at dinner, Aretino gave Titian an orange. When Titian protested that he had nothing to give the writer in return, Aretino said he needed nothing. He pulled open the top of his mistress the lascivious Angela Zaffetta's dress and said: "Have I not the sun and the moon right here?"

When Cecilia died, Aretino comforted the great artist by bringing the most beautiful courtesans to his house and getting them to strip off, then giving him a guided tour of their best features. Many of them became Titian's models. But Titian did not jump on them straight away, as Aretino did. He liked to savour their naked beauty first. This slow sensual approach to the female nude was what made Aretino suppose that Titian did not fool around. But everyone else assumed that Titian was sleeping with his models.

And he was good to his models. One of his favourites was the courtesan Tullia d'Aragona. In later life, she went on to become a famous poet, got married and moved to Florence. The law there said all courtesans and former courtesan must wear a yellow stripe in their veil. Now a famous artist, Titian accompanied her through the streets of the city and backed her petition to be spared this humiliation. It was granted.

But his greatest comfort was the beautiful Lina, who also posed nude for him. When he asked her to be his Venus a second time, she said he could only paint her back because she was engaged to be married. He laughed and told her that he was old enough to be her father. But she insisted and that is why she adopts such an awkward pose in Titian's *Venus and Adonis*. The marriage fell through and Lina resumed her duties as Titian's model. The sight of her naked body, full frontal, kept him going well into his seventies.

8

Dutch Chaps

Rubens was a student of Titian's and it was in Venice that he learnt to paint his fleshy nudes. But although he was Flemish, he was not uptight about sex.

He may have inherited his liberated attitude from his father Jan Rubens who was financial advisor to the beautiful, blonde, twenty-six-year-old Anne of Saxony whose husband, William of Orange, was away at the time trying to wrest the Netherlands back from the grip of Spain. Anne got pregnant. Jan went to jail.

Or Rubens might have learnt the lax ways in the court of Countess de Lalaing where, as a youth, he was a page. The Countess liked to dress her pages up as girls to entertain her female guests.

When he went to Venice to learn to paint, Rubens indulged himself freely with Italian actresses and prostitutes. He also had an affair with an unnamed aristocratic Roman lady.

But once he had learnt his craft, he forswore hot-blooded Italian women and returned, via Spain, to Antwerp where, in 1609, he married a heavy-looking Flemish girl named Isabella Brant. He was thirty-two; she was eighteen.

She was the daughter of the sister of Marie de Moy, whom Rubens' brother Philip had just married. Her father was the town secretary of Antwerp and an alderman. The wedding could hardly have been more respectable. Except for one thing.

SEX LIVES OF THE GREAT ARTISTS

The epithalamium – a written version of the best man's speech – composed by his brother Philip. It was called *Invocation to Hymen*.

Invocation to Hymen

You, mediator of divine love, we call upon you to this night of my brother's greatest happiness, this night for which he has yearned so ardently, and for his young women whom you have also called. Your virginal impatience is restrained today, but tomorrow you can say that tonight bore you away to a beautiful awakening... But already the god Hymen is impatient to light the nuptial candle, and to penetrate the domestic sanctuary, where the marriage bed can be glimpsed, Venus's arena of gentle struggles... May your wife soon count the days and months, when she rejoices to see her womb grow round and, before the sun with its golden halo has accomplished its annual round, she will swell with pride with a child who resembles her husband.

Amen
.

But after fifteen years of marriage, and five children, Isabella died in the outbreak of plague that hit Antwerp in 1626. Rubens was devastated. In his grief he turned to stoicism. He even banned nude models from his studio for a time.

Nevertheless, he found time to have a year-long affair with Suzanne Fourment, the lush model in his famous painting *Chapeau de Paille*. When Suzanne married another man, the fifty-three-year old Rubens married her buxom sixteen-year-old sister Helena. He abandoned his stoicism and started living the life of a *bon viveur*. Justifying his marriage to such a young girl, he said that he did not look down on pleasure. He simply preferred to indulge in it with God's blessing.

Helena was a real beauty. Her breasts were high and round; her eyes as bright as stars; her neck ivory; her shoulders velvet and "the beauty of her form only surpassed by her charming nature, her spotless simplicity, her innocence and her modesty". She was his favourite model and he gloried in painting her nude. She is often depicted being raped or in sexual rapture and she bore him five children.

His marriage seems to have opened the floodgates. There

was talk that he seduced other models and that he kept a mistress who was a prostitute. But his most frequent sitter was still Suzanne. He painted her no fewer than seven times. Four pictures of her, he kept in his private collection.

Rembrandt was the painter of dark rooms and stout women. He also painted a number of self portraits, which show him to be an ugly cove. He had ears like jug handles, a bulbous nose and coarse, sensual mouth. Nevertheless, three women loved him devotedly.

The first was Saskia van Ulenborch, whom he married in 1631 when he was twenty-four. Her father, the Burgomaster of Leeuwarden, died when she was twelve, leaving her a wealthy woman.

A fashionable artist, Rembrandt took on pupils. One day the great artist found one of his pupils naked with one of the nude models. The pupil said that they were Adam and Eve. So Rembrandt drove them out of the house with the biblical exaltation: " Because you are naked you must get out of Paradise."

After eleven years of marriage, Saskia died. She was just thirty, but worn out by childbearing. She left him with their only surviving son, the infant Titus.

Rembrandt promptly consoled himself with the child's nurse, the widow Geertge Dircx. Saskia's will stipulated that he would lose the income from her estate if he remarried. Nevertheless Rembrandt and Geertge lived together. Geertge helped him out financially and Rembrandt made a bit on the side selling lascivious etchings in the then puritanical Amsterdam. His etching *Het Ledekant* takes a particular pleasure in showing a young couple making love.

Then Rembrandt went and spoiled it all by falling in love with their young serving maid Hendrickje Stoffels. The *ménage à trois* was stormy and Geertge was eventually ousted from the house. She promptly sued the great artist for breach of promise. The Commissions' Book of Disputes of 16 October 1648 in Amsterdam records:

"The plaintiff declares that the defendant made an oral promise to marry her, in token of which he gave her a ring; she said moreover that he slept with her more than once; she requests that she may be married to the defendant, or otherwise be supported by him."

On the other hand:

"The defendant denies having promised to marry the plaintiff, declares that he is under no obligation to admit that he slept with her, and adds that the plaintiff would have to come with proof."

The court found against him and he was ordered to pay her 200 guilders a year, money he could ill afford.

He got his own back by accusing her of promiscuity and stealing some of his wife's jewellery though, in fact, he had given it to her it when they were together. He won the case in 1650 and paid for her transportation to a house of correction in Gouda. She was sentenced to eleven years hard labour, but was released after five and began suing him for unpaid alimony. The situation was only resolved when she died eighteen months later.

Despite his money worries Rembrandt was happy. Hendrickje was younger and prettier that either Saskia or Geertge. He frequently painted her nude and portrayed her as a courtesan, things he had not done with his wife. This caused outrage among the good burgers of Amsterdam. Seven months pregnant with Rembrandt's child Hendrickje was hauled in front of an ecclesiastical court and charged with living in whoredom. The great artist was not a religious man and did not bother to accompany her.

The record shows that she confessed "to fornication with Rembrandt the painter". She was sentenced to penitence and denied communion. However, this was lifted when the child was born so that it could be baptized.

9

Mad About Majas

Goya was mad about *majas* – the young women he saw on the streets of his native Spain. In 1800, he made one famous by painting her in the same pose nude and clothed. But while her beautiful body is remembered, the world has forgotten her name.

In the eighteenth century, French influences dominated Spain. The *majas'* male counterparts, the *majos*, stood as the self-appointed guardians of Spanish virility and tradition. They dressed sprucely, in tight waistcoats and breeches, tied their hair back in a colourful hairnets, affected the walk of gentlemen, but looked blunt and menacing. Eschewing the genteel habit of snuff-taking, they smoked large black cigars and put down those whom they saw as effeminate Frenchified aristocrats with a dry wit.

The *majas* were street women of brazen manner, who usually earned their living as market vendors, maids or fruitsellers. In his book *The Modern State of Spain*, the French ambassador Jean-François Bourgoing described their charms: "Language, attitudes, walk, all have in them a perfect air of effrontery and licentiousness; but if you are not over scrupulous as to the means of exciting voluptuousness, you may find in them the most seductive priestesses that ever attended the altar of Venus; their alluring charms inflame the senses of the wisest, and promise at least pleasure if they do not inspire love."

For Goya, these street women became muses.

In his early career, he seems to have been a run of the mill painter, twice being refused a scholarship to the Academy of San Fernando in Madrid. But in 1771 he took a bold step. He went to Venice to study the work of Titian, Tintoretto and Veronese. After a romantic entanglement with a nun, he headed for Rome to study Raphael and Correggio.

To finance these travels, he worked as a con artist, styling himself the Marquis of d'Aglaita. In partnership with the Sicilian fraudster Giuseppe Balsamo, aka Count Alessandro Cagliostro, Goya put his artistic talents to good use forging bank notes, treasury bonds, wills, letters of recommendation and Rembrandt etchings.

He squandered his money in taverns and brothels. This incited the jealousy of one Otavio Nicastro who reported him to the police. Goya escaped Rome disguised as a monk, leaving Balsamo to face the music. When Balsamo caught up with Goya back in Spain, the great artist, who had established his reputation by then, handed over what remained of their ill-gotten gains in return for Balsamo's silence.

Goya married and settled down. But then, in 1800, he did the most shocking thing. He painted *The Clothed Maja* and *The Nude Maja*, at a time when possessing a nude was forbidden by the Inquisition. The pair were painted for Manuel Godoy, a government minister and sometime lover of Queen Maria Luisa.

Godoy was a collector of nudes, which were kept in a secret room in his palace. His mistress, the Duchess of Alba, had given him the great artist Velázquez's *Venus at the Mirror.*

Great artist though he was, there is little record of Velázquez fooling around, despite a propitious beginning. He was born in Seville which, at the end of the sixteenth century, was renowned as a city of pleasure. The citadel there was known as the School of Love. At the age of nineteen, Velázquez married Juana de Miranda, the daughter of his art teacher, the painter Francisco Pacheo. If he did not fool around, he certainly had a lot of opportunity. At twenty-four, he moved to Madrid as court painter to Philip IV. Although the young king was married, he was a sucker for women and competing ministers kept him well supplied with mistresses. There was more amorous intrigue when the Duke of Buckingham and the Prince of Wales, who went on to become Charles I, turned up to woo the king's sisters. And the court grew even more lively when the king, at forty-four, took as his second wife his fourteen-year-old niece. Working alongside Rubens, Velázquez took a great deal of pleasure in painting the women of the court and, shocking in strict Catholic Spain, nudes.

For a long time it was thought that Goya used the Duchess of Alba herself as the model for the *majas*. Another candidate was Godoy's new mistress the lovely Pepita Tudo, whom he later married. Goya painted her portrait and her face bears a striking similarity to that of the *majas*. But it is very unlikely that Godoy would have allowed either of his mistresses to pose nude for the artist.

At the time the *majas* were painted, it is thought that Goya was staying at the home of the Duchess of Alba at Sanlucar, where there would have been a number of young ladies that he could have sketched nude or scantily clad, lying on an unmade bed.

Whoever *The Nude Maja* was, she was quite a gal. Her pose is brazen, her breasts full and, shocking for the period, she has a full crop of pubic hair. The painting was considered so lascivious that it did not go on public display until 1901, over a hundred years after it was commissioned.

10

The Thinker

We do not know what Auguste Rodin's *The Thinker* is thinking about. But we do know what is passing through the great artist's mind. Like most men he thought of only one thing. Sex. Sex. Sex. He was the first great artist to sketch and sculpt women with their legs open. His work showed women as sexual creatures and specifically depicted their sexual parts.

He loved to touch his models. He could not keep his hands off them. He would bend down and kiss his nude model on her stomach. The dancer Ruth St Denis said that, when she posed for him, she had trouble getting her blouse back on because the great artist was smothering her with kisses "from wrist to shoulder" and muttering endearments. Gladys Deacon, the second wife of the Duke of Marlborough said that he "precipitated himself on every woman he met, hands all over you".

Even the casual visitor would get the same treatment. According to one account, "in the course of a conversation his hands would caress and crush every breast and phallus within reach".

Over 80 per cent of his late drawings of the female figure show the women with their legs spread. His work focused on their genitals. This presented a problem for journalists from family magazines who would arrive at this studio, only to be confronted with his private collection of gynaecological studies or a number of young nude women adopting acrobatic positions.

Women were eager to model for him. His atelier offered the best working conditions in Paris, it was said. Rodin would say: "Don't hurry in taking your clothes off." Then he would watch greedily.

"A woman undressing," he said. "What a glorious sight."

He would get his models to masturbate for him or get naked women in twos or threes to caress each other. Lesbian love was an established theme in nineteenth-century art as, traditionally, men and women did not pose nude together, but women would readily pose nude with other naked women.

His models were not just the working class girls and prostitutes other artists of the period used. Society women would pester him. The Countess Anna de Noailles posed nude for him. Although she was shocked to see drawings of a woman "so shameless as to take her melancholy pleasure in front of him", when he fell on his knees before her, took her by the feet and spread her legs she found it "totally natural".

Even women with their clothes on felt his sexual power. Once he dined at the Monets' home. Monet had four beautiful daughters. Rodin looked at them so intensely that, one by one, they felt obliged to get up and leave the table. Other women would simply offer themselves to him or deliver roses to his door.

Rodin worshipped women. He was very close to his mother, a peasant woman who never learnt to read. He also idolized his sister, Maria, a progressive, educated woman. Their relationship was so close that it could have been misinterpreted. She became a nun rather than marry and died of smallpox in 1862.

In 1864, Rodin employed the eighteen-year-old Rose Beuret as a model.

"She attached herself to me like an animal," he said.

Rodin was awkward and shy as a young man. But he was already adept at persuading pretty young women to take their clothes off, for the sake of art.

"Only the nude is well dressed," he said.

What he loved about Rose, he said, was that she had the firm flesh of a peasant's daughter. She modelled for him, then moved in. By the spring of 1865, she was pregnant. She named her child, naturally, Auguste.

Despite Rodin's countless infidelities, they stayed together until her death in 1917. She even colluded in his affairs. Rose often helped persuade girls to pose nude for him. But although he married Rose just sixteen days before she died, Rodin never recognized her child as his own.

Eighteen sixty-five was a very good year for the nude. Manet's *Olympia* had brought the female nude back into fashion. This was great for Rodin, who modelled himself as a sculptor on Michelangelo, though their other interests were very different.

As well as his model, Rose worked as his studio assistant and willing helper. He had no other female friends. But principally she was a body to him. She would not wear any underclothes so, whenever he sought inspiration, he could throw her dress up over her head and examine her naked figure.

In 1882, he took on a group of students, all of whom were female. Rodin immediately fell in love with one of them, the beautiful and talented Camille Claudel. He was forty-six; she was just eighteen. He called her *ma féroce amie* – my ferocious girlfriend – and his letters to her are tortured.

"You would not believe my suffering," he wrote when she would not see him. "Death would be sweeter... I can't go another day without seeing you. Atrocious madness, it's the end. I won't be able to work any more. Malevolent goddess! And yet I love you furiously." And he begged her to run away with him.

He set her up in a rented house not far from his atelier. She said she did not mind that he maintained another home with Rose, but she drew some savage drawings of a nude Rodin with his shrivelled mistress.

The real problem was that Rodin could not give up fooling around with his other models, no matter how much Camille reproached him. Now he was famous, he could afford the sexual freedom he had been denied when he was younger and he was going to enjoy it. It was rumoured that he had four children by various mistresses.

Nevertheless, his feelings for Camille were intense. When she went to visit a friend in England, he went after her. While he was away, Rose took the opportunity to have a little fling herself.

Returning to Paris, Rodin practically gave up sculpting men and concentrated all his efforts of the female nude. He crammed his atelier with models and filled notebooks with their names and addresses. All his work was done directly from models. His favourites at this time were a couple of Italian sisters, one dark and one blonde. He liked to get them to pose together.

His success as a sculptor allowed him to become what was then called *un érotique* – a collector of interesting women. And it was said that he could not get enough of gazing at the nude bodies of the gloriously beautiful models he employed.

"These lovely creatures with their elite forms could not pass through the ateliers with impunity," wrote the journalist Emile Bergerat, "for beauty cannot 'pose' without being exposed to the love with it inspires."

Even models who were used to the casual demands of the artists they posed for were shocked by the urgency of Rodin's behaviour. Younger and more handsome men were uncomfortably aware of him as a rival.

"I met a charming little model on the Boulevard St Germain," relates poet and novelist Pierre Louÿs. "She became my mistress and moved in with me. She never left my side and went with me everywhere. I was just becoming seriously attached to her when, one night, she disappeared. First I was worried, then irritated, then angry at her unexplained departure."

Louÿs asked around, but no one had any news of her. Then he dropped by at his old friend Rodin's atelier.

"When I entered the studio, I let out a scream. There before my very eyes was my little mistress, posing completely nude, hiding her face behind her arms. I made a terrible scene. She burst into tears."

Louÿs insisted on taking her home with him, but Rodin would not let her go. There was a row. Louÿs was furious that Rodin had kept her away for a week.

"Why didn't you let her come back to me?" he asked the sculptor.

"I knew you would be jealous and would have kept her with you," he said.

"But, good God, she is mine."

"That's precisely the reason," said Rodin.

Then Louÿs saw the figure that Rodin had been working on.

"Her image, already alive, was rising out of the clay," he recalled. And his anger subsided.

Rodin asked him to understand.

"If you were in my place you would have done the same thing," he said. "This little girl whom I met at your apartment, she has a magnificent, unique body. She is indispensable to me."

Louÿs grudgingly accepted defeat and said goodbye to his model. Rodin smothered the nude girl in kisses and said with joy: "You are going to stay with me. Pierre has given his consent."

Around this time, Rodin sculpted the *Crouching Woman* also known as the "Frog". It shows a woman squatting, with her legs parted and her sexual organs openly displayed. The model, Adèle Abruzzezzi, had plainly established more than a rapport with the artist. Rodin frequently said that suggestions for the pose came from the models themselves. However, many critics say that, although Rodin may have been looking at Adèle Abruzzezzi with her legs open while he was working, he was thinking of Camille.

Of course, Rodin would not have had Camille strutting brazenly around his atelier or squatting like Adèle, but he frequently sculpted her face. She appeared as *Dawn, Thought, France* and *St George*. At one time, he promised to keep her as his only student. He was so desperately in love that he even promised to stop sleeping with his models. But the one model he would not give up was Rose. So Camille left him. She went on to have an affair with the great composer Claude Debussy and became a celebrated sculptor in her own right. Her theme was the same as Rodin's. She worked from nude models and when one critic saw her sculpture of a group of waltzing couples, he said: "They seem to want to finish the dance so they can go to bed and make love."

But Rodin did not forgive Camille for leaving him. When she wanted a sculpture cast in bronze at the state's expense, Rodin opposed it. The plaster model had been exhibited at the spring Salon. It showed a naked man walking into the open arms of death, while a young woman implores him not to go. Rodin, as the premier sculptor in France, got his way and the bronze was never cast.

The critic Octave Mirbeau told the writer Edmond de Goncourt that Rodin was capable of anything, committing "a crime, if it was for a woman". Rodin, he said, was "the beast of a satyr that you see in his erotic sculptures". The truth was that Rodin was a workaholic as well as a satyr. Both in his work and in his private life he found it impossible to say no.

After breaking with Camille he took up with the painter Hélène Porgès Wahl, wife of Albert Wahl, the chief engineer of the French navy. They shared models and he opened his heart to her.

"The tyranny of passion seems to be passing," he said of his parting from Camille. "It is not that I love women less than before, but I love them differently. Lastly, I can call you my divine sisters and admire you for the delicacy of forms in which you have been made. In body and heart, the Great Founder who made us all endowed you with a better patina than he did us."

Rodin explicitly expressed his relationship with his models in *The Sculptor and his Muse*, which shows the sculptor's head enwrapped in the naked muse's hair. The muse is also holding the sculptor's penis. He may have developed some of these ideas from his friend, the great writer Victor Hugo to whom a woman's breasts, thighs or better still "*la forêt*" were sources of inspiration. To Rodin, it was "the Eternal Tunnel". Rodin paid tribute to this with his figure *Iris*. Originally intended for the

Monument to Victor Hugo, it shows a headless Iris, the messenger of the Gods, with her legs spread. According to Rodin's preliminary sketches, her crotch was supposed to appear directly over the poet's head. After all, Rodin said, a man's desire for women was "willed by God and, after Him, the strongest thing there is in the world".

Seeing *Iris*, his assistant Jean Alexandre Pézieux said: "He's never made a woman like this before, it's wonderful. And it's only a beginning... he's so dominated by his prick, the brute."

At the height of his fame, Rodin was pursued by a posse of attractive women – the English artist Emilia Cimino, Malvina Hoffman, Ernestine Weiss, Judith Cladel, Sarah Hallowell and Loe Fuller, star of the Folies-Bergère.

Young Polish émigré Sophie Postolska wrote begging to model for him. She was an aspiring artist herself, but was happy to disrobe for him, provided that they were "alone". For three years, they had an intense affair. Friends disapproved, saying that she was only trying to further her own ambitions by being intimate with the great artist. But she became obsessed and fiercely jealous of all the women who threw themselves at him. She even attempted suicide, before moving to Austria.

In his sixties, Rodin exhibited the sexually explicit *Gates of Hell*. One critic said this was "an audacious exhibition of marbles and bronzes seemed to have escaped from the private collection of the Marquis de Sade". Others praised him for rescuing the nude from cold academia and giving it voluptuousness and passion. He had, they said, "discovered the eternal Venus in every woman".

In 1900, Rodin met Sophie von Hindenberg, daughter of the German ambassador, and her twenty-three-year-old Helene von Hindenburg. He travelled to Italy with them. Although Helene was thirty-eight years his junior, he plied her with flowers and they spent a lot of time alone together. Their letters speak of an intense passion.

"God is too great to send us direct inspiration. He speaks to our weakness and sends us earthly angels," he wrote. "For the artist, a soft woman is the most powerful message. She is holy.

THE THINKER

She rises in our heart, our genius and our potency. She is the divine sower who sows love in our hearts so we can return it a hundred-fold in our work."

This passionate correspondence continued even after she married. He wrote of the struggle between suffering and voluptuousness and called her his muse. He had already shown the world what a muse was supposed to do.

After the turn of the century, Rodin could afford to keep on a number of models – Suzie Langlois, Renée Couchet, Yvonne Odero, Fenella Lovell, Carmen Damedoz, Dourga le Hindu, Nora Falk, Maguerite de Fontenay, Julia Benson and Juliette Toulmonde. He paid them well and looked after them when they got into trouble.

"He draws them by day and cuddles them by night," the novelist Emile Zola remarked, "though the term cuddle is too mild."

He would heap praise on their naked beauty, "caressing them with his eyes and sometimes with his hand". He would kiss them and fondle them and make drawings of them for his private delectation. It was an effort, he said, to understand "female sexuality". Critics noted that the principle of Rodin's work was sex – "sex so conscious of itself that it finds a desperate energy to attain the impossible". The bodies he portrayed, it was said, were "agitated either by the memory of sensual pleasure or its anticipation". The central pivot of his female nudes was their sex.

He found that young athletic girls could perform the kind of modelling he required best. They often seemed to enjoy it. Some people, including the writer Anatole France, condemned his fascination with the female sexual organs as obsessional. Others were riveted by his drawings of naked women touching each other. He drawings are full of longing and he was the first artist to make women's sexuality important. Until then the female nude had been sexless and passive. And his models did what they did, not just for the money, but because of his sexual charisma.

Augustus John's sister Gwen fell completely under his spell.

She gave up England, her family, her art, everything to model for him. She thought his models should be intelligent as well as beautiful. He would make love to her after the posing sessions and the other assistants were gone. In her letters, she recorded her blissful sexual awaking at his hands. Soon she saw herself as his muse.

They sometimes had a threesome with Finnish sculptress Hilda Flodin, but it was Gwen who fell in love with him. Even when she was completely worn out, she begged for him to make love to her some more. Soon she was getting thin, too thin for him to model. But, she complained: "I rarely have time to eat".

Another of his models, Judith Cladel, dismissed Gwen as one more of the "hysterical models" who surrounded the master because of his rapacious sexuality. Making love for Gwen was an act of worship. But he had other altars to pray at. Too much lovemaking, he warned her, turned people into brutal animals. And he insisted that she begin painting again. Soon he was visiting her for just an hour or so, once a week.

He missed out with the young Isadora Duncan though, when the dancer found herself in awe of his work and sought him out.

"My pilgrimage to Rodin resembled that of Psyche seeking the God Pan in his grotto," she wrote in her memoirs, "only I was not asking the way to Eros but to Apollo."

She was very impressed when he took two small lumps of clays and pressed them in his palms. He breathed hard and heat steamed off him. Then in two shakes of a duck's tail he had modelled a pair of tits.

As she explained her theory of the new dance, she realized that the old goat was not listening.

"He gazed at me with lowered lids, his eyes blazing," she wrote, "and then, with the same expression that he had before his works, he came toward me. He ran his hands over my neck, my breast, stroked my arms and ran his hands over my hips, my bare legs and feet. He began to knead my whole body as if it were clay, while his emanated heat scorched and melted me. My whole desire was to yield to him my entire being and, indeed, I would have done so if it had not been that my absurd upbringing caused me to become frightened and I withdrew, threw on my dress over my tunic and sent him away bewildered. What a pity! How often have I regretted this childish miscomprehension which lost me the divine chance of giving my virginity to the Great God Pan himself, to the Mighty Rodin. Surely Art and all Life would have been richer thereby."

When Rodin travelled to London in 1904, he could not stay at any of the posh hotels, but rather a seedy joint in Jermyn Street. This was because of the hordes of ladies who came to see him who did not want to give their names.

Although feminists attacked him, even they saw that he did not depict women as prey, but rather individuals with desires of their own, both animal and noble at the same time. Rodin, it was argued, made women feel more comfortable about their bodies. He celebrated their physical and emotional reality.

However, Rodin was not comfortable in women's company. Not when they had their clothes on at least. And still the offers kept coming. Isabelle Perronnet, the mistress and model of Robin's rival Alexandre Falguière, wrote to Rodin the day after Falguière's funeral, asking for a position. Rodin took her on and her clothes off.

Women pursued him at every turn. He got a letter from nineteen-year-old Minna Schrader de Nygot, saying that she had lost her parents and would soon be reduced to prostitution or suicide. She offered to model for him, explaining that she had never done such a thing before but "I am put together in a manner more or less digestible. My chest is even quite nice."

Rodin took a look for himself, agreed and took her on. But he turned others down. His biographer Judith Cladel longed to be "immortalized in the fragile human flesh that I am" again. But, frankly, she did not match up to the vision of young fresh female beauty that Rodin idolized.

At the age of seventy, Rodin fell in love again. The woman in question was Claire Coudert, Marquise de Choiseul. She was an American of French extraction, in her forties and the wife of the Marquis de Choiseul, from whom Rodin was buying some seventeenth-century busts. Claire was soon writing billet doux, signing herself "your little wife". The affair drove Gwen John into paroxysms of jealousy. Rose Beuret was not pleased either, especially when Claire's husband wrote to her, saying: "Madame, it is unendurable that you tolerate the state of things that I can no longer bear. I refer to the constant presence of my wife in the atelier of Monsieur Rodin."

Out of deference to Rose, Rodin stopped seeing Claire. But when he got a note from her maid saying she was not eating and was in "a terrible state", he relented. They spent the Christmas of 1908 together in Dijon. The Marquis was good enough to send a Christmas card.

Despite the Marquis's title, he did not have any money. Rodin helped him out financially, in exchange for open access to his wife. On his own initiative the Marquis elevated himself to Duc, and Rodin continued his relationship with the Duchesse. Claire busied herself selling his work to rich Americans, while he modelled her bust. She installed herself in his life to the exclusion of other acquaintances. Rodin soon grew unhappy with the situation. She shared his life like no other woman had, decorating his house, selecting his clothes, travelling with him and mixing in Parisian society.

At the prompting of the Duchesse, Rodin turned out for the première of Debussy's *L'Après-midi d'un faune*, where Nijinsky in spotted tights pursued nymphs around the stage who wore nothing under their flimsy tunics, and got himself caught up in the controversy it spawned. Soon he was ridiculed in the newspapers. One cartoon depicted him sketching one nude girl sprawled across a bed while another naked nymphet asks: "Where can I put my togs?"

Rodin and his Duchesse rowed over a third woman, Marcelle Martin, Rodin's secretary whom the Duchesse herself had hired. Marcelle was fired, but Rodin decided to rid himself of the Duchesse as well. Friends thought that she had for too long dominated his life and, to pay for her extravagance his work, had become unaffordable.

Rodin went to Brussels, leaving a friend to get his keys back from the Duchesse. Distraught, she fled to Brittany to stay with the Comte de la Belinaye.

She wrote, complaining: "My suffering is beyond endurance."

Rodin's response was the promise of a monthly payment of a thousand francs, although his correspondence shows that he never stopped loving her.

In the last year of Rodin's life, the great artist suffered a stroke. It affected his memory. One day he was sitting with Rose Beuret and he asked: "Where's my wife?"

"I am here," said Rose. "Aren't I your wife?"

"Yes," said Rodin. "But I meant my wife in Paris – has she any money?"

It is generally thought that it was not the Duchesse Rodin was talking about but Camille Claudel. But by this time, Camille was in an insane asylum. In 1913, she had smashed up her studio, destroying much of her remaining work. She had to be forcibly removed. Rodin tried to a visit her in the asylum but was refused admittance. She remained there for the next thirty years, until her death in 1943.

Before he died in 1917, Rodin remarked to a friend: "People say I think too much about women. Yet, what is there more important to think about."

11

The Dirty Diaries of Delacroix

Eugène Delacroix was a prodigious and frank diarist. He was also the greatest painter of the Romantic era. There is certainly a good deal of romance surrounding the circumstances of his birth.

According to the *Journals* of the Goncourt brothers: "There is an old woman going around, who says that Delacroix [*père*], Minister of Foreign Affairs during the Revolution, begged Talleyrand to give his wife a genius as a child, that Talleyrand graciously consented and as a result Eugène Delacroix was born."

The truth was that Charles Delacroix, the great artist's father, had an enormous growth on one of his testicles which had made him impotent for years. On 12 November 1797, after a series of five operations undertaken without an anaesthetic, it was removed and his sex life resumed. By then though, his wife was already two-and-a-half months pregnant.

Fortunately, Charles Delacroix was not around when the baby was born. Talleyrand, a former bishop and formidable womanizer, had taken over at the Foreign Ministry and posted Delacroix senior to an obscure part of Holland.

Delacroix *père* was also away when the official organ of the Revolution, *Le Moniteur*, of 24 Germinal, year six of the Revolutionary calendar, carried a story about the operation on his balls. The story said that it had taken place on 27 Fructidor (14 September 1797) and that the success of the operation had been confirmed by the birth of Ferninand-Victor-Eugène Delacroix on 7 Floréal (26 April 1798). Had the date of the operation given by the newspaper been true, it would have been just about possible for the diplomat Charles Delacroix to be the father of the great painter. As it was, no one was fooled and the rumour that Talleyrand was Delacroix's father was widespread in his lifetime.

Nevertheless Delacroix was proud of his nominal father. He boasted in his diary that, after the fourth of the five operations on his balls his father had treated the surgical team to lunch and, over the hors d'œurve, said: "Well gentlemen, that's Act Four over... Let us hope that the fifth will not end in tragedy."

It seems his Uncle Riesener told him that story. Uncle Riesener's wife, incidentally, had once been a lover of Napoleon's.

Delacroix certainly did not look like his brothers and sister. They were chubby and bovine. He was slim, delicate and handsome. At school, he took a stab at writing a Romantic novel. It had the regular quota of maidens, mistresses, bastard children and transvestism for the period.

Although he gave up literature for art, he continued to write. In *A Sentimental Journey through France and Italy*, he declared his love for "Eliza", a married woman named Elizabeth Draper. His letters also tell of the seduction of his sister Henriette's English maid, Elisabeth Salter. One day, while his sister was out shopping, he had laid his head on Elisabeth's breast, only to be interrupted by a knock on the door. The "friend of virtue" who knocked on the door was his sister. He did not open it.

"It is foolish to be disappointed when you come to a door that people are making love behind," he wrote. "But what the hell. People must make love and later for killjoys."

Another of Henriette's maids, he noted, had a backside "worthy of drawing the goddess Diana's chariot".

Then on 3 September 1822, he began his famous *Journal*. It begins promisingly enough with a flirtation with his brother's maid Lisette, whom he managed to kiss in a dark passage that ran through the house.

The models who posed nude for him were more forthcoming. On 15 October, he "risked syphilis" with a girl called Marie who sat for him.

"I saw Sidonia [one of his models of *The Massacre at Scio*], last Tuesday," he wrote on 15 April 1823. "What ravishing moments! How lovely she looked lying naked on the bed. It was mostly lovemaking and kisses. She is coming back on Monday."

He still pursued housemaids though. Young Fanny let him kiss her again and again. She did not try to push him away and only said she was afraid of being seen. Ought he to have gone further? He kicked himself for not trying it on.

Then there is Madame de Puysegur's maid, whose well developed figure he could not get out of his mind. One day he saw her with another maid. He wanted them both. Again he chided himself for not seizing the opportunity to have two housemaids at once.

Then, on 7 April 1824, tragedy struck. Suddenly his dirty diaries became droopy diaries.

"This morning, Hélène came," he records. "Oh, for shame, I could do nothing."

On 1 June, he visited Dr Bailly to consult him about his impotence. The good doctor could do nothing. The problem was in his soul and he knew it.

"The chaste sisters have been more harmful to you than courtesans; the perfidious delights they offer, more illusory than the pleasures of the flesh," he tells himself. "Your soul has crippled your understanding and your lack of youthfulness at twenty-five years old, your ardour that has no strength to support it."

His impotence was caused by the fact that he was tortured with guilt. The year before, his friend the painter Charles Soulier asked him to pop around and see that his mistress was okay. Naturally, Delacroix beds Darling J., "*la cara*". He tried to break it off and wrote a letter to her ending the affair, but he could not quite bring himself to send it.

THE DIRTY DIARIES OF DELACROIX

He need not have worried. There were always models and working girls. By 14 June, he complains: "I need a mistress to keep my flesh in proper subjection."

Thankfully, Laure was due the next day.

On 19 June, he notes: "Great want of sex. I am utterly abandoned." And he begged his mistress, "the loveliest of women", to see him Thursday. It was so difficult to concentrate when he was painting naked thighs.

Delacroix indulged himself, in true Romantic fashion, with his working-class models and took on a mistress in the form of Madame Eugénie Dalton, "*la bonne petite amie de la rue Godet*", who invited him round to dinner and to bed. And by April 1830, he was so well restored that his friend, the writer Prosper Mérimée, reported his behaviour at a sex orgy as frantic.

Love was taking its toll though.

"The life of lovers, especially when the lover loves two or three women, tends to take up all his energy," he wrote. And love is expensive. He had trouble finding the money to keep it up.

In 1832, Delacroix went to Morocco where he fell for a Scottish girl called Miss Drummond-Hay, was excited by belly dancing, had his first experience of hashish and went to a Jewish wedding in Tangiers and a brothel in Algiers.

Back in Paris, entirely refreshed, he fell for Joséphine de Forget, the daughter of a count. She toyed with him.

"There's a lot of pleasure to be had from flirting," he noted. But he had his usual fallback. "As for Madame Dalton, I find myself in the usual situation, except that there's a greater sense of reality and excitement."

Occasionally, Delacroix had to break off from Madame Dalton – that is, whenever her husband turned up. Even then, she made no effort to be faithful. Once Delacroix foolishly asked Soulier to convey a kiss to her and his friend got him back for his dalliance with Darling J.

Joséphine de Forget was a much more serious prospect though. She had been married at the age of fifteen. By the time

Delacroix met her, she had two children and was separated from her husband. After the initial flirting, they became lovers. And for years, they poured out their great love in a series of torrid love letters. They could not live together, but had sex at least twice a week. They were often seen together at the same salons. Otherwise he was discreet. There are very few mentions of Joséphine in his *Journal*.

At the same time, Jenny Le Guillou moved in with Delacroix, first as his maid, then as his model, then as his mistress. She displaced Madame Dalton when she moved into his bed. Madame Dalton had put in ten years service as Delacroix's mistress. Now surplus to requirements, she emigrated to Algeria and took up painting.

Jenny probably had an illegitimate child by Delacroix. But the artist could not give up fooling around with his nude models. And his affair with Joséphine de Forget was still going on.

"Jenny loved a lot and must have forgiven a lot," wrote a friend.

In 1839, Delacroix let a young pupil, Elise Boulanger, drag him off to Holland ostensibly to study Rubens' nudes, but he did not inform his other mistresses of the trip. They split up in Antwerp. Three years later, she wrote to him telling that she had "decided, to punish you, not to write to you that I love you". He did not respond.

He moved house to be near to Joséphine in the fashionable rue de Notre-Dame-de-Lorette. It was also handy for another lover, the voracious transvestite writer Georges Sand. He later painted Sand with her new beau the great composer Frederic Chopin.

Delacroix also took a little cottage outside Paris at Champrosay, where he would entertain attractive young women. Joséphine became suspicious about the amount of time he spent down there. Suspicions turned to jealousy. However, they never broke off their relationship completely and their passionate affair cooled into an abiding friendship – as did his relationships with all his women. So the dirty diaries became dreary diaries.

THE DIRTY DIARIES OF DELACROIX

"Without doubt," wrote the great writer Charles Baudelaire, "he loved women very much in the agitated days of his youth. But long before his death, he had excluded women from his life. Like a Muslim, he would not have chased them from his mosque, but he would have been astonished to see them enter, unable to understand what sort of communication they could have had with Allah."

12
Manet the Man

In 1865, Édouard Manet outraged Paris with two nudes. One, *Olympia*, was a picture of a courtesan looking brazenly out at the viewer as if the spectator were her customer. The other, Le *Déjeuner sur l'herbe* shows a naked woman picnicking with two clothed maleartists. Again she looks brazenly at the viewer. It was his nudes' lack of modesty that made them revolutionary. But Manet came from a deeply conservative background. He was the son of a long line of landowners. What turned him into a rebel in a frock coat? The answer, as usual, is in his sex life.

As a youth, he travelled to Brazil and was very impressed by the fact that the black women there went about naked to the waist. He notably used a black serving woman in *Olympia* – the one Gauguin sought out.

In 1850, at the age of eighteen, Manet began studying under Thomas Couture, who thoughtfully supplied his students with nude models. Then Manet longed to get the nudes out of the studio and, if not into the street, at least into the countryside.

He also began studying the piano. His music teacher was Suzanne Leenhoff, the daughter of the organist of Groove Kerk, the Gothic cathedral at Zaltbommel. She had left her family and moved to Paris on the advice of the great composer Franz Liszt. Both her sisters married artists. She was no great beauty, slightly overweight and looked older than her nineteen years – Manet portrayed her ample figure nude in *The Surprised Nymph*.

MANET THE MAN

As a student, Manet was totally dependent on his father's money. He could not afford prostitutes. But his father was paying for the piano teacher anyway. She was lonely and compliant, so much so that Manet's father Auguste dallied with her too. Well, he was paying the bills.

Manet was a diligent student and, on 29 January 1852, Suzanne gave birth to a son. The child could not be acknowledged, but Manet was registered as the godfather on his baptismal certificate. Manet and Suzanne married ten years later.

By that time, Manet had fallen under the influence of Baudelaire and painted his syphilitic mistress Jeanne Duval. Syphilis was rife largely because, during the mid-nineteenth century, Paris was awash with prostitutes. The trade was tightly regulated though. There were stringent laws against unregistered practitioners, who were fined and jailed. Nevertheless, unregistered *filles de boulevard* worked out of furnished rooms under false names and were organized by pimps. Below them in the pecking order were the *filles de cité*. They were the very dregs.

Registered girls were confined to *maisons closes*, first floor brothels who windows were sealed. *Filles de maison* either worked as *filles d'amour*, working just for their food and board, but they were allowed to keep what they made on their day off. Or they became *pensionnaires* and got a share of the house's take. Otherwise, four or five young "Arthurs" – nineteenth-century Paris's version of today's "Johns" – got together to support a *lorette*, the illegitimate daughter of a bourgeois family who they would use for their entertainment. Only the very best lorettes aspired to become one of the *grandes horizontales*.

However, unlike in London, medical inspection of Parisian prostitutes was lax. This led to an epidemic of syphilis. It did not matter to the girls much. They would almost certainly die of tuberculosis first, long before their syphilis had reached its third and final stage. Their clients did not much mind either. Having the pox was seen as a badge of virility. A popular student song of the day had the joyful refrain: "Who gives a damn about getting the pox, as long as you get laid."

Vulcanized rubber condoms were sold in brothels, but they were not used consistently. In 1857, Manet's father suffered a stroke, probably caused by syphilis. Baudelaire died of it and Manet himself suffered from the wretched disease.

Manet's model for *Olympia* and *Déjeuner sur l'herbe* was Victorine Meurent. Her unashamed nudity and her unabashed gaze picked her out from other women. She was certainly the antithesis of his wife Suzanne in *The Surprised Nymph*. Manet clearly doted on her. While other artists portrayed prostitutes as Eve, Venus or other figures from mythology, Manet painted Victorine as a real woman. In *Portrait of Victorine Meurent*, he even went to the trouble of identifying her. To heighten the effect of her nudity, he put her with two clothed male figures in *Déjeuner sur l'herbe* and put a ribbon around her neck, a bracelet on her arm and a silk mule on one of her feet in *Olympia*. The pose of *Olympia* is borrowed, of course, from Titian's *Venus of Urbino* and is clearly influenced by Goya's *Naked Maja*.

The name *Olympia* came from Olympia Maldachini, mistress of Pope Innocent X. She had already been immortalized in paint by Velázquez.

Manet first saw Victorine model in Thomas Couture's studio, but met her later in a dance hall and got her to pose for him in his own studio. By then, he was safely married and would have been expected to take a mistress. More than likely, Victorine did the honours. Manet certainly did not fancy Suzanne any more and had taken to portraying his wife as a shapeless mass. He married her out of duty, rather than love. He also took the precaution of marrying Suzanne in a Protestant church in Holland. So technically Manet, a Catholic, would not have been considered married in France.

Although he never became a bohemian, Manet adopted many of Victorine's lower-class mannerisms. He listened to her comments on his paintings. She knew the art world well, having posed for other artists previously and taken some of them as her lovers. When she gave up modelling in 1876, she began to paint and was certainly not without talent. But it was as a model she had the greatest effect on the history of art.

When *Olympia* and *Le Déjeuner sur l'herbe* were exhibited in 1865, they were mocked by the critics, condemned by the public and denounced by the very men who used courtesans. But the art world closed ranks behind Manet, recognizing these paintings for the masterpieces they were. By that time, Manet himself was already suffering badly from the effects of syphilis and, having watched his father die of the disease, was witnessing Baudelaire go through a similar terminal decline.

Manet took on two young female pupils Edna and Berthe Morisot, who also modelled for her. There seems to have been a particularly close relationship between Manet and the attractive Berthe. She posed for *The Repose*. This was a revolutionary painting too. It was not done then to portray respectable young women reclining. He also painted *Berthe Morisot with a Black Hat and Violets* at a time when violets were a symbol of love. The violets were tucked in her open bodice and seemed to indicate that something was going on between them. Just exactly what it was we cannot be sure of as much of the correspondence between Berthe and her sister Edna has been lost. The letters that survive expressed her unrestrained joy in Manet's presence and they instruct the reader to burn them like the others.

Later, when he took on a new younger student Eva Gonzales and began to paint her instead, Berthe grew jealous and became anorexic. Eventually, Berthe married Manet's feckless brother Eugène. This allowed her to hang around the great artist's studio without raising eyebrows and she signed herself "Madame E. Manet" – as she would if she had married Édouard.

During the Franco-Prussian War, Manet sent his wife and son out of Paris to safety at Oloron-Sainte-Marie. Even though Paris soon found itself under siege, Manet, like many of the other grass widowers left behind, went out on the town.

He sent Eva out of town too. In his letters to Eva, he often mentions his wife. But in his letters to his wife, he never mentions Eva. He also complained of pains in his legs and ulcers on the foot caused by his syphilis. Although he went to the doctor often, in those days, little could be done.

SEX LIVES OF THE GREAT ARTISTS

Manet began attending the salon of Méry Laurent, who was known to all as the lover of the poet Stéphane Mallarmé. At that time, the salons of courtesans were glittering affairs. Méry was not a fabulously wealthy courtesan like Païva or Cora Pearl, but she did have an income of over 100,000 francs a year provided by an American dentist called Dr Evans, another principal lover and smaller gifts from others. Manet became a permanent fixture and occasional lover.

Evans was famous as the man who proposed to Napoleon III the building of a new broad avenue in the Bois du Boulogne where society ladies and the mistresses of their husbands would parade, while gentlemen on horseback could pick out new lovers. The Avenue Thomas W. Evans was named after him. Despite this distinction, Dr Evans was a little put out to find that Méry was entertaining the great artist Édouard Manet behind his back.

Manet was drawn more into the demimonde of courtesans. He used a number of them as his models, including Louise Valtesse, Comtesse de la Bigne, who was one of the models for the central character in *Nana*, Emile Zola's book on the demimonde. But Manet did not look down on prostitutes as Zola did. There is nothing in his portrait of Louise Valtesse to suggest what she did for a living.

Manet's self portraits were another matter. The symptoms of syphilis were plaguing him to the extent that, he began portraying himself as a corpse.

His interest in life was briefly renewed by a new model, Isabelle Lemonnier. He painted her six times in 1879 alone. But the progress of the disease was inexorable.

For five months he suffered "torture" in a clinic in Bellevue, confiding details to his friend, the great writer Marcel Proust. But the treatment proved useless. Death came in 1883. For the next seven years, the first white lilacs of the season appeared on Manet's grave. They were put there by Méry Laurent, who had become increasingly devoted to him in his later years.

Asked why she did not leave Dr Evans, especially when the income he endowed on her was secure, she told the English writer George Moore: "That would be ignoble. It is enough that I deceived him."

"Is there one of her many lovers," Moore asked after her death in 1900, "who forgoes an idle hour to lay flowers on her grave?"

13
The Wrong Impressionists

The Impressionist painters suffered from bad eyesight. You can see it clearly from their paintings. And we all know it makes you go blind.

Pierre Auguste Renoir was extremely prudish in old age, but he had been a bit of a lad when he was young. His first love seems to have been a girl called Berthe from Picardy, who had come to Paris to be a housekeeper for a relative. When that proved to be no fun, she let an old gentleman install her in an apartment.

This left her with plenty of money and time on her hands. She took the penniless painter to a glittering ball. In exchange, he took her to the woods at Meudon where she effortlessly robbed him of his virginity. Soon they were doing it back at her apartment. In later years, he would reminisce about the excitement of hiding in the wardrobe when her old gentleman came round.

His advice to his son, the film-maker Jean Renoir, was to play around as much as possible when he was young. The danger of syphilis added piquancy to sex. Any cure would "take the fun out of the fast life," he said.

"It's not much fun to spend a night with a whore," he told Jean. "The best part is what leads up to it. Later, it's ghastly. But there's always the risk. It's the risk that adds spice to the affair."

THE WRONG IMPRESSIONISTS

Renoir loved the girls from Les Halles, especially as they had not succumbed to the prudery spreading from England and still let their breast show above their bodices.

One particularly attracted him, a forceful Spanish girl. After he had sex with her, he went straight around to see a doctor, who was a friend of his sister, Lisa.

"Your sister tells me you are a great painter," said the doctor when he examined Renoir. "A great many geniuses have been syphilitic. Perhaps I ought to wish you had caught the disease."

Instead, he gave him a clean bill of health. So Renoir went straight back to his Spanish lady. When he could not afford to pay her for sex, she persuaded him to paint her. Soon after, he quit his job and began painting full time.

Although Renoir painted a number of bouncy nudes, he claimed that he avoided sex with his models and felt sorry for libidinous men who were always chasing women.

"On duty day and night, what a job," he told his son. "I've known painters who never did any good work because, instead of painting their models, they seduced them."

This is disingenuous. In later life, he told the great artist Modigliani: "You must paint with joy, the joy with which you make love to a woman. Before I paint, I caress the buttocks for hours…"

One of his models was Suzanne Valadon, who had worked as a prostitute before she got a job bare back riding in the circus. With the other girls, she put on special shows where the girls went bare backed as well as the horse in a nude spectacular for a specially invited audience. She posed nude for Renoir and became his mistress. Her son was the painter Maurice Utrillo. She went on to become a lover of Toulouse-Lautrec, companion of Degas and a famous painter in her own right, particularly renowned for her rendition of female nudes. She set up home with her favourite male nude model, André Utter, but domestic conflict between Utter and her son pushed Utrillo into his slow descent into alcoholism.

From 1865 to 1872, Renoir lived with his model Lise Tréhot. Then in 1881, at the age of forty, he met Aline Charigot.

She was just nineteen. He advised her that, with her looks, she should find herself a rich man. But she loved to pose for him. Naturally, he painted her as Venus. Her mother heartily disapproved. She did not want her daughter throwing herself away on a penniless painter. The lovers parted. Renoir went to Algiers. Aline tried to forget him, but failed. When he returned to Paris, she was waiting for him at the station. They married and were to remain together for the rest of their lives.

A great artist who shared Renoir's love of the theme of nude bathers was Paul Cézanne. Having bathed nude with friends as a child near his home in Aix, he hankered to recreate the sensation, but living out in the countryside models were hard to come by. Besides, he was scared of naked women.

"I paint still lives," he told Renoir. "Women models frighten me. You have to be on the defensive the whole time."

One woman who would model for him was Marie-Hortense Fiquet, a lively young Parisian bookbinder ten years his junior. They met when he was thirty. He overcame his fear of women enough to take her as his mistress. They had a son. But his conservative provincial family deeply disapproved of the relationship.

They disapproved even more when, in in 1885, at the age of forty-six, he suddenly fell in love with a serving girl called Fanny. She was a strapping lass who could lift a wine cask and was said to be "just like a man". He wrote her a fevered love letter and gave her a painting. When his family found out, she was sacked.

Cézanne was so distraught that he ran away to Gardanne, a small town five miles from Aix, where he comforted himself in the brothel. This convinced his family that it was high time he married. Even though they disliked Hortense, who had been his mistress for over sixteen years, there was no one else to hand. So on 26 April 1886, they married.

But they spent little time together. While Hortense and their son established themselves in Paris, Cézanne remained in Aix, where he concentrated on landscapes. However, it is said, that he "married his hills to the curves of women".

THE WRONG IMPRESSIONISTS

Camille Pissarro fell for his mother's maid, Julie Vellay. Not only was she from the wrong class, she was not Jewish. She fell pregnant, but miscarried. His family cut off his allowance and they were forced to live in his studio together. They had a son in 1863 and a daughter in 1865, but they did not bother to get married until 1870, by which time they had been together for twelve years and she was about to give birth to their third child.

Like Pissarro, the English Impressionist Alfred Sisley married his long-standing mistress and mother of his children. His wife Eugénie Lescouezec had come to him as a model and, when she got pregnant, moved in. Thirty years – and two children – later they married. Interestingly, in his early masterpiece *The Engaged Couple*, Renoir depicts Seurat with his own mistress Lise Tréhot.

Georges Seurat had a mistress named Madeleine Knobloch, who bore him a son. But her existence remained unknown even to his intimate friends until after his death. He painted her, clothed, in *Young Woman Powdering Herself*. And his nudes betray not one hint of sexuality.

Claude Monet preferred horticulture to whores. He took up with Camille Doncieux in 1865. Along with Renoir's mistress, Suzanne Valadon, she had modelled for Manet and other artists of the period. They married just before the outbreak of the Franco-Prussian War in 1870, when their first son was three years old. To escape being called up for military service, Monet, like many of the Impressionists, fled to England, leaving Camille and his son behind in France. On his return, he was taken up by the wealthy patron of the arts Ernest Hoschedé and, when Camille was pregnant with their second son, Monet seduced Hoschedé's wife of thirteen years, Alice. Alice was soon pregnant too.

Hoschedé went bankrupt, but was still prepared to help his friend and cuckolder. The Monets moved in with the Hoschedés in their modest house at Vétheuil. Hoschedé was away most of the time, trying to restore his fortunes, so Monet was left alone with the two women who both had young babies to look after.

After three years of this *ménage*, Camille died. Eleven years later, Ernest Hoschedé died too, and, after a decent interval, Monet married Alice. They stayed together until she died in 1911. Monet was already seventy-three. He lived on for another thirteen years, painting his garden at Giverny. He died in 1926, after several unsuccessful operations on his cataracts.

So the Impressionists were the marrying kind. In most cases, they were even one-women men – one at a time, at least. Compared to the other great artists we examine in this book, they were a relatively a chaste lot. But in the chastity stakes, none of them could match Edgar Degas. Even though he did a series of pictures of brothels and was renowned for his nudes, Degas was celibate.

"Marry? I could never bring myself to do that," he said. "I would have to live in mortal fear of my wife saying: 'That's a pretty little thing' after I had finished a picture."

Some have put forward the theory that he was a repressed homosexual. But he took a bristling attitude towards pederasty. When he met Oscar Wilde in 1885, he took an instant dislike to him.

Wilde tried to compliment Degas by saying: "You know, you are very well known in England."

"Fortunately, not as well known as you are," Degas, not known for his wit, snapped back.

However, around 1876-7, Degas drew a penis transformed into a canon. Two sketches show penises as cats with their tails lifted. And when he imitated the signature of the composer Ernest Reyer, he turned the flourish into a penis and a pair of testicles.

Manet developed the theory that Degas was sleeping with his maid. But when a group of artists cross-questioned the girl, she said: "He isn't a man. I once went into his bedroom while he was changing his shirt, and he said: 'Get out of here, you wretched girl.'"

Not even the ever-accommodating Suzanne Valadon turned him on.

Manet told Berthe Morisot, he had concluded that Degas was "incapable of loving a woman, even of telling her so". But

THE WRONG IMPRESSIONISTS

Degas did have tender feelings and expressed his amorous thoughts in poetry. One of his poems read:

> Lively, sensitive, a little coquettish
> Let's follow glory and pleasure
> She is a rose caressed by the breeze
> She flares up, she calms down
> She smiles and weeps in turn
> And still she is a French woman
> And constant in her love.

He particularly liked black women. On a visit to New Orleans in 1873, he said: "I like nothing better than negresses of all shades... the pretty women of pure blood and the pretty quadroons and the well-set-up negresses."

But even there he did not indulge. It seems that he may have had a sexual encounter when he was twenty-two. His notebook for the spring of 1856 records: "I find it impossible to say how much I love that girl, since for me she has..."

Whatever happened, Degas did not like it. The notebook continues: "Monday, April 7. I cannot refuse to... how shameful it is... a defenceless girl. But I'll do it as little as possible."

And doing it as little as possible meant, in practice, not doing it at all – although, in later life, he lived in awe of other men's sexual adventures.

It was not that he did not have the opportunity. In the later 1870s and early 1880s, he made over fifty drawings and pastels of brothel scenes. During the Second Empire, there were over forty thousand prostitutes in Paris – including waitresses, shop girls, laundresses and other willing amateurs – far more than in other European cities. Men of Degas' class used the *maisons de tolérance* – the fifty-nine state regulated brothels – much as they went to restaurants and cafés. A directory called the *Guide Rose* was published annually. During school holidays, regular customers had to be dropped because of the influx of adolescents.

Degas depicted the girls happily lolling about naked, or encouraging clients. In one print he shows a girl servicing a lesbian customer. In *The Client* he depicts himself being grabbed by a naked girl. Elsewhere he shows himself looking on while the girls are in bed or ogling up at a nude girl while she is taking a bath.

He liked to depict girls naked in the bath, or astride the bidet. Even the hardened models of the Montmartre were a little shocked by the things he got them to do. And although, he treated his models as if they were animals, it is noticeable that he always picked pretty ones.

The obvious conclusion to draw is that Degas was a voyeur. But there is no evidence to suggest that he crept around Paris at night, peeping through windows or peering through the peepholes found in brothels. All these depictions of nude woman at their toilet were done from life, posed in the studio. The strange thing is that they are so true to life. One of the great joys of living with a beautiful woman, I have found, is to glimpse her through an open doorway taking a bath or combing her hair naked, exactly as Degas pictures them. But Degas never lived with a woman. So how can he have known how to get them to pose?

Degas certainly had bad eyesight. During the siege of Paris, he joined the National Guard as an infantryman, but was transferred to the artillery after he was sent for rifle practice and it was discovered that he could not see the target. Well, if you spent all day in the studio surrounded by naked young girls, what would you be doing in the evenings? Ask any bloke. It's enough to give you hair on the palms of your hands.

Degas may have been the least sexual of the Impressionists. But, although the rest of them had mistresses, not one of them was exactly what you would call a real ladies' man. With the luscious nudes they painted though, the Impressionists seemed to be striving to give the wrong impression.

14
England Expects

The English are supposed to be a cold race. But there are great English artists who can be every bit as racy as those naughty Frenchmen.

Thomas Gainsborough, for example, was the great painter of the English landed gentry in the eighteenth century. A pillar of respectability? You would have thought so. But the briefest scan of his artistic output reveals that he is much happier painting women than men. As in art, so in life – by his own confession. He says in a letter to John Henderson in 1773: "Deeply read in petticoats am I."

On 15 July 1746, at the notoriously lax Mayfair Chapel, Gainsborough secretly married a Scots girl called Margaret Burr, who was the "natural daughter of Henry, Duke of Beaufort". She was very beautiful and Gainsborough already considered himself a connoisseur of beautiful women. The marriage was kept secret because his parents objected to him marrying a woman who was illegitimate. Margaret was also pregnant at the time, although the child died on 1 March 1747 according to the parish register of St Thomas's Church, Holborn.

However, Gainsborough's great incentive to marry Margaret was money. Her father the Duke had generously settled £200 a year on her, a considerable sum in those days. This put a considerable strain on the marriage. So did his sexual adventures. His younger daughter Margaret said that his debauches "often exceeded the bounds of temperance and his health suffered from it, being occasionally unable to work for weeks afterwards".

They had other consequences. At nineteen, Margaret fell severely ill with a mental condition caused by syphilis inherited from her father.

Gainsborough had left his native Sudbury in Suffolk to learn his art in London. It was there that he began to develop the art of drinking and loose living. In his cups, he frequented brothels. In one brothel, he met the artist William Hogarth, who was his own rake's progress. Together they watched two whores having a wine fight. Later, Gainsborough fell in the gutter. His boozing companion the actor James Quin told him not to bother getting up as the watch would soon be along to arrest them.

On another night, Gainsborough records falling down in the street and waking in a strange woman's bed. He gave her £30 for her kindness.

Meanwhile, the thirty-two-year old Hogarth eloped with the twenty-year-old daughter of his painting teacher Sir James Thornhill, Sergeant-Painter to King George I. This post was taken over by Thornhill's son John, then by Hogarth himself. Despite his marriage and his elevated position, Hogarth saw no reason to turn from "the usual gaieties of life", which in eighteen-century London meant the tavern and the whorehouse.

Gainsborough moved to Bath, a louche spa town, where his neighbours included William Pitt and Clive of India.

"I might add perhaps in my red hot way," he wrote to his friend, the composer, William Jackson in Exeter, "that damn me Exeter is no more a place for a Jackson, than Sudbury in Suffolk is for a G--."

His daughter mentioned that he "had two faces, his studious and domestic" one and "his convivial one".

In Bath, the convivial one ran amok.

"I have done nothing but fiddle since I came from London," he wrote from Bath in 1774, "so much was I unsettled by the continual run of pleasure which my friend Giardini and the rest of you engaged me in, and if it were not for my family, which one cannot conveniently carry in one's pocket, I should be often with you, enjoying what I like up to the hilt."

Gainsborough uses the expression "up to the hilt" in other letters and it clearly meant the penetration of women. Indeed he told William Jackson: "If you were a lady I would say what I have often said in a corner by way of making use of the last inch. Yours up to the hilt. T.G."

But he paid for his pleasures. Even as early as October 1763, he was so ill from his excesses that *The Bath Journal* mistakenly announced his death.

"I have kept to my bed five weeks tomorrow, excepting two hours sitting up for the last three days of a most terrible fever," he wrote, the week after the death notice appeared. "My life was dispair'd of by Dr Charleton after he tried all his skill, and by his own desire Dr Moisey was call'd in when in three days my faintings left me and I got strength. I am now what they call out of danger."

The treatment, he had been told, was six glasses of good old port a day.

"The truth is, I have apply'd it a little too close for these five years," he wrote.

There can be no doubt that the cause of his malady was venereal.

"Oh my dear friend, nobody can think what I have suffer'd for a moment's gratification," he rued. Despite the cause of his illness, his wife stood by him. "My dear good wife has sat up every night... I will never be a quarter good enough for her."

Not even an eighth. As soon as he was well again, he was out playing away once more. His wife was more than a little annoyed that he had given £20 to a woman he claimed not to have known. And once, when he had packed his wife and the children off to the countryside for a holiday, they came home unexpectedly as, Gainsborough records: "Madam is afraid to trust me alone at home in this great town."

Not without good reason. Her premature return prompted

him to write to one Mary Gibbon saying that he could send her any money as he would not be able to "receive anything privately" now his wife was home.

Fortunately, commissions to paint portraits meant that he spent long spells away from home, often in the easy-going city of London.

After his daughter became mentally ill, Gainsborough told his friend Samuel Kilderbee that he regretted his dissolute life, adding though, that when people assessed his life: "They must take me altogether, liberal, thoughtless and dissipated."

In 1772, Gainsborough had a row with Sir Joshua Reynolds, President of the Royal Academy, when he refused to hang his portrait of the Countess Waldegrave, who was having an indiscreet affair with the Duke of Gloucester, brother of George III. Gainsborough refused to send paintings to the Royal Academy Summer Exhibition for the next five years. When he resumed, he caused another brouhaha with two portraits of well-known courtesans, Clara Haywood and Grace Dalrymple.

In 1782, his portrait of Mrs Perdita Robinson, the mistress of the Prince of Wales, had to be withdrawn after the press alleged she was blackmailing the prince over some salacious letters he had written to her. Reynolds cheerfully hung his own portrait of Mrs Robinson in its place.

Reynolds himself never married but *Town and Country Magazine* reported that he carried on love affairs with his aristocratic sisters and kept a mistress. His name was linked with those of a number of ladies and he is said to have thrown himself on his knees in his studio and proposed to one Mary Hamilton. His mistress, it was said, was a Miss J—ngs, the daughter of "a gentleman of the navy". She had previously been the mistress of Lord F. who dropped her when his discovered her affair with Reynolds. Reynolds was then obliged to offer her "his purse and his person".

"Her present situation would not let her refuse either, as it would have been ridiculous to have laid claim to virtue," *Town and Country* said. "As the knight had already made a very favourable impression on her, she, with seeming reluctance, yielded to his proposal, and since that time there is great reason to believe they have been mutually happy."

His dealings with Reynolds and the Royal Academy meant that Gainsborough had to move back to London. There, he helped a young girl forced into prostitution.

"A poor wench whom I used to speak to in Bath, came to London with some worthless ungrateful villain, who left her to go abroad, in some poor state indeed, and it is a person of that merit that if her heart was bad enough would have no occasion for my help," Gainsborough wrote to his sister. Of course, he says, his wife must know nothing of this act of charity. Nor was the young woman in question about to spill the beans. "The creature would rather die than hazard my domestic happiness by making any request to my house, and it was by chance that I went to afford timely relief."

He found a large house in Pall Mall. The east wing of the house was given over to Dr Graham's Temple of Health, where a dubious clientele enjoyed mud baths and massages. It was a high-class brothel and from his windows Gainsborough could observe the clients going in and out. It was said that Emma Hamilton, the mistress of Admiral Lord Nelson, posed for the statue of the Goddess of Health in Dr Graham's establishment and that Gainsborough used her as the model for the naked nymph in his picture *Musidor*.

Most of Gainsborough's letters, according to his old friend Kilderbee, were "too licentious to be published" and his heirs destroyed them.

Gainsborough's oldest daughter Mary's marriage lasted only a matter of months. The mentally impaired Margaret never married. When Gainsborough and his wife died, Mary looked after Margaret who, by this time, was suffering from the delusion that the Prince of Wales was in love with her. There's nothing new under the sun.

The sex life of John Constable, the master painter of the English countryside, seems tame by comparison, though still waters run deep. In 1800, when he was twenty-four, he met twelve-year-old Maria Elizabeth Bicknell. She was visiting her grandfather the wealthy Reverend Doctor Durand Rhudde, who was the Rector of East Bergholt, Constable's Suffolk home.

It is said that it was not until nine years later, when she was twenty-one, that he started wooing her. There is no record that he saw any other woman during that time. Maria's parents were all for the match but, however upright, uptight and godly Constable was, Reverend Rhudde took against him and threatened to write Maria out of his will if she married the painter. He also warned he would leave East Bergholt, if the couple married and settled there, thereby causing a scandal.

Constable did everything he could think of to get around the old man. He even gave him a drawing of East Bergholt Church inscribed "presented in testimony of respect to Durand Rhudde D.D., the Rector".

Dr Rhudde accepted the gift enthusiastically, but in his formal letter of thanks enclosed a banknote so that Constable could buy himself "some little article by which you may be reminded to me, when I am no more".

How Constable must have longed for that day. In February 1816, just before his fortieth birthday, he wrote to Maria, saying "never will I marry in this world if I marry not you".

Constable did his cause no good by giving Johnny Dunthorne, the sixteen-year-old son of a friend, a holiday in London. Dr Rhudde warned that Dunthorne was "a destitute of religious principle...if not dangerous, at least a most melancholy associate".

Later in the year, when his father died, Constable decided to marry come what may before the year was out. And when Maria's mother died, she too found the strength to defy the Reverend Doctor.

They married on 2 October 1816 in St Martin-in-the-Field in London. It was a lonely affair. But back in East Bergholt there was rejoicing that someone had stood up to the tyrannical Dr Rhudde and they received numerous messages of congratulations.

The couple honeymooned in Dorset and soon Maria was pregnant. But Dr Rhudde still would not unbend. It was only when she miscarried in February 1817 that he softened, redrafting his will to provide for any children of the couple. And when he died in 1819, he left Maria an unexpected legacy of £4,000.

By this time Constable had a mistress who lay before him while he unveiled her considerable charms.

"Landscape is my mistress," he said. "'Tis to her I look for fame."

The painter J.M.W.Turner also loved a good landscape. He never married, but the nudes he sketched in his notebooks show that he had a lively erotic imagination.

He also wrote erotic poetry. One poem asks: "By those hairs which hid from my sight... I prithee dear Molly be still." It contains the verse:

> By the lips quivering motion I ween
> To the centre where love lies between
> A passport to bliss is thy will
> Yet I prithee dear Molly be still.

He made furtive trips to Wapping where he, among other things, made drawings of "sailor's women... in every posture of abandonment". The critic John Ruskin testified that a number of sketchbooks containing "grossly obscene drawings" were burnt at the behest of the National Gallery Trustees in his presence in December 1858. They had, Ruskin said, been "drawn under conditions of insanity" – but Ruskin himself was no sepulchre of sanity when it comes to sex. One drawing that survived the conflagration shows a Swiss girl in bed with a companion, her national dress on the floor beside her. The rendition is detached and voyeuristic.

A respectable member of the Royal Academy, Turner was very secretive about his sex life. In 1796, he seems to have fallen in love with a girl whose surname was White. She was the sister of a former school friend. "Vows of fidelity" were exchanged. But he left on a trip and did not write. When he returned, she had taken up with someone else.

By 1798, he was having an affair with Sarah Danby, widow of the composer John Danby, though they had met before

Danby's death. She was a Catholic and nine years his senior. Some of his nude studies showing the torso from the shoulder to the knee are probably of her. They had two daughters, Evelina and Georgina, to add to the four Sarah already had by Danby. His two children used the name Turner, though in his will he only dared refer to them as Evelina and Georgina T. They all lived together in Turner's house in Harley Street, London.

The relationship was stormy and came to and end around 1820. Sarah Danby was soon replace by Mrs Sophia Caroline Booth, whose house Turner had lodged at in Margate. She was "a tall, lusty woman". Later, she moved into Turner's house in Chelsea, ostensibly as a "housekeeper". But around Chelsea, he was known as Mr – and sometimes Admiral – Booth.

Then along came the Pre-Raphaelite brotherhood as a reaction to the stylized painting of that period, particularly what they considered the "sloshy" work of Sir "Sloshua" Reynolds. The young John Everertt Millais, William Holman Hunt and Dante Gabriel Rossetti declared that nothing good had been produced since the Renaissance.

One of the leading figures in the movement was John Ruskin. Despite the romantic gush of his letters, Ruskin could not handle the physical side of love. At sixteen, he was romantically attached to fourteen-year-old Adèle Domecq, the daughter of his father's French partner. The affair was sustained by correspondence alone and foundered after four years.

Eight years later, Ruskin thought he would try his hand again and in 1848 he married his beautiful Scottish cousin Effie Gray. Unfortunately, when he discovered, on his wedding night that, unlike marble statues, women had pubic hair, he could not rise to the occasion.

Effie explained later that "he was disgusted with my person that first night". She herself was naive about these things.

"I had never been told the duties of married persons to each other and knew little or nothing about their relations in the closest union on Earth," she said.

However, she did know that *something* was supposed to

happen and the frustrated bride cited the biblical injunction to procreate.

"He then said it would be sinful to enter into such a connection as, if I was not very wicked, I was at least immature and the responsibility that I might have children was too great, as I was quite unfit up bring them up." Nice guy.

He told Effie that he would do his marital duty when she was twenty-five, a full five years away. And when she reached that age he unilaterally extended the deadline.

Meanwhile, he got her to model for Millais, in the hope that she would give him cause to divorce her. She certainly found the artist very attractive.

"He is so extremely handsome, beside his talents, that you may fancy how he is run after," she wrote.

Soon they were deeply in love.

Effie's every move was watched by Ruskin and his parents. But Effie then had a stroke of luck. She discovered that an unconsummated marriage is not legally binding.

"I have therefore simply to tell you," she wrote to her parents, "that I do not think I am John Ruskin's wife at all – and I entreat you to assist me to get released from the unnatural position in which I stand to him."

Worse than being impotent, he was a brute.

"If he had only been kind, I might have lived and died in my maiden state, but in addition to his brutality – his leaving me on every occasion – his threats for the future of a wish to break my spirit – and – only last night when I bade him leave me he said he had a good mind to beat me."

Her mother whisked Effie away from London. The afternoon they left, she sent Ruskin her wedding ring, her house keys and a petition for the annulment of the marriage on the grounds of impotence.

A few weeks later, Effie returned to London for a humiliating medical examination that certified that she was a virgin with no "impediments on her part to a proper consummation of the marriage". The annulment was granted in 1854.

Millais was overjoyed and, the following year, they got

engaged. They married in Perth on 3 July and raised eight children.

Meanwhile Ruskin look for hairless perfection elsewhere. He indulged his yen for pube-less nymphets by teaching at Winnington Hall girls' school. And he fell for a nine-year-old Irish girl called Rose La Touche who had been brought to him for art lessons.

When Rose was eighteen, Ruskin, then forty-seven, asked her to marry him. She accepted, but they had to wait until she was twenty-one. She counted the days. But in the nick of time, Effie heard about the match and wrote to Rose, warning her against it. When Ruskin was asked whether it was true that he could not get it up for Effie, he denied it, saying he had not been in love with her when he married her but was sure the he would have been up to it once he had fallen in love with her.

The marriage did not go ahead, but Rose never got over her disappointment. She became mentally unstable and bedridden. She died five years later.

After she died, Ruskin attended a seance which, he said, led him to a lost love letter from Rose. He carried it in his breast pocket, preserved between two gold leaves, for the rest of his life.

The Pre-Raphaelites always had problems finding models. They would comb Tottenham Court Road for them, but were generally too afraid to approach women in case the women thought they had mistaken them for prostitutes.

So they mainly shared accommodating Lizzie Siddal. Millais painted her as *Ophelia*. She had to pose lying in a bathtub with lamps beneath to keep the water warm. Millais was so engrossed in his work, he did not notice that they had gone out. Numb with cold, Lizzie caught a severe cold and her father demanded £50 damages. Millais paid her doctor's bills and Lizzie soon recovered.

Holman Hunt painted *The Awakening Conscience* as a condemnation of loose sexual morals. But both Rossetti and another Pre-Raphaelite Ford Maddox Brown fell in love with their models. Brown eventually married his model, Emma, but

ENGLAND EXPECTS

Rossetti drew back from marrying Lizzie Siddal, whom he had inherited from Millais, despite the urgings of – of all people – Ruskin.

Hunt set off to Egypt, searching for models of his own.

"There are beautiful women here," he wrote home. "In the country the fellah girls wear no veils and but very little dress, and those in their prime are perhaps the most graceful creatures you could see anywhere. In prowling about the village one day I came face to face with one of them and could not but stop and stare."

He had left Annie Miller, behind in England, a barmaid who had posed for *The Awakening Conscience*. He had arranged for her education in his absence with the unspoken aim of making her his wife, or at least saving her from a life of shame.

He returned to discover that part of her education was a comprehensive study of London's racier night-spots, courtesy of Rossetti. Neither Hunt nor Lizzie was amused.

Lizzie then demanded marriage. When Rossetti refused to set a date, Lizzie absconded to Bath. Rossetti chased after her and patched things up. But not for long. He had fallen out of love with her and soon they split up.

Edward Burne-Jones, William Morris and the poet Algernon Swinburne joined the Pre-Raphaelite cause and they soon began adopting Swinburne's habit of calling beautiful women "stunners". One stunner Rossetti found was seventeen-year-old Jane Burden, the daughter of a stableman. He painted her as Guinevere. Then Morris took her over to pose for *La Belle Iseult*. He was shy with women so, to declare himself, he wrote on the back of the canvas: "I cannot paint you, but I love you."

Swinburne thought that Morris's plan to marry his stunner was insane – "to kiss her feet is the utmost man should dream of doing". But the wedding went ahead in 1859.

Meanwhile, Burne-Jones was living with his fiancée Georgina "Georgie" Macdonald. Rossetti had found a new model, the buxom, blonde-haired Fanny Cornforth. She was a prostitute, plying her trade on the streets. When Rossetti met her, she was "cracking nuts with her teeth and throwing the shells about. Seeing Rossetti staring at her, she threw some at him. Delighted with this brilliant naiveté, he forthwith accosted her and carried her off to sit for him."

Rossetti also celebrated the occasion with a poem, though discreetly replacing her "Fanny" with "Jenny":

Why, Jenny, as I watch you there –
For all your wealth of loosened hair,
Your silk ungirdled and unlac'd
And warm sweets open to the waist
All golden in the lamplight's gleam –
You know not what a book you seem,
Half-read by lightning in a dream!

He painted her as *Bocca Baciata* – "The Much-Kissed Mouth" – adding the legend: "The mouth that has been kissed loses not its freshness; still it renews itself as does the moon."

Burne-Jones moved in on Fanny. He took her to the Argyle Rooms at Piccadilly circus and then to supper at Quinn's.

"She was in considerable trepidation lest Rossetti should come in," Burne-Jones wrote in his journal, "and lo! he did so."

Suddenly Burne-Jones and Georgie announced they were going to get married as soon as possible and the Brotherhood was stunned when Rossetti said that he was going to do the decent thing by Lizzie. They married in Paris in 1860. By this time Lizzie was ill, hopelessly addicted to laudanum. After two miscarriages, Lizzie OD-ed. Rossetti found her, but it was too late.

Lizzie was buried in the Rossetti family plot in Highgate Cemetery with a bunch of his poems in her hands. But she did not rest in peace. Rossetti had her dug up seven years later when he wanted his manuscript back. Despite a large wormhole through the centre, the poems were published in 1870.

Rossetti moved to a larger house in Chelsea where he lived with Fanny. Under the influence of the fun-loving Fanny, Rossetti's paintings grew sexier. The prudish Holman Hunt protested that this violated the ideals of the brotherhood.

"I tell you," he told Rossetti, "the people you are associating with are ruining you."

ENGLAND EXPECTS

Rossetti compounded the offence with a portrait of William Morris's wife Janey and an erotic poem in her honour. This sparked a passionate affair.

In his distress, Morris turned to Burne-Jones – only he was having an affair with his model Mary Zambaco, one of three Anglo-Greek girls, known as "The Three Graces", whom half the artists in London were in love with.

He promised to elope with her, then changed his mind. She proposed a suicide pact and then threatened to drown herself. In desperation, Burne-Jones passed her on to Rossetti, who was now living discreetly with Janey. Meanwhile, Morris comforted himself with Aglaia Coronio, Mary's cousin and another of The Three Graces.

As divorce was unthinkable, Morris found a bigger house, where he, Janey and their children could stay, and Rossetti could "visit". As soon as they had all moved in, Morris took off for Iceland. But the strain of this arrangement proved too much for Rossetti. He withdrew into paranoid schizophrenia. Janey stayed loyal for a while, then patched it up with Morris.

Along with Morris in the Arts and Crafts movement was Eric Gill whose *Stations of the Cross*, say the Christian Survivors of Sexual Abuse, should be removed from Westminster Cathedral because of his paedophile tendencies and incest. But that was not even the worst of his excesses.

From his countryside childhood, he had been fascinated with the sexual organs of animals and would examine animal semen under the microscope comparing it with his own. One day when the bull failed to mount a cow that had been brought for service, the vet prescribed a medicine. Instead of giving it to the bull, Gill gulped it down himself and proclaimed next morning that it was no good.

Animal experimentation did not end there.

"Expt with dog in eve," ran an entry in his diary and five days later: "Continued experiment with dog after and discovered that dog will join with man."

From when he was a youth, he liked to pick up prostitutes. What their pubic hair was going to look like was, for him, a matter of burning curiosity. He complained that his dick was too big for one prostitute he picked up in Bond Street. It hurt the poor girl.

He told his future wife Ethel, whom he was courting at the time, about his experiences and his need for regular masturbation. He asked her to sleep with him to keep him safe from temptation and sent her a diagram outlining the principles of contraception.

He considered seeing women naked in the life class a privilege. It excited him so much that he took Ethel to a hotel in Fleet Street and watched her take her clothes off.

"Then for the first time I saw that she was a woman," he wrote. "I saw the dark full growth of hair on her belly. I touched it and kissed her. By now she was naked. Her breasts – her little tender nipples were against me – her hair down and covering my face – our lips kissing. So we lay together for the first time."

After they were married, Gill found Ethel the perfect sexual partner.

"The roundness and largeness of her legs and thighs and hips, the sudden smallness of her waist and the splendid fatness and softness of her buttocks, the thick hair on her belly are beautiful and very exciting," he said.

She was as enthusiastic as he was and wrote about his "dear body" and "dear penis". This continued throughout their lives together. Gill's diaries are full of remarks such as "great time in bed" and even "discoved a new *façon de faire*". According to his diaries they made love almost every day.

But that was not enough. The casual encounters with prostitutes continued. One night after leaving prominent Bloomsburyite Lady Ottoline Morrell he picked up a girl in Guildford Street and went home with her. After hearing a lecture by the writer Hilaire Belloc, he gave a woman two shillings to feel between her legs.

"No connection," he noted. "No orgasm. Am I mad!"

Even on holiday, he had no compunction about dropping Ethel back at their hotel and going out to pick up women.

This did not just happen outside the home. When Ethel fell pregnant, Gill asked their maid Lizzie to help him out.

"I said to her would she let me lie with her as Ethel was with child," he wrote. "She agreed."

The following year he took his one publicized mistress, Lillian Meacham, a "New Woman". He was quite open about the affair and suggested setting up a *ménage à trois*.

Lillian and Ethel did not hit it off at first. But after he took Lillian on holiday to Chartres, he took her on as an apprentice.

As well as formal brothels, Gill liked casual encounters in Turkish Baths. He once took Ethel and his brother-in-law Ernest along. On another occasion Ethel allowed Ernest to "play with her body" in bed.

Gill did not mind being the other corner of the triangle in a *ménage à trois*. He seduced Moira, the wife of his friend a patron Robert Gibbs. The three of them liked to get naked together and kiss and fondle.

"Bath after supper and dancing (nude)," he wrote in his diary. "R. and M. fucked one another after, M. holding me the while."

And the experimentation continued.

"A man's penis and balls are very beautiful things and the power to see this beauty is not confined to the opposite sex," he wrote. "The shape of the head of a man's erect penis is very excellent in the mouth. There is no doubt about this. I have often wondered – now I know."

However, he considered homosexuality to be "the ultimate disrespect both to the human body and to human love".

Gill did not like to use professional models for his work, preferring to get people he knew to strip off. He often depicted couples copulating. One drawing shows two men entering one woman.

He was particularly adept at stealing other people's women. He always made a move on friends' wives and girlfriends. It was as if he considered all the women in the world to be his. In particular, he swiped the lady friend of fellow typographer Stanley Morison, Mrs Beatrice Wade. She modelled nude for him, begining an enduring affair.

When Joseph Cribb, Gill's apprentice, announced his engagement to sixteen-year-old farm girl Agnes Weller, Gill drew their double portrait to celebrate the event. He could not resist seducing her though. It was simply the *droit de seigneur.*

Sixteen-year-old Daisy Hawkins got the same treatment from fifty-year-old Gill. He had known her as a child. But when she came to live with the Gills as a servant, he used her as a model for his *Twenty-Five Nudes* and made her his mistress. The affair continued for two years. His secretary Mrs Colette Yardley also succumbed.

But it is for having sex with his three daughters that Gill has been most harshly criticized. Once they were pubescent he loved to portray them nude. Sex with them, again, was conducted in a manner of experimentation. For example, when his daughter Betty was sixteen, he recorded one afternoon that he had made her come. And she had performed the same service on him. While they did it, he told her to watch the effects on the anus. Why should it contract during orgasm, he asked. And why should a woman's anus behave the same as a man's?

He would also visit his younger daughter's bedroom at night.

"Stayed half an hour – put p. in her a/hole," he wrote in his diary. "This must stop."

A Catholic convert, Gill confessed to Father John O'Connor. But the priest knew so little about sex that Gill ended up doing a series of "fucking drawing and diagrams for Fr. O'C". Gill's brother, another a Catholic convert, went one better and seduced a nun.

In Gill's defence, it must be said that, despite his jealousy when they began to take lovers of their own, his daughters grew up to be well adjusted and led contented married lives. Incest was commonplace in the Gill family when he was a child. Even though his father was a priest, nudity was an everyday occurrence when Gill was young. One day, while out walking on the Downs with his sisters, they suddenly flung off all their clothes and continued naked, much to the amazement of a passing shepherd. He had sex with his older sister Cicely and her friend "Bunny" Browne.

Sex with his sister Gladys, who was eight years older than him, continued throughout their lives. He liked to watch her with other men. She and her husband Ernest Laughton were the models for a carving Gill called *Fucking*. Now in the Tate Gallery, it has been renamed euphemistically *Ecstasy*.

As to the *Stations of the Cross*, Westminster Cathedral has stood firm. Gill's masterpiece is to stay.

15
Little Big Man

Despite being a dwarf – a little under five feet tall – Henri Toulouse-Lautrec boasted that he was remarkably well endowed. He was described himself as the "little coffee pot with the large spout". He was also known as the "prick on paws" and the "prick on wheels" – and also, majestically, as "the tower".

With his foreshortened limbs and his distorted face, Lautrec identified himself with the myth of Vulcan, the crippled blacksmith who had enormous sexual prowess. He also took after his libidinous father, an aristocrat of normal height with a well-deserved reputation as a seducer.

Lautrec's sexual development was retarded by his dwarfism and he was fourteen before he showed any signs of puberty. As soon as he could, he grew a beard as a symbol of his virility. As a youth, he fantasized that his pretty young cousin would come and sit by his bed. In his mind's eye, he contrasted her beauty and his ugliness, comforting himself with the tale of *Beauty and the Beast,* which he would later illustrate.

In 1882, Lautrec went to Paris to study in the atelier of Ferdinand Cormon. He was famed for having three mistresses at the same time. The atmosphere was riotous with the students singing obscene songs and boasting about their sexual exploits, usually with shop girls. Like most boys in France at that time, they would have been taken to the brothel at the age of fourteen or fifteen. But Lautrec, having been a sickly child, was still a virgin at twenty-three.

After working in at Cormon's all morning, the students would hire models, usually young Italian girls they found in the *marché aux modèles* in the Place Pigalle, and take them back to their studios for painting sessions that often turned into orgies.

Lautrec would accompany his friends to bawdy dancehalls, scandalous student balls and the brothels. Soon he shrugged off the academic style he learnt at Cormon's. In *Etude du nu* for example, he depicted naked women dressed only in black stockings – hardly a classical touch. Most of the women who modelled were not particular about the circumstances in which they took their clothes off. Compared to the pious women he had been brought up with, they were a revelation.

A fellow student at Cormon's, Charles-Edouard Lucas, arranged for the shy and defensive Lautrec to lose his virginity. He arranged for a young model named Marie Charlet to seduce him. She was an inspired choice. She was just sixteen, but had a broad range of sexual experience behind her. Sexually abused by her drunken father, she had left home, supporting herself by nude modelling and casual prostitution. She was randy and uninhibited with an insatiable sexual curiosity. Lautrec's dwarfism intrigued her. This was very satisfactory from Lautrec's point of view too. Marie introduced him into the world of sex and to the type of women who would give him pleasure. And she left him with few illusions about the relationship between men and women. He told a friend that he would like to "find a woman who had a lover uglier than me".

In 1884, Lautrec moved to Montmartre, where he would be surrounded by prostitutes. Belatedly his father, like all good fathers at the time, had introduced him to the brothels there. Lautrec stayed with his friend René Grenier and his wife Lily. Among his surviving erotic drawings, there is one of a nude Lily giving Lautrec a blow-job. There is a look of enormous satisfaction on his face. Although it is not known whether such a thing actually took place, she did pose for him. But then, she also posed nude for Degas.

He was also obsessed with the Polish heiress Misia Godebska who married his friend the publisher, Thadée Natanson. In one picture of her, he painted in the background their pretty young housemaid, dressed in pink as if she were a prostitute. One evening at dinner, he got drunk and made such gross overtures to the poor girl the Natansons had to ask him to leave.

Frequently he was seen out on the town with beautiful women. They would mother him and he would pretend that he really was their lover. Indeed, at one time, he really did have a beautiful lover, the model turned artist Suzanne Valadon who had once been the mistress of Renoir. It was Lautrec who gave her the name "Suzanne" – she had been born Marie-Clémentine Valadon. When they met in 1882 at a riotous party in the studio of the artist Louis Anquetin – so riotous that the police were called – he said: "You pose naked for old men so you should be called Suzanne."

Suzanne and the Elders is the theme of any number of classic studies of the female nude.

She was eighteen, stunningly beautiful and would often pose for him. She would act as hostess at parties in his studio. He encouraged her to draw, supervised her engravings and organized her first one-woman show.

She denied ever being his lover. But she lied about a lot of things in her life, including the paternity of her son. She was wildly promiscuous but they stayed together, off and on, for at least ten – probably fifteen – years.

In a letter to him in 1890, she invited him to "come and sleep over when you want only not before half past midnight". And signed off the letter: "I give you a kiss on your (little bedroom slipper etc)…"

Lautrec's mother thought they might marry. Mistakenly, she thought Suzanne was from something approaching the right social class.

"What you say about the chic young lady is of no interest to me," Lautrec wrote back caustically. "It's just another absurd mistake made by whoever cooked up the idea. The girl in question is a tart. She used to work in a bakery."

Suzanne and Lautrec got on well together, though there were occasional scenes. One day, Lautrec burst into the studio of his friend, the artist François Gauzi, saying that Suzanne was threatening to kill herself unless he married her. The two of them rushed to Suzanne's apartment and, hesitating at the door, overheard Suzanne in conversation with her mother.

"You've done it now," said the mother. "You've scared him off and he's never coming back. A lot of good it's done you."

"He wouldn't go for it," said Suzanne. "I've tried everything."

After that, his relationship with Suzanne cooled.

Another beauty who gave herself to him was Jane Avril, a dancer at the Moulin Rouge who worked under the name La Mélinite – "The Explosive". She was famed for her "Botticelli-like" beauty and, though she feigned prudery, her décolleté descended nearly to the waist. She also had the reputation of being a lesbian.

He got her to pose for him often, partly because she was a favourite of other artists and partly because she would do whatever he asked, no matter how lewd. Although she was the maîtresse en titre of another man at the time, it is said that Lautrec asked her to go to bed with him and she accepted, just once, "as friends".

Lautrec would sometimes try to use his pencil as a tool of seduction. In Le Rat Mort – the restaurant where he ate – when he spotted a pretty woman, he would not hesitate to go over to her and sketch her as a way of introducing himself. Le Rat Mort means "the dead rat", it also means bored stiff. But many of the great artists of this period, Degas particularly, called their models rats. As well as being a hangout for artists – Le Rat Mort appears in works by Degas, Manet and Forain – it had a large gay and lesbian clientele. The poet Arthur Rimbaud cut the wrist of his homosexual lover Paul Verlaine there for a dare. Later Rimbaud was stabbed three times in the thigh in Le Rat Mort.

There is an element of sexual display in all Lautrec's artistic output. He wanted to lure women to him with his art, because they wanted to be models or because they wanted to be close to someone who was famous.

He would ask any woman he found attractive to come and pose for him, usually with the aim of seducing her. If that failed, he would still have the pleasure of caressing their bodies with his brushes on the canvas.

Sometimes, when drunk, he would ask attractive women whether he could sit behind them. That way he would have the pleasure of looking at them, without them suffering the pain of looking at him. He loved simply to be in the world of "female odours and nerve-endings". Women held a deadly fascination for him. There was something suicidal in the way he pursued them.

Sometimes he won through by sheer persistence. One evening, he was observed at a fashionable salon trying to flirt, with little success, with an attractive aristocratic woman. When he finally gave up and got up to leave, the woman caved in and agreed to meet for lunch the next day. She explained to a friend that he looked so sad that she was afraid to refuse him.

"It seemed, at any cost, I had to give him a reason to go on living until lunchtime tomorrow," she said.

Normally, Lautrec did not feel at home in society. One evening at an elegant party, surrounded by deep *décolletage*, he was asked if he was enjoying himself.

"Marvellous," he said. "You'd think we were in a brothel."

Due to his deformity, Lautrec spent a lot of his time in the brothels where he could get what he wanted for cash.

"The brothel is the only place where you can get your shoes shined without listening to a lot of nonsense," he said.

He would eat, drink and sleep with the girls there, only venturing out to ogle the scantily clad dancers at the Folies Bergère. The madams would make sure he was well fed and served the finest wines. He would also entertained there.

"What you do expect?" he said when someone was shocked by an invitation to meet him in a *maison close*. "I just feel more at home there than anywhere else."

At least five brothels rented him a room where he stayed as

if it was a hotel. And in 1899, when he travelled to Bordeaux, he wrote ahead to a brothel there, reserving a room.

His mother was outraged when Lautrec introduced his young cousins to the delights of the *maison close*. But the girls would treat him like family. They would call him "Monsieur Henri". He would chat with them, listen to their problems, play cards with them when they were not busy and give them gifts. He would also use them as his models, both off and on duty.

He loved nude female flesh so much that he would not sketch without being overwhelmed with the desire to caress it, cuddle it and press himself against it.

"The body of a beautiful woman is not made for love," he once said. "It is too exquisite."

But, of course, he would sleep with them. Under the circumstances, they could hardly refuse. But some of them got to know him well enough to overcome the revulsion that other women felt.

He depicted the prostitutes with great sympathy at work, or bathing, often with a male figure in the background observing. He, the observer, is always fully clothed. Lautrec also picked up commissions in the brothels from other clients eager to have some memento of the time they spent there.

When asked why he liked to use prostitutes as his models, he explained that they were less self-conscious with their clothes off. He also said that he liked to study the female nude in its natural setting.

Lautrec showed the brutal side of brothel life too – the girls lining up, naked from the waist down for their weekly medical inspection or lying back exhausted with their legs apart, ready to be used again.

He had no time for love.

"The men most loved by women have nothing but vice in their eyes, vice in their mouth, vice in their hands, vice in their bellies and women too," he told cabaret singer Yvette Guilbert. "You can sing about love in any key you want, but hold your nose my dear. Now if you sang about desire, we would understand each other, and about the variety of its explosions, we would have fun... but love, my poor Yvette ... there is no – such – thing."

Lautrec liked to watch while other people made love.

"You should see the faces they make," he said.

He kept an album of lovers in the throes. And, as if to get his own back for the trick that nature had played on him, when he depicted lovers, he horridly deformed their bodies. He often hung out in lesbian bars and, bizarrely, liked to proposition the women in what he considered his lesbian harem. I suppose rejection did not come so hard from them. He also enjoyed depicting lesbian lovers, even in bed. When *Dans le Lit*, which shows two women in bed kissing, went on show, the police were called. Usually, his lesbian works were sold privately.

But more than anything it was women themselves he loved, redheads especially. His women did not have to be pretty and young, just as long as they were thin. He loved their skin particularly in the little nooks of the body, such as those behind the knee and elbow, where the skin was "made of living silk that never wears out". He would play with a woman's hand for hours, pressing it against his cheeks, ears and nose, smelling its dampness without ever quite letting his lips touch it. He raved about women's mouths, the colour of the faces, their thighs and their breasts. He would smell their hair and the pits of the elbows and knees. He would smell the stockings that his model had just taken off, but most off all he loved to smell their armpits called "tobacco shops". He even smelt the armpits of women past their prime because, he said, it brought to mind their past splendours.

Lautrec loved all things feminine – perfumes, jewellery, corsets, hats, underclothes. He liked cross dressing and was often photographed dressed up in the clothes of female friends.

When Oscar Wilde was exiled to France, Lautrec sought him out, not because he had any homosexual tendencies, but because he was an anglophile and considered Wilde a fellow outsider.

His love of prostitutes brought with it, inevitably, gonorrhoea, then syphilis. He caught it, probably, from a woman named Rosa La Rouge. He had been warned that she had it, but Lautrec was not a man who could contain his impulses.

Soon he was "a martyr to the Big S". Degas said that even Lautrec's art stank of syphilis. He suffered from all the major symptoms, and was treated by Dr Henri Bourges, author of *L'Hygiéne de syphilitique*. But could not quite bring himself to tell his mum, though he hinted about it in his letters to her.

Lautrec turned to drink for consolation. He was one of the first in France to take up the American fad for cocktails. He drank to forget about his ugliness. He drank because it made his dreams come true. He drank because, in his drunkenness, he could believe that any woman he desired passionately might allow themselves, for a moment, to be tempted. He drank to forget about his syphilis and, while drinking, he forgot about his treatments for the disease. In short, he drank himself to death – in 1901 at the age of thirty-six.

There was no autopsy so there are no official statistics on the size of his organ. In fact, some of his acquaintances – one can hardly call them friends – contradicted his boasts and said he suffered from microgenitalism, that is he retained the penis of a young boy. Others say that his penis was a normal size and only looked big in comparison with his short legs. Whatever the truth, when you look at his art you know he was a big man.

16

Prickasso

More than any other artist, Picasso put sex into his art. His friend the poet Max Jacob said that he would have rather won fame as a stud than as a great artist. The Spanish bull claimed that his sex life started as a child and that he moved directly from childhood to manhood. According to legend, he knew more about sex by the time he was sixteen than most men will ever know. This may have been Andalusian braggadocio, but then he was still making the most explicit sexual etchings when he was ninety.

When asked about his sex life, he said he started when he was quite small – "obviously I did not wait for the age of reason or I might not have started at all".

He may have begun in his hometown of Corunna. He was certainly in love there, with one Angeles Méndez Gil. Her parents were the local nobility. They did not approve of the match and sent her away to Pamplona.

More likely he lost his virginity when he moved to Barcelona to study painting at the age of fourteen. According to the Dada poet Tristan Tzara, Picasso had his cherry popped by the young girl who drew wine in the bar below his studio.

"She was a tall slim girl, not like the buxom women most male virgins hanker after," Tzara said. "But she had a bawdy sense of humour and made him laugh. She said that one day while they were laughing together, he got her up against a barrel and 'made a man of himself'. Looking at her thin body and red hair, he said to a friend it had been like 'screwing my father'."

Picasso was introduced to the brothels of the Barrio Chino in Barcelona by his friend and teacher Manuel Pallarès. Picasso and Pallarès went to Barcelona's February Carnival of 1897 in drag. Pallarès attracted a male admirer who was so persistent that the only way to get rid of him was to fell him with a punch. It is not known whether Picasso scored.

Picasso certainly had a close relationship with a gypsy boy. They met on a painting trip to the Ebro valley and went native, living naked in a cave and sleeping on a huge bed of hay they had cut themselves. They cut themselves and mingled their blood. But eventually the gypsy boy left, telling Picasso he was leaving because "I love you too much".

In Málaga for the summer, Picasso spent hot afternoons watching a woman in a neighbouring apartment going from room to room "wearing nothing but her corset", much to the amusement of his family.

Picasso soon became a regular of the whorehouses of the Barrio Chino. It is not known how he paid for his pleasures. Pallarès may have treated him. Some of the more motherly prostitutes may have been taken in by his boyish charms. Or he may have produced a quick sketch in exchange for sexual favours.

The experience cannot have been a particularly romantic one. A visitor to a China Town brothel in 1948 explained the system. Forty or so women in their bra and panties sat on a raised dais, shouting their sexual specialities. A mob of about a hundred men, all smoking, would hang around until they saw or heard something they fancied. The woman would lead the client to a grilled window where he bought a three-part ticket. He would get one part, the woman another and the stub would be retained by the cashier. They would then go up one side of a staircase divided down the middle with a banister. When their business was done, they would come down the other side, so their descent would not impede oncoming traffic. The woman would go back to the dais. The man would go home, or pick another girl for another turn. Picasso would spend hours in the brothels of the Barrio Chino and first caught syphilis there.

By the time he was fifteen, he had a mistress – Rosita del Oro, a well-known circus performer. This did not mean that he neglected his studies. He worked hard La Llojta art school, especially in the life classes, and rewarded himself for solid days sweating over his nudes with torrid nights of sexual pleasure.

He moved on to the Academy in Madrid. After a few disillusioning days at the Academy, he began to explore the girls of Madrid who, he said, "left the prettiest houris of Turkey in the shade".

On his first trip to Paris when he was nineteen, Picasso set up house with Pallarès, the Catalan artist Carles Casagemas and three easygoing "models". This was a satisfactory arrangement. They gave up going to the brothels of the rue de Londres and were in bed each night at ten. Everything was done to schedule – eating, sleeping, painting, sex. This caused a problem. The six of them ate, slept, painted together in one big room. But Casagemas was a little shy found that he could not perform in front of other people – especially the priapic Picasso. The girls mocked him for his impotence and he became increasingly mentally unstable.

The whole thing ended in tears. Although Picasso persuaded Casagemas to return to Spain with him, the Catalan became increasingly obsessed with Germaine Pichot, the randiest of the three girls, and asked her to marry him. He wrote to her twice a day from Spain. Germaine responded by going back to her husband, whom she had quit for the *mènage* in the studio.

Casagemas gave Picasso the slip and returned to Paris. He caught up with Germaine in a crowded restaurant, pulled out a gun and shot. He missed, but Germaine fell to the floor and played dead. Casagemas then turned the gun on himself and blew his brains out.

Picasso painted two pictures of the dead Casagemas. In one, he places beside his death friend's head a candle whose flame looks very much like an incandescent vagina. Picasso, it seems, was mocking his dead friend's impotence beyond the grave.

Although Casagemas's death haunted him, Picasso happily slept with Germaine on his next trip to Paris. In the meantime, Pallarès kept her warm. However, for a while, Picasso's paintings lost their overtly sexual tone. There were no more nudes in stockings, streetwalkers and frenzied cancan dancers and he entered what became known as his Blue Period.

In his biography of the young Picasso, Norman Mailer speculates that another reason for the absence of sex in Picasso may have been because he had syphilis at that time. It would account, Mailer says, for "his new-found interest in the women's prison at Saint-Lazare, where prostitutes were treated for the same disease". Picasso painted Germaine wearing a headscarf like those the syphilitic prostitutes of the Saint-Lazare were forced to wear. It would also have accounted for the fact that he painted a frieze depicting the Temptation of Saint Antony around the walls of his studio. St Antony is supposed to protect the faithful from the plague. And "St Antony's fire" was once a euphemism for syphilis.

Due to the disease or not, Picasso plunged into a new "Blue Period". It was not blue in the sense that he used blue paint, but because of the content. Much of his work from this period shows women with their legs spread. Some are opening the lips their vaginas with their fingers. One dreamy nude had the tentacles of an octopus entering her. On another drawing of a female nude Picasso scrawled: "When you want to fuck, fuck."

Picasso, who considered himself another martyr to the big S, even portraying Christ on the cross in the mouth of a vagina. Male nudes of this period are portrayed without genitals.

It is worth remembering – for those of you who have not experienced it – that when you suffer from any venereal disease the organ is itself is both stimulated and inflamed. It is full of desire and highly dangerous. The only thing you can think about is spreading the contagion. In one sketch, Picasso portrays himself as the devil.

But Picasso was never down for long. Soon his work is full of erect penises again and couples making love manually, orally and genitally. There was only one thing for it – move back to Paris permanently.

In 1904, at the age of twenty-two, Picasso took a studio the Bateau-Lavoir in Montmartre. A beautiful Frenchwoman called Fernande Olivier, who was separated from her husband, a sculptor who had gone insane, also lived there. They met at the communal tap. On a humid afternoon, Picasso invited her up to see his etchings.

Once Fernande had warmed him with her love, his blue period turned not so much pink as flesh coloured. He seduced a model named Madeleine and made her pregnant. At his behest, she had an abortion.

There was also Alice, who was living with a mathematician named Princet. Picasso got her into his studio to show her a pornographic book named *L'Anti-Justine* he had just borrowed. He caught her likeness on paper as the book put the appropriate thoughts in her head.

Then Picasso found out that, at that time, she was also sleeping with another Spanish painter called Joaquim Sunyer. With his ego bruised, Picasso took a short trip to Holland where he took pleasure in the large Dutch girls.

"Fernande is a big girl," he told a friend. "But those Dutch women are enormous. Once you got inside them, you could never find your way out."

He brought back several studies of Dutch girls. The models who had posed nude for him had caused quite a scandal in their village. In turn, Fernande took her revenge by posing nude for a Dutch artist.

The poet Guillaume Apollinaire introduced Picasso to opium. Soon he and Fernande were spending a lot of time together in bed, smoking. Soon Fernande found she was in love. Up to this point they had not been living together. After a year, Picasso finally persuaded her to move in with him. They lived together for the next eight years.

At first, Fernande was shocked by the terrible conditions in Picasso's studio and set about tidying it up. His only contribution was to make in an alcove a shrine to love which bordered on the obscene.

PRICKASSO

She spent much of her time around the home naked. When he was not making love to her, he was using her as a model. He often worked naked too. Picasso genuinely loved Fernande. His drawings of them making love reveal an extraordinary passion. He wanted to marry her and, whenever he made a few francs selling a canvas, he would buy eau de cologne, because he knew she loved scent. But he liked to keep Fernande indoors. He was proud of her and intensely jealous. He insisted that she stop modelling for other artists. He knew for himself the temptation of having an attractive female nude in the studio. This caused problems for Cormon and François Sicard who were working on large canvases featuring the nude Fernande. Sicard wrote to Picasso saying that he only had two weeks work left on his painting and invited him to the modelling sessions. Picasso refused.

The great artist would not even let her go out and do the shopping in case she saw other men on the street. She was only allowed out when her charm was needed to persuade the local merchants to extend their credit.

Picasso, of course, came and went as he pleased, particularly at night when he went to paint the pimps and whores of the Pigalle. His rumbustuous nightlife caused few problems because Fernande liked to sleep a lot. His acquaintanceship with the ladies of the night does not seem to have bothered her either. His painting *Demoiselles d'Avignon*, the brothel scene that made Picasso's name, passes without mention in her memoirs.

But then she was not really interested in art. She did not like or understand Cubism, so Picasso discussed his new vision of painting with the painter Georges Braque, who became known, behind his back, as "Madame Picasso".

Fernande's role, aside from being his model and mistress, was there to look after him on the domestic level. And he needed some looking after.

"I never met a foreigner less suited for life in Paris," she said.

But then she found herself just as much out of her depth when Picasso took her to Spain on holiday after he had sold his thirty canvases for what he then considered the princely sum of two thousand francs.

But they were usually so short of money that they would have to go without food so Picasso could buy paints. Once a dealer came to see him and offered him seven hundred francs for three canvases. Picasso furiously refused. He returned a few days later and offered five hundred francs for the same three canvases. Picasso was incandescent with rage and again refused. A few days later the dealer called again. This time Picasso was forced to settle for just three hundred francs.

Picasso's temper was legendary. Once a German poet bored him so much with the verse he was reciting that Picasso pulled a gun and shot a hole through the roof of the cab they were riding in, then ran off leaving the poet to face the police.

Fernande was often on the receiving end of his temper. In a jealous rage he tried to burn the studio down. He often locked her in the flat so she could not go out. If she managed to escape and caught up with him in a café or bar, she would often find him with another lady friend perched on his lap.

When the *Mona Lisa* was stolen in 1911, Apollinaire was arrested. Picasso was also a suspect. Fernande was on hand to give succour. But when the real villain was caught, a deranged nationalist who thought the painting should be returned to Italy, Picasso went back to his womanizing ways.

In 1912, Picasso and Fernande split up. Fernande ran off with the futurist Ubaldo Oppi. The loss of his beloved did not stop Picasso painting. In fact, it heralded a renewed bout of creativity. Besides he was already seeing Marcelle Humbet, whom he called Eva, the mistress of the sculptor Louis Marcoussis.

He made no bones about the fact that there was a new woman in his life. He had painted a picture of her with the words *Ma Jolie* – "My Pretty" – in the corner. "Ma Jolie" was the name of a love song popular at the time. It may have been that Fernande had gone off with the young and charming Oppi to try and make Picasso jealous. As it was, he was relieved and went off to Avignon with Eva. He only had one problem. He wrote to Braque: "Fernande ditched me for a futurist. What am I going to do with her dog?"

PRICKASSO

By that time, Picasso had hooked up with the lesbian writer Gertrude Stein, mentor to the young Ernest Hemingway. Under her influence, Picasso's nudes became sexually ambiguous and took on Stein's stocky build and her facial features.

Eva was small, dark and passionate, unlike the tall red haired girls he had been with since he lost his virginity to the wine girl in Barcelona. Eva looked like Picasso's mother.

"At last he has stopped screwing his father," a friend remarked.

In bed, Eva found Picasso surprisingly gentle. Unlike Fernande, Eva helped him with his art. She found him patrons, encouraged his experimentation in Cubism and got him to move to Montparnasse, so that he would not be distracted by his favourite bars and cafés far away in Montmartre. His studio there overlooked the cemetery. After three years of domestic tranquillity, in 1915, Eva died of cancer. By that time, his canvases were fetching high prices.

As Eva lay dying, Picasso began an affair with Gaby Depeyre. She was a twenty-seven-year-old night-club singer, a classic beauty and the lover of a minor American-born artist and poet whom she eventually married.

They took a brief holiday together in the unspoilt fishing village of Saint-Tropez, where they would go skinny-dipping together. When they returned to Paris, he was deeply in love and wanted to marry Gaby. But that did not stop him having a brief affair with Baroness Hélène d'Oettingen, the Russian lover of Leopold Survage.

Gaby turned Picasso's proposal down which, not doubt, hurt his pride. Eva was now dead and Picasso was very much alone. He consoled himself with the model Elivire Palladini, whom he called "You-You", and drew her naked offering herself up to him. But when she later refused him and locked him out of her apartment, he threatened her with a gun.

He also had an affair with Emilienne Pâquerrette, a fashion model at the haute couture house Poiret. She was tall, cool and stylish. Models were all very well, but Picasso was looking for a wife. He picked on Irène Lagut, the mistress of the Russian

Serge Férat, step-brother of Hélène d'Oettingen and reputedly also her lover.

Férat was serving with a Russian ambulance unit on the Western Front. The last night of his leave in Paris, he had to go and see Hélène and asked Picasso to take Irène to the local cinema, where he had a private box. This made seduction all the easier.

Unfortunately, Irène was bisexual and currently had six lovers. Among them were a Piedmontese clown, a soldier who had lost an arm in the war and Ruby Kolb, mistress of Apollinaire. Irène and Ruby had gone off for a holiday together in Brittany, where Apollinaire joined them for a blissful *ménage à trois*. The affair between Ruby and Irène continued back in Paris, though Ruby married Apollinaire six months before he died.

When Irène refused to marry Picasso, he simply abducted her and kept her locked in his apartment. But she escaped and made her way back to Férat. Picasso then used blackmail to try and get her back. He threatened to show Férat photographs he had taken of her in the nude. Irène was unmoved.

"He's the vilest man one could possibly imagine," she said.

Her rejection of him made Picasso suicidal. Apollinaire had to lock him in a closet to prevent him harming himself.

When Férat found out about the affair he forgave Picasso, so great was his respect for the artist. Apollinaire blamed Irène for the whole thing. She was constantly leading Picasso on, then rejecting him. Even after the abduction and the blackmail attempt, she resumed her affair with him.

In 1917, Nijinsky and the Ballet Russes were all the rage. The artist Jean Cocteau and Picasso went with them to Rome, where Picasso was to design the curtain for Diaghilev's new ballet *Parade*. Picasso wrote home to Gertrude Stein: "I have sixty dancers. I go to bed late. I know all the Roman women."

It was not true. He was already stuck on just one of the dancers. Her name was Olga Koklav and she was the daughter of a former colonel in the Russian Imperial Army.

Seduction was no easy matter. French was their only common language and Olga spoke it no better than Picasso did. She was an aristocrat by upbringing, though the Russian Revolution had put paid to that. Although, by this time, he was famous and well off, Picasso's origins were distinctly middle class.

Cocteau was so fascinated by their affair that, for a moment, he dropped his homosexuality and began dating another ballerina so that they could join Picasso and Olga on double dates. Meanwhile, he was flirting with Diaghilev, who was busy with Nijinsky and his Italian valet.

Although Olga was flirtatious, she resisted Picasso's advances.

"No, no, Monsieur Picasso," she was heard to say from her hotel room. "I will not let you enter."

Diaghilev warned Picasso that, if he wanted to have his way with a Russian girl like Olga, he would have to marry her. And that is what he did.

He took her to Barcelona to meet his mother. Then, in Paris, they married in a Russian Orthodox service as well at the statutory civil ceremony. He had married Olga, he said, because she was pretty and an aristocrat. The loss of the haughty Angeles over thirty years before still smarted. They honeymooned in Biarritz.

After their marriage Olga gave up dancing but she continued her ballet practice to preserve her slender figure. It did not work. On 21 February 1921, she gave birth to a son, Paulo.

Although Picasso was content to settle into a fashionable marriage, Olga became increasingly jealous of the women he had known in his past. She tore up letters that made the slightest references to them. Just the mention of their names sent her in to a tormented rage.

On 8 January 1927, seventeen-year-old Marie-Thérèse Walter was emerging from the Metro near the Galeries Layfette when a man grabbed her by the arm.

"I am Picasso," he said. "You and I are going to do great things together."

Marie-Thérèse did not even know who Picasso was. But her mother did and she encouraged the liaison.

"I resisted for six months," Marie-Thérèse said. "But you don't resist Picasso."

On 13 July 1927, her eighteenth birthday, he took her to bed, an event he commemorated seventeen years later in a letter to her.

"Today, 13 July 1944, is the seventeenth anniversary of your birth in me, and twice that of your birth in this world, where, having met you, I began to live," he wrote.

While he kept his new love secret, he celebrated it in numerous nude portraits of her. Fortunately his wife, Olga, never came to his studio above their apartment. Perhaps the reason was that, on the door, he had hung a sign saying: "*Je ne suis pas un gentleman.*"

Picasso was nearly thirty years older than Marie-Thérèse and she called him her "wonderfully terrible" lover. He gave her a thorough *education sentimentale* and subjugated her with his passion. When the family went on holiday to the South of France, she would be sent ahead to stay at a children's camp. Then, when he had had his fill of frolicking with even younger girls, he would come and vent his ardour on her.

His frenzied sexual relations with Marie-Thérèse and the secrecy that surrounded it sparked a period of intense creativity. For Picasso, sex and creativity went hand in hand. Explaining his working methods, Marie-Thérèse said: "He first raped the woman, as Renoir said, and then he worked. Whether it was me or someone else, it was always like that."

Their clandestine unruffled affair continued for eight years until, in July 1935, Marie-Thérèse fell pregnant. Olga found out and it prompted an acrimonious separation. Marie-Thérèse was delighted. But once Olga had gone Picasso moved on. While Marie-Thérèse was giving birth to his daughter, Maïa, Picasso found his wife's replacement.

Her name was Dora Maar. He saw her sitting at the next table at the *Café Deux Magots*, the meeting place for André Breton and the Surrealists. The poet Paul Éluard introduced them. She was the twenty-eight-year-old mistress of Georges Bataille, a painter and photographer, the intellectual muse of the Surrealists and she spoke fluent Spanish.

Picasso repaid Éluard's kindness by seducing his wife Nusch. Éluard forgave the great artist, honoured that Picasso had made this sexual bond with him. Meanwhile, Picasso moved in with Dora and took over her life. And while Dora became his *maîtresse en titre*, Marie-Thérèse was kept on as his secret concubine.

Picasso became increasingly frustrated with Marie-Thérèse. Although she was blonde and beautiful, there was no life in her. His domination of her had left her no room for a personality of her own. She was completely in his thrall. And after Maïa was born, his sexual passion for Marie-Thérèse waned.

"Every time I change wives I should burn the last one," he said. "That way I would be rid of them and they would not be around to complicate my existence."

By destroying the past, he thought, he could recapture his youth. Being around someone young would keep him young. Dora certainly did that. As love grew deeper, it rekindled his ardour for Marie-Thérèse and sent her a torrent of passionate letters.

And Dora was not the only youthful influence on his life. On a trip to Cannes with her, he found two beautiful young sisters. Inès was a chambermaid in a small hotel and Sabartés was a jasmine picker. He took them on as housemaid and cook respectively.

Every aspect of this was celebrated in his art. He even depicted himself as a minotaur – half man, half bull – carrying off a limp, nude Marie-Thérèse, watched by Dora, Inès and Sabartés. Marie-Thérèse had no choice but to accept the situation. She had depended on him for so long, she had nowhere else to go. While Dora was thrilled to be seen by the world as his official mistress, she had to accept that she was not the only one. And Inès and Sabartés needed their jobs. But something had to give.

The confrontation between Marie-Thérèse and Dora came while Picasso was painting *Guernica*, his masterpiece depicting the German air attack on the defenceless Basque market town during the Spanish Civil War. Dora was one of the models for *Guernica* and was photographing the work in progress, when Marie-Thérèse turned up in Picasso's studio.

"I have a child by this man," she told Dora. "You can leave right now."

Dora replied that, although she had not had a child by him, she did not see what difference that made.

"I have as much right to be here as you do," she said.

Picasso kept on painting. He liked them both and saw no reason to choose between them, so he told them that they had better fight it out.

"So they began to wrestle," he said. "It is one of my choicest memories."

Perhaps he savoured the irony of scene: the great artist at work on the twentieth century's most powerful image decrying the horrors of human conflict while two women slugged it out in his studio.

Of course, the fight settled nothing. He told both of them that the other one meant nothing to him – and continued seeing them both. Not that they were the only ones. He continued his affair with Nusch Éluard, while mocking the cuckolded Éluard in his paintings. Holidaying at Mougins, a small village near Cannes, he added Rosemarie to his harem. She would drive Picasso and Dora to the beach bare-breasted.

Picasso was now over fifty and his sexual adventures became increasingly competitive.

"Compared to me," he said, "Matisse is a young lady."

At that time the artist Henri Matisse had moved to Venice with his "secretary" Lydia Delektorskaya, the woman with whom he would spend his declining years.

World War II came as something of an annoyance to Picasso. He had exhibitions around the world, including a huge retrospective in the Metropolitan Museum, New York. As France mobilized, he was having his picture taken for *Life* magazine.

The American Embassy invited Matisse and Picasso to come to the US. Both refused. Picasso would not leave his mistresses.

As the Germans invaded France, Picasso, Marie-Thérèse and Dora sought refuge in Royan. He put them up in separate establishments and hired a studio for himself which they were both forbidden to visit.

Back in Paris, the Germans were not amused by *Guernica*.

PRICKASSO

"Did you do this?" they asked him.

"No," said Picasso, "you did."

Marie-Thérèse found a flat for herself and Maïa not far from Picasso's apartment in the rue des Grands-Augustins, right around the corner from Dora's. Picasso visited Marie-Thérèse on Thursdays and Sundays. The other five days she kept a room in the flat locked and told Maïa that her father was at work in there. He was not to be disturbed.

"We were happy," said Marie-Thérèse. "No one else counted. I knew nothing would get better, but at least despite the whole world and whoever else was around, there were the two of us. Not even the children, not even Maïa."

The rest of the week they maintained a passionate correspondence.

"Without your letters I am sick," he wrote. "You are the best of women... I love only you."

Meanwhile another of Picasso's women, Inès, was installed with her husband in a small apartment below his in the rue des Grands-Augustins.

As if this arrangement was not hard enough for Marie-Thérèse to bear, Picasso sent her clothes identical to those that Dora picked out. This inflamed her to the point where she rushed around to rue des Grands-Augustins uninvited.

Marie-Thérèse demanded that he regularize the situation, a divorce from Olga and marry her as he had long promised. Picasso said that it was not so easy. There was a war on. In the midst of this, Dora walked in. She put her tuppence worth in and insisted it was she that Picasso loved.

"Dora Maar, you know perfectly well that the only one I love is Marie-Thérèse Walter," he said, putting his arms around Marie-Thérèse.

Marie-Thérèse now felt on top of things and ordered Dora out. Dora refused to go. Again they fought. Marie-Thérèse managed to push Dora out of the door. Picasso rewarded her with five kilos of coal, which was rationed during wartime, and sent her home. He made up with Dora later.

Picasso painted Dora as the weeping woman. Women were

suffering machines, he thought, and he was about to increase Dora's burden of suffering.

In May 1943, they were dining together in a Catalan restaurant Picasso frequented when his eye alighted on two beautiful young women. They were Geneviève Aliquot and Françoise Gilot.

The two women had been childhood friends and had become romantically obsessed with each other during their adolescence. Picasso introduced himself. The dark-haired Geneviève, he decided, was a Greek goddess. Françoise was a Florentine virgin.

"Not the usual kind of virgin," said Geneviève. "A secular one."

Picasso pricked up his ears. He asked what the two girls did. They were painters, they said. So he invited them back to his studio. As the Nazis considered Picasso's work degenerate art, it was not on show anywhere in occupied Europe. So this was an offer they could not refuse. But when they got there, all he showed them was his hot water system and invited them to come round and have a bath any time they fancied.

They became regular visitors. Picasso went to see their work, which was on exhibition in a gallery and he encouraged them. Then one day in his studio he kissed Françoise on the mouth. When she made no protest, he said: "That's disgusting. At least you could have pushed me away. Otherwise I might get the impression I could do anything I wanted to do."

Although she was still a virgin, Françoise said that anything he wanted to do was okay by her.

"How can you expect me to seduce anyone under these conditions?" he protested. "If you are not going to resist, it's out of the question."

Later, he took her into his bedroom, gave her a copy of a book by the Marquis de Sade and asked her if she had read it. Françoise said she had not. She did not need to, but he obviously did. Besides, how could he talk about de Sade and his sadistic sex games when so many people were being tortured by the Nazis for real.

At the end of June, he took her up on the roof to show her a seven-foot phallus some workmen had painted on the building opposite. Gently he cupped her breasts in his hands. Again she was ruffled. But he simply took his hands away.

"Not suddenly, but carefully, as though they were two peaches whose form and colour had attracted him," she said, "he had picked them up, satisfied himself that they were ripe, but then realized that it wasn't time for lunch yet."

Françoise and Geneviève went to the country for a break. It was there that the twenty-one-year-old Françoise Gilot realized that she was in love with the sixty-two-year-old Picasso. When she told her parents, her father was furious. To escape his wrath, she ran to her grandmother's house. But her father caught up with her there and beat her. When the old woman interceded, he threatened to have them both committed. It was an empty threat.

Françoise stayed with her grandmother. Cut off without a penny, she found work giving riding lessons in the Bois de Boulogne and began visiting Picasso's busy studio almost every day. But still he made no move on her.

Then in February 1944, he said that the next time she came, there would be just the two of them and he would teach her engraving. She arrived in a chic black dress.

"Is that the kind of thing you wear to learn engraving?" he asked.

"No," she said, "but it is appropriate for what you have in mind."

"Couldn't you at least pretend to be taken in?" he said. "The way women generally do."

They looked through some of his more erotic engravings together. Then he took her upstairs. In the bedroom, he told her that he wanted to see if her body corresponded to the mental image he had of it and undressed her. When she was completely nude he stood back nine or ten feet and examined her.

When he was satisfied, he sat down on the bed and pulled her down on to his knee. He spoke to her reassuringly. Then he laid her on the bed he began moving his hands gently over her body like a sculptor working over marble.

Françoise found the loss of her virginity to this master thoroughly satisfactory. Afterwards he explained that they must not see too much of each other.

"Everything exists in limited quantities," he said, "especially happiness. If a butterfly's wings are to keep their sheen, you must not touch them."

Just six weeks after the Liberation, Picasso exhibited at the Salon d'Autome. His wartime canvases caused an uproar among the older academicians. Françoise had to stand guard on them. Instantly, he became both a national institution and the darling of the young. Bevies of young schoolgirls flocked to pay homage the master – and to be deflowered. One of them was Geneviève Laporte, who came to interview him for her school newspaper.

"I am a woman," he told her. "Every artist is a woman and should have a taste for other women. Artists who are homosexual cannot be true artists because they like men, and since they themselves are women they are reverting to normality."

The rest of the action did not make the press.

Françoise knew nothing of these dalliances. She thought that Marie-Thérèse was a thing of the past and that Dora was her only rival. When Dora heard about Françoise, she accepted she had been supplanted by a "schoolgirl... in bed, but not at the table". This remark prompted Picasso to invite Françoise to dinner.

She brought with her the artist André Marchand, who had painted her portrait many times and was obviously in love with her. Dora was taken in. She began inviting Marchand to dinner in the hope that he would bring Françoise with him, believing that, if Picasso saw them together often enough, he would go off her. Of course, it had the opposite effect.

Picasso took Françoise to the Bateau-Laval and showed her the studio where he had started out. Nearby, they visited a gnarled, toothless old lady, sick in bed. It was Germaine Pichot, the model Casagemas had shot himself over.

Although the affair with Françoise was serious, she was not his only interest. He still tried to seduce every woman who walked into his studio – and often succeeded. Dora fought back with an exhibition of her own paintings. Françoise ran away. But Picasso always chased after her, bedded her and brought her back. All this began to take its toll on Dora. Suddenly, she got religion.

"As an artist you may be extraordinary," she told Picasso, "but morally you are worthless."

One day, she burst into Picasso's studio – from which she had been banned – and tried to get Picasso and Éluard to get on their knees and beg forgiveness. Picasso called a doctor, who took her to a clinic where she received electric shock treatment. She was released to the treadmill of analysis.

Plainly Dora needed a holiday, so Picasso took her to the South of France. He invited Françoise to come too, but she refused to humiliate her rival further and took off to Brittany. In the Midi, he got rid of Dora by giving her a large house which he had bought for one still life, sight unseen.

Françoise then became the *maîtresse en titre*, much to Marie-Thérèse's chagrin. When Picasso teased her about what a great rider Françoise was, Marie-Thérèse took to riding in the Bois de Boulogne too. It did no good.

When Françoise broke her leg, Picasso sent her to the South of France to recuperate. She invited Geneviève to stay with her, who told Françoise, for her own good, she ought to leave Picasso. When Picasso got wind of this he drove down to the South of France for a confrontation. In a jealous tantrum, he threatened to burn Françoise's face with a cigarette.

Then there ensued a tug of love between Geneviève and Picasso over Françoise. Picasso told Françoise that her best friend had tried to seduce him behind her back. He gave her an engraving and promised her children. After all, he said, he did not have long to live and he deserved a little bit of happiness. Geneviève offered her safety and sanity. He won the day.

"You are sleepwalking your way to destruction," Geneviève told Françoise when she got on the train to go home.

Picasso had now decided that Françoise should live with him. She refused, saying that Dora Maar was still in his life. To prove that she was not, Picasso took Françoise and Dora out to dinner. He took pains to enthuse about every word Françoise said, while ignoring Dora's most sparkling repartee.

When that did not work, Picasso took Françoise around to Dora's flat to get her to say that they had broken up.

"There is nothing to left to break up," Dora said. And she told Picasso: "You have never loved anyone in your life. You don't know how to love."

When Françoise was still not convinced, he threatened to throw her in the Seine. He pushed her to the edge of a bridge and forced her head over the parapet, while she taunted him, begging him to throw her in.

Nevertheless, Françoise did move into the rue des Grands-Augustins, much to the displeasure of Inès who had long ruled the roost there. Picasso got Françoise to pose for him and for a time it was idyllic. Then he took her on holiday. They stayed at the house he had given Dora. It was not the happy honeymoon she had been expecting, especially as he still received passionate letters from Marie-Thérèse every day.

He even read passages out to her.

"I don't see you writing letters to me like that," he said. "That woman really loves me."

His letters in reply were no less passionate.

All Françoise could think of was escape. She tried to hitchhike to Marseilles where she intended to pick up a boat for Tunisia. But, when she got out on the road, the first car that stopped for her was Picasso's.

Françoise did not want to have children. But Picasso decided that having them was the only solution. Soon she was pregnant. Françoise said that Picasso got women pregnant to make them more dependent on him. Picasso disagreed. He said that getting a woman pregnant was one way to destroy his feelings towards her.

"You can't imagine how constantly I feel the need to free myself," he told Geneviève Laporte, the schoolgirl–reporter whom he was seeing again.

When Nusch Éluard died of a stroke, Paul Éluard asked Picasso if he could marry Dora. Picasso said yes, but Dora refused.

"After Picasso," she said, "only God."

PRICKASSO

Françoise gave birth to a son, Claude. Picasso discovered that being a father again did not slow him down. He flirted with any woman who visited and when women asked him for an autograph he said he would prefer to paint on their naked flesh. Françoise also had to bear Olga following them around wherever they went, often hurling abuse at them. Picasso pretended to find this annoying, but what could he do? However when a senator suggested that Picasso take out French citizenship so that he could divorce his wife and marry Françoise, he went ballistic.

Olga began physically assaulting Françoise, who begged Picasso to move to another house so she would not be able to find him. On the day of the move, Picasso said: "I don't know why I am going through with this. If I had to move house every time women started fighting over me, I wouldn't have much time to do anything else.

The new house was at Vallauris. It had a large studio and Picasso encouraged Françoise to take up painting again. But it was open house, with people turning up from all over the world to see him. The only time that Françoise was left undisturbed was when the sculptor Albert Giacometti visited. Picasso would buy pornographic magazines and they would take them down to the local café like two smutty schoolboys.

Otherwise, Françoise grew discontented with this very public life. But Picasso knew the cure for that. By the end of the summer, Françoise was pregnant again.

When Picasso went to Poland to attend a Communist conference, he got his chauffeur to send a telegram to François daily. The chauffeur misspelt her name and always signed off with the working class salutation: *"Bons baisers."*

Interestingly, special arrangements had to be made when Picasso travelled, because he did not have a passport. Despite living in France for seventy years, he never naturalized as a French citizen. And he would not accept one from the Fascist government in Spain. But he was so famous he could travel without one.

When Picasso returned home, Françoise slapped his face, saying: "That's for *bons baisers*."

It was a deliberate insult, she concluded. She was getting to the end of her tether.

"If I am willing, out of love, to be a slave, I am the slave of love, not your slave," she warned. "If my love ends, so does my slavery."

But the new pregnancy and her fuller figure brought them closer again. That ended at term. Picasso was due at a Peace Conference, advertised by his famous dove, in Paris when Françoise was advised by her doctor to check into the maternity home. Picasso refused to give up his car and driver to take her, nor would he take a detour to drop her there on the way. Instead, after he had driven Picasso to the conference, the driver had to go back for her. She arrived at the clinic at five o'clock. At eight, she gave birth to a girl, Paloma.

"She will be the perfect woman," said Picasso, observing the sleeping child. "Passive and submissive, the way girls ought to be. They ought to stay asleep like that until they are twenty-one."

Soon after he became a grandfather. Paulo, his son with Olga, sired an illegitimate son called Pablo, who Picasso called Pablito. Living under the shadow of his father, Paulo had become a drunk and a drug addict. One night he had picked up a couple of girls and taken them back to small hotel. When he got bored with them, he tried to throw them out of the window. He was arrested and was released only because he was the son of the great artist.

Picasso sent Françoise to get him. When she returned with him, Picasso threw everything that he could lay his hands on at Paulo who sheltered behind Françoise. It made no difference. How could anyone even conceive of throwing a woman out of a window? demanded Picasso. Paulo said that anyone familiar with the works of the Marquis de Sade should have no problems with such a peccadillo.

Picasso maintained his routine of seeing Marie-Thérèse every Thursday and Sunday. Even when he and Françoise were away from Paris, Marie-Thérèse would be lodged conveniently near by.

PRICKASSO

Françoise wanted to put an end to this artificial situation, so Picasso invited Marie-Thérèse to visit.

"With any luck, you two will come to blows," Picasso said.

The immediate beneficiary of this move was Maïa, who was now thirteen. At last, she discovered the truth about her father and she got on well with Françoise, Claude and Paloma.

But trouble was brewing. Françoise had not recovered well from giving birth to Paloma. She was haemorrhaging and she could not fulfil the sexual needs of the sixty-eight-year-old Picasso. He left her at Vallauris with the kids and headed back to Paris where he tried to seduce Françoise's grandmother.

At Vallauris, he mused on how wonderful it would be to have as many children as Oona O'Neill had given Charlie Chaplin – they had eight. But in fact, he spent little time with his children and his trips to Paris became increasingly frequent. He was seen in his studio at the rue des Grands-Augustins with Pierrette Gargallo, daughter of the sculptor.

When Paul Éluard married again, Picasso said: "If Paul thinks that I am going to honour him again by going to bed with his new wife, he is wrong."

He simply did not fancy Dominique Laure, the new Mrs Éluard. So next time, Éluard came to Vallauris, he brought with him Geneviève Laporte, rekindling that affair. Soon Picasso was telling her that he had never loved Françoise but he could not leave her because he was too afraid of hurting people.

Meanwhile he was telling Françoise that she had let herself go since giving birth to Paloma and she looked like a broom. When she cried, he chided her for that too. And four-year-old Claude was told that he was the son of a mother who always said "no".

Geneviève Leporte was certainly not a woman who said "no".

"With her, it's all sweetness and honey," Picasso said. "She is a hive without bees."

Meanwhile, Picasso was supplementing his diet with women of every age, size and rank along the Côte d'Azure. Françoise was told of one he had installed in Saint-Tropez, with whom he planned to elope to Tunisia.

When Françoise confronted him, he said the story was just malicious gossip. Soon the newspapers were full of stories of the affair. He still denied everything.

The death of Françoise's grandmother and the newspaper stories of Picasso's affairs heralded a reconciliation between Françoise and her father and she visited him. When she returned to Vallauris, it was obvious that Picasso was been sleeping with Geneviève Laporte. If there was a third person in their relationship, Françoise said, he should be honest about it. Picasso continued to deny everything.

In a last ditch attempt to save their relationship, Françoise suggested they buy a big house where everyone could live – all his mistresses and their children. Picasso and Marie-Thérèse were shocked at the suggestion. She still thought that Françoise would go and finally Picasso would be all hers.

When Picasso heard that the artist Marc Chagall's wife had left him, he laughed.

"Don't laugh," Françoise said. "It could happen to you."

Picasso said that was the most ridiculous thing he had ever heard.

"Nobody leaves a man like me," he said.

Next time Picasso set off on one of his jaunts to Paris, Françoise asked to go with him, otherwise she might not be there when he got back. It was an empty threat. She was still there when he got back, but her love for him was dead and sex with him became repugnant.

Now in his seventies, Picasso began a new bout of sexual promiscuity, returning home tired and haggard. He was not even discreet. He would often book into a hotel with his latest amour under his own name. The next morning the paparazzi would be waiting and Françoise would be treated to the juicy details of his latest sexual adventure on the front page of the daily newspapers.

Things reached a head when Picasso began an affair Jacqueline Roque, a hazel-eyed sales girl from the local pottery. Picasso called her Madame Z. Françoise took off to Paris, where she had been commissioned to design the costumes and sets for a ballet. She wrote to Picasso from there, begging him, for once, to come clean. He rushed to Paris. Praising her for her beautiful letter, he admitted everything and, with tears in his eyes, begged her forgiveness.

To prove that he was a reformed character, she should come with him that minute to a restaurant around the corner where Geneviève Laporte was waiting. He was going to tell her it was all over.

However, in Françoise's mind this only proved that Picasso was beyond reform. On the way from Vallauris, he must have stopped to arrange the rendezvous with Geneviève.

Picasso did give up Geneviève though. Each night, when Françoise passed the restaurant, she saw Geneviève waiting there, alone. She could not believe that Picasso had dumped her. Like all the other women in his life, Geneviève believed that she was his one true love.

Back at Vallauris, Françoise threw herself into her work and made little time for Picasso. This drove him into deep despair and he threatened suicide.

"That would certainly be an effective solution for all your problems," Françoise told Picasso and she said she would do nothing to stop him.

With the ballet commission, now it was her turn to take trips to Paris, leaving him at home in Vallauris with the kids. While she was away, she began an affair with the Greek existentialist philosopher Kostas Axelos.

When she returned to Vallauris, Axelos bombarded her with letters and telegrams. When Picasso asked Françoise what was going on, she told him she was leaving him.

"Nobody leaves a man like me," said Picasso again. This time he was wrong.

Françoise took the children to Paris, where she resumed her affair with Axelos. Picasso did everything from bombast to self pity to get her back. They could resume life at Vallauris together as friends, he said, no questions asked. Meanwhile, he consoled himself with a pretty young English blonde who agreed to pose for him.

Friends told Françoise that, at his age, Picasso should not be left alone. She faltered and returned to Vallauris only to find that her clothes had been worn. Some had even been altered. Jacqueline Roque, Madame Z, had been spending a lot of time at the house, it seemed.

Picasso complained of the solitude he suffered with her gone. Although they had had their problems living together, it was even harder living apart. Françoise was moved.

But then he started his old tricks again. He began making portraits of a pretty young blonde named Sylvette David. This was supposed to make Françoise jealous. Instead, she urged him on and kept out of the way when Sylvette was around.

Picasso complained. His former lovers had always been fiercely jealous when a new woman appeared in his work, he said.

"You are a monster of indifference," he told Françoise.

Indeed she was. She left him again, promising to come back for a month in July with the children.

Soon after, Picasso bumped into Dora Maar at a friend's house. She was with her historian friend James Lord.

"Are you two married?" he said sarcastically.

"No, only engaged," said Dora.

Picasso scowled.

"I'd rather see a woman die, any day, than see her happy with someone else," he once said.

Over dinner, he lamented the fact, rather pointedly, that he was without a woman. After dinner he drew Dora aside. The room was full of his paintings and he led her to a far corner. He left her there, and left. Dora was very upset.

But there were still plenty of women in Picasso's life. Madame Z was with him almost constantly, until the beginning of July when she was packed off back to the village.

When Françoise had returned with the children, he was determined to show her a good time. He took her to bullfights and night-clubs, sometimes partying all night and on through the next day. Often Jacqueline Roque would tag along. She kicked up a fuss one night in Bandol, when Picasso insisted on sharing a hotel room with Françoise. And she was deeply humiliated when Picasso got Françoise to perform, on horseback, the opening ceremony of a bullfight held in his honour.

Afterwards, Picasso told Françoise she was wonderful.

"Now you will have to stay," he said.

She left the next morning.

What Picasso had lost in quality, he made up for in quantity. There followed a procession of young women, many supplied by friends who were worried about him being on his own. They got younger and younger. The press published pictures of likely candidates. Picasso drew and painted them, naked in increasingly pornographic positions.

Jacqueline Roque became more and more desperate. She threatened suicide. But eventually she reconciled herself to accepting every humiliation, just so she could be around the great artist. This suited Picasso just fine. He even took her with him to Paris to use as a model and lover whenever there was nothing else to hand. She was useful to him. She had had one child before she had met him, but the birth had left her infertile so he could make love to her without the bother of contraception.

Jacqueline found herself the model for all the whores in Picasso's numerous reworkings of Delacroix's *The Women of Algiers*. He was just finishing the series when he heard that Olga had died of cancer in a hospital in Cannes. He did not attend the funeral.

Then came a worse blow. Françoise was going to get married to the artist Luc Simon, two years her junior. She came to Picasso's studio in person to tell him. He exploded. How could she be so selfish? Then she noticed that the door to the sculpture room was ajar. It was plain that they were not alone. Having lost the moral high ground, Picasso calmed down and offered Françoise a tangerine.

In a more measured tone, Picasso pointed out that, while another man might not have his faults, he would not have his virtues either. And instead of giving her his blessing, he said: "I hope your marriage is a fiasco, you ungrateful creature."

He grew even more fiercely jealous when she went to Venice

on her honeymoon with her handsome young husband. He looked after the children and refused to return them until she had handed over all the drawings and etchings in her apartment. When he heard she was pregnant, he was determined to destroy her. He used his considerable influence in the art world to demolish her artistic career. Her contract was terminated and no galleries dared show her pictures.

Now that Olga was dead, Picasso was free to marry Marie-Thérèse. He called her up and told her so. But it was only another cruel tease to humiliate Jacqueline who also thought she was in with a chance.

Up until the 1950s, Picasso had kept in touch with all his old lovers, including Fernande. When he had heard she was in hospital with pneumonia, he had sent her an envelope stuffed with money. But slowly he began to cut himself loose, even from Dora and Marie-Thérèse.

In the summer of 1959, he began a new series of brothel pictures. The following year, Françoise pressed Picasso to have their children legitimized. Picasso used this a tool to recapture her. In January 1961, the courts awarded Claude and Paloma their father's name. In February, Françoise asked her husband for a divorce, clearing her way to marrying Picasso. But in March, in the utmost secrecy, Picasso married Jacqueline Roque instead. Twelve days later, Françoise opened the paper to discover that the man she was divorcing her husband to marry had married someone else.

Jacqueline then became Picasso's "*maman*". But she was still his model as well. He made more than seventy pictures of her in 1962, one hundred and sixty in 1963. Most of all, though, she was his unquestioning slave. He grappled with mortality by brutalizing her body on canvas. But he still made up for this tenderly at night. Sex became, more than ever, the dominant theme of his work. His later work is full of women with their legs spread and couples copulating. Distinguished critics became concerned about his pornographic obsession.

At eighty he was still as randy as an old goat. At his birthday party he made a pass at a pretty young journalist from

PRICKASSO

Paris-Soir. Françoise Gilot got her own back for his cruel mistreatment of her with the publication of her book *Life with Picasso*. Picasso tried to have it banned as an unwarranted intrusion into his privacy. The courts decided against him on the grounds that, with stunts like having himself photographed naked in the bath, he had already "exposed himself to public curiosity".

As he withdrew further behind the electronic gates of his house in the South of France, Jacqueline began to get the upper hand. She excluded his children and got him to cut off the allowance that he had been giving Marie-Thérèse for more than thirty years. When an art dealer interceded for Marie-Thérèse, Jacqueline castigated her as "that woman you slept with once in a while on Thursday afternoons" and said in a rage: "If she needs money why doesn't she hire herself out as a *femme de ménage*."

After Jacqueline had stormed out, Picasso shrugged and said: "What can I do? Jacqueline would never forgive me, so that's that."

Marie-Thérèse eventually went to a lawyer. After protracted negotiations, her allowance was not just restored but increased.

Although Claude and Paloma now carried their father's name, Françoise fought on to have them fully legitimized. Meanwhile, Picasso began to satirize Degas as a voyeur in his etchings.

The end came quickly, on 1 April 1973, he wrote to Marie-Thérèse telling her once more that she was the only woman he had ever loved. On 5 April, he phoned the artist Edouard Pignon who was putting on an exhibition called Red Nudes.

"Paint nudes, nudes and more nudes," said Picasso, "mountains of breasts and bottoms."

Three days later, Picasso was dead, of a heart attack. Perhaps he had surfeited on nudes at last, buried under a mountain of breasts and bottoms. What a way to go.

17
Modeldigliani

Modigliani could not get enough of nude models. Even in his religious paintings, the girls had to strip off. In 1917, the only exhibition of his work during his lifetime, consisting almost entirely of nudes, was closed by the police. His nudes are extraordinarily seductive probably because he took the precaution of bonking the model first and then, some say, bonking her again afterwards.

Amedeo Clemente Modigliani was born in Livorno on 12 July 1884 in a bed piled high with valuables. His father had just gone bankrupt and an ancient Roman law prevented the bailiffs taking anything from the bed of a woman in labour.

After attending art school in Livorno, Modigliani knew where his calling lay. In 1902, he enrolled in Fattori's *Scuola de Nudo* – the School of Nude Studies – in Florence. When he was seen out on the town, there was always a beautiful young woman on his arm. Modigliani was very handsome. Conquests were almost too easy and women pursued him remorselessly.

He moved to Venice where, for a time, he had a regular girlfriend, Albertina Olper, who had the type of elongated oval that characterize his paintings. Then he decided to go to Paris. On the train on the way, an old woman and her pretty young daughter invited him to sit with them. Modigliani charmed the old lady with her politeness and flirted outrageously with the daughter every time the old lady's back was turned.

MODELDIGLIANI

The first thing that Modigliani did when he arrived in Paris was to join a life class at the Académie Colarossi. He befriended Picasso who advised him to move to Montmartre. This was more to Modigliani's tastes, especially as the can-can girls on the street corners taking a break from the shows were only too glad to show off the fact that they were not wearing any underwear.

Soon well-bred virgins as well as washerwomen and street girls were queuing to pose for him. He had them all in the same casual fashion. He became a bit more serious about a svelte girl called Mado. She was one of Picasso's cast-offs and he thought making love to her frequently might imbue him with some of the master's genius.

Modigliani befriended Utrillo, Suzanne Valadon's son and championed him when everyone else dismissed him as a drunk. Modigliani would go drinking with Utrillo to get away from the swarms of pretty girls that pursued him.

He tried painting the acrobats and harlequins that were fashionable at the time. But he could not resist doing nudes. So, in emulation of Picasso's blue period, he got girls with syphilis to model for him. Although he called these paintings "sorrowful", the joy could not help bursting out of him. One Parisian lady recalled seeing Modigliani with his mistress Elvira, a ravishing courtesan who worked under the name *La Quique*, dancing naked in a garden.

The painter Severini invited Modigliani to join the other Italian artists who had just published the Futurist Manifesto. Modigliani declined. The Futurists condemned the painting of nudes. They were, said the Manifesto, "as sickening and tedious as the adulterer in literature" and they called for a ten-year ban on nudes. But Modigliani could not give them up and continued to take life classes as long as he lived. Once he remarked to the Russian poetess Anna Akhmatova while passing the *Venus de Milo* in the Louvre that "women of a beauty worth painting or sculpting often seem encumbered by their clothes".

Twenty-two-year-old Anna, beautiful, romantic and recently married, took the hint and posed for him. He was a perfect gentleman, she said. He never mentioned previous love affairs.

Modigliani sold few paintings during his lifetime, but his reputation around Montparnasse was high. Once when a dealer was beating him down on a series of drawings from ten francs to five, Modigliani simply took a knife made a hole in the corner of the drawings and hung them on a hook in the toilet.

Modigliani smoked hashish. He found it gave him a greater insight into his work. It also put his models in the mood. He also used pornography and was a great fan of *Les Chants de Maldoror* by Isidore Ducasse, who used the *nom de plume* Comte de Lautréamont to avoid prosecution. In the book, the protagonist Maldoror copulates with a female shark, a beautiful young girl is violated by a shepherd's dog and God visits a brothel.

Always penniless, Modigliani found that even the most mercenary women would cook, clean and wash for him – as well as pose nude for free. And it was not just ordinary working girls. When Modigliani was commissioned to paint the portrait of the wife of a prominent businessman, the businessman came home to find his wife posing nude. Mad with jealousy, the businessman tried to throw Modigliani out of the house. The painter resisted so ferociously that the businessman fled. But when Modigliani returned to see his mistress again, the woman had been abducted and the painting was gone. It is said that Modigliani had introduced her to drugs and she died in an insane asylum.

His success in love and his easy access to free models caused no end of jealousy in Montparnasse. So, for a break, Modigliani returned to Livorno where he did some sculpting. When the time came to go back to Paris, he asked his friends from the art school whether there was anywhere he could store his sculptures. They chorused with one voice: "In the moat."

And that is where they remain to this day.

But Modigliani's work did not go entirely unnoticed. Augustus John bought one sculpture. Modigliani was so grateful that he threw in his well-thumbed copy of *Les Chants de Maldoror* for free. The dealer Paul Chéron was so impressed that he sent his own wife to model for Modigliani. But she was not to Modigliani's taste and he took Chéron's pretty young maid instead.

When Chéron and Modigliani had a falling out, the dealer stole the painter's clothes to keep him indoors working. The Rumanian sculptor Constantin Brancusi had to buy him a jumper and a pair of trousers so he could go and see his mistress Gaby, the thirty-year-old *maîtresse en titre* of a prominent lawyer.

When the lawyer got to hear of their affair, he summoned Modigliani to met him at the Café Panthéon on the Boulevard Saint-Michel. Modigliani turned up smartly dressed and ordered an expensive bottle of wine. He rattled on about Gaby's beauty and charms without allowing the lawyer to get a word in edgeways. Then he produced a picture of Gaby nude. He had painted a series of them, he said. Some day they would be worth thousands and he pressed the painting on his rival in love.

The two men got drunk, united in their love for one woman. Gaby was so flawless, they agreed, that no man of taste and discernment could help falling in love with her. At the end of the evening, they went reeling into the night, arm in arm, swearing eternal friendship.

In 1912, the young British artist Nina Hamnett came to Paris. She was eating in Rosalie's, a cheap restaurant recommended to her by the sculptor Jacob Epstein, when Modigliani came up to her and said: *"Je suis Modigliani, Juif, Jew."*

He showed her some of his work and every morning they would go to La Rotonde, a hangout for artists, and sell his drawings at five francs each. They were both chronic exhibitionists. She loved to dance naked in public places. He would strip off too and chase her up the street. Nina went to bed with Aleister Crowley, but "the Beast" himself could not get it up. Crowley then became convinced that her then lover, the Polish artist Waclaw Zavado, was trying to kill him and sent three of his concubines to warn him off.

When Epstein was in London in 1914, he met Wyndham Lewis's lover, the fiery feminist Beatrice Hastings at a party in

Soho. She was also the lover of Alfred Orage, co-editor of the short-lived arts journal *The New Age*. Then thirty-five, Beatrice was a thoroughly modern woman. She wore Liberty smocks and smoked in the street. She was also slim with high breasts. She said she wanted something to write about. So Epstein recommended that she go to Paris and look up Modigliani. And that is exactly what she did.

Nina claimed to have introduced them at La Rotonde. But Beatrice said that she met him when he whistled after her in Rosalie's. She introduced herself as a poetess; he as a drunk.

Beatrice was soon obsessed with Modigliani, but she was also committed to the Feminist cause. She was appalled to discover than there was no suffragette movement in France.

"The women count money all day and make love on Sunday," she wrote.

But her column in *The New Age* was soon brimming with the name of her new lover – Modigliani. While she briefly returned to England, Modigliani entertained himself with Marevna Vorobiev, who went on to become the lover of the great Mexican artist Diego Rivera. When Beatrice came back to Paris, Modigliani moved into her studio and drew and painted her nude and as a courtesan.

The First World War was on, and against the background of nightly bombings, Modigliani and Beatrice made love and fought. According to the writer Blaise Cendrars, they were well matched. One night, alarmed at the commotion, the concierge knocked on the door of Beatrice's apartment. Modigliani answered and promised her nothing untoward was going on.

"I am merely chopping firewood and beating my mistress like a gentleman," he said.

Apparently Beatrice had bitten his balls.

She used to wind him up, playing him off against Max Jacob, Picasso's gay friend. Modigliani got so angry with her at a party once, he picked her up and threw her through a closed window. According to Marevna, the blooded Beatrice was carried back into the house and laid on the sofa. She wept while Modigliani repeated over and over: *"Non mea culpa."*

But their relationship was not without its moments of tenderness. One night they were invited to a ball and Beatrice did not have anything to wear. Modigliani told to her put on an old black silk dress.

"But everyone has seen that a hundred times before," she complained.

He told her to put it on and he would make her the best-dressed woman at the ball. He drew a floral pattern on it and got her to cut the *décolleté* to a line he had drawn. When she entered the ball, the dress drew a gasp. Beatrice danced the tango with numerous admirers. Modigliani got drunk and when Beatrice went a little too far with her flirting, he tore the dress to shreds.

Behind his back, Beatrice had a sly affair with the Italian sculptor Alfredo Pina who lived close by. At the same time she kept Modigliani locked up so that he could not see other women.

The painter Moïse Kisling invited Beatrice to pose for him. Modigliani prevented it. When Kisling asked why, Modigliani said: "As far as I am concerned, if a woman poses for you, she gives herself to you."

Eventually, Modigliani lost Beatrice to Raymond Radiguet, the teenage author of the romantic best-seller *Le Diable au Corps*, whom Modigliani had introduced her too. She was forty; he was eighteen.

The pretty French Canadian blonde Simone Thiroux stepped into the breach. She modelled for a number of the artists of the Montparnasse and had had her eye on Modigliani for some time. One night, she found him drunk in La Rotonde, took him home, put him to bed and got in with him.

Modigliani's new dealer Leopold Zborowski was away in the South of France and returned to find that Modigliani had painted three portraits of his wife in the nude. To prevent it happening again, Zborowski set up a studio for Modigliani and hired models for him. Naturally, he had to peep through the keyhole every so often to see that he was getting his money's worth fron the artist and his model.

Hanging out with Utrillo had taken its toll. Utrillo himself had already ended up in a lunatic asylum through his alcoholism. Modigliani now drank almost constantly and often turned up to parties or salons covered in mud. Although his paintings did not sell, his drawings found ready buyers. But Modigliani frequently gave them to the sitter or handed them over the bar in exchange for drinks, to the exasperation of Zborowski who had to pawn his suit to keep the artist going.

In 1917, at the height of the slaughter in the First World War, Modigliani painted a series of nudes – shop girls, waitresses, models. They were openly sexual women in the flower of their youth. These suddenly found a buyer. Zborowski was so delighted to have found someone who appreciated Modigliani's work that he gave the first canvas away free.

Simone became pregnant, but Modigliani refused to admit paternity of the child and the affair ended there. The gossip around Montparnasse was that, now Modigliani's works were selling, Simone had decided to have a Modigliani of her own. Others said that Modigliani had caught her in bed with another painter. She was well known to have shared her favours around, so the child probably was not his anyway.

In 1917, Modigliani found a new model. She was nineteen-year-old art student Jeanne Hébuterne. Although the Japanese artist Foujita claimed they had been lovers, friends insist that Jeanne was a virgin when she met Modigliani. She only had eyes for him and he was to paint her more than twenty-five times.

Soon they were seen walking in Montparnasse hand in hand like two teenage lovers. Modigliani was then thirty-three. To the outrage of her respectable Mass-going parents, Jeanne moved into a seedy hotel room with the penniless drunken drug-taking Jewish bohemian.

If that was not bad enough, only months after she had moved in, his scandalous one-man show opened. And on the cover of the catalogue was a drawing of Jeanne, nude, with a very prominent triangle of pubic hair.

Numerous celebrities attended the opening. A magnificently inviting nude in the window attracted a crowd. It also attracted the police. When they entered the gallery to ask for it to be taken down, they found that the walls were crammed full of nudes equally magnificent and inviting. The commissioner of police himself ordered that the exhibition be closed on the grounds that Modigliani's nudes had pubic hair.

The scandal may have been an embarrassment for Jeanne's parents, but for Modigliani it was a triumph. Although he had sold only two drawings for thirty francs each during the brief run of the show, its closure sent his name buzzing around Paris and his paintings were suddenly much sought after.

At the beginning of 1918, the Germans redoubled their air raids on the city. And Paris was now under attack from the German supergun Big Bertha. Meanwhile Modigliani was back in the studio painting more nudes. However, the bombing and shelling meant that almost anyone who could afford it left the city to seek safety in the South of France. With them went the art dealers and art buyers.

Modigliani followed his market. He took Jeanne, who was pregnant, with him. Jeanne's mother, concerned about her twenty-year-old daughter, tagged along. Just to make Madame Hébuterne really at home, Foujita and his wife Fernande Barrey, who boasted of having started life as a prostitute, also joined the party.

To make her feel a little better, Modigliani publicly acknowledged paternity of the child and promised to marry Jeanne. But it was wartime, they were a long way from home, he had no time for officialdom, so when this was going to happen was anyone's guess.

In Nice, he continued to paint Jeanne and any other woman who he could get to pose for him. Madame Hébuterne cursed his art and the tension became so bad that he had to move out of the house Zborowski rented for them and into a hotel.

Cendrars came to Nice to work on a film script and decided to look up Modigliani. When he found him, he was looking terrible. For two or three months, he had been off the booze. Cendrars was concerned and insisted that he start drinking again. He left a thousand-franc note on his bedside table and told the bell hop to get him anything he wanted. For several days the note lay there untouched. Then one day Cendrars found it gone. He went to look for Modigliani – and found him dead drunk, asleep in the middle of the Place Iéna.

When his daughter was born, Modigliani set off for the Town Hall to register the birth but never arrived. He got drunk on the way.

And there were other troubles. Modigliani had to move hotels after he fell out with a local pimp whose girls were posing for him for free.

During his time in the South of France, Modigliani visited Renoir who made his famous remark: "Before I paint, I caress the buttocks for hours…"

Modigliani said: "I don't like buttocks" and walked out.

It is true. Modigliani's nudes are always shown full frontal.

In 1919, Modigliani returned to Paris leaving Jeanne and their baby in Nice. He found a seedy hotel room which was no place to bring up a baby. But Jeanne was eager to be with him and Lunia Czechowski, a friend of the Zboroskis and one of his models, offered to look after the child until they found somewhere more suitable.

Back in Paris Jeanne saw little of Modigliani. Utrillo was out of the sanatorium and they went on a bender together. One night at Rosalie's they ordered a meal that they could not afford, so in lieu of paying the bill they decided to paint a mural on the wall. No art connoisseur, Rosalie saw two drunks making a mess of her wall and ordered them to clean it off with turpentine and rags.

Fourteen-year-old Paulette Jourdain began posing for Modigliani and Jeanne grew jealous. Although she did not interrupt the sittings, she got Modigliani to sign a note promising to marry her "as soon as the papers arrived".

Twenty-year-old Thora Klinckowstrom turned up from Sweden and was appalled to find what a squalid pit the legendary La Rotonde had become. But when she met Modigliani she eagerly volunteered to model for him. She also introduced him to her friend Annie Bjarne, another Swede, who also modelled. Jeanne, pregnant again, tried to keep an eye on the sessions, but there was little she could do about it.

Throughout the sessions, Modigliani swigged copiously from a rum bottle. It was for his cough, he said. And the cough was getting worse. Soon he was coughing up blood. He went to hospital and on 20 January 1920 he died of tubercular meningitis.

It is said that on his deathbed he suggested that Jeanne join him in death "so that I can have my favourite model in paradise and with her enjoy eternal happiness".

The day after his death, the heavily pregnant Jeanne leapt from a fifth floor window and killed herself, mutilating the beautiful body he had immortalized.

After his death, his figure work began to fetch high prices. But they retain their power to shock, not only because they are open and inviting. They are also, plainly, sexually satisfied. Even as late as 1949, when *Life* magazine ran a feature showing Modigliani's nudes, readers rang in from all over America to cancel their subscriptions

18

Salvador Darlíng

Surrealist painter Salvador Dalí's sex life was – well – surreal. He loved to shock. But what was most shocking was that, despite all the overt sexual imagery in his work, he was a bit of a soft watch.

Dalí was fixated on the anus. When he was a child, he liked to conceal his turds in the most inaccessible places around the house. He would wet his bed deliberately until his father promised to buy him a red tricycle to stop. And he made public announcements about his bowel movements on the most inappropriate occasions to humiliate his father who was a civil servant.

As he grew up, he turned to other people's bottoms. At school, he fell in love with a blue-eyed boy called Butchaques.

"His buttocks were squeezed too tightly into trousers that were too small," he recorded. "But despite my embarrassment an unconquerable curiosity made me look at his tight trousers every time a violent movement threatened to split them wide open."

The effete painterly Dalí even enjoyed his military service because he was assigned to clean the latrines.

But there were other pleasures to be enjoyed in the lavatory as he learnt at school. Friends enjoyed a solitary pleasure that they called "it". The young Dalí did not know what "it" was and would rather have died of shame than ask. One day he discovered for himself what "it" was. After that, there was no stopping him.

"One could do 'it' all by yourself," he discovered. "'It' could also be done mutually, even by several at a time, to see who could do 'it' quickest."

Whenever he felt sexually aroused he would go to the lavatories and jerk off. It gave him intense pleasure, but afterwards left him depressed and disgusted with himself. And he repeatedly vowed to give it up. He never did.

Dalí was a lifelong masturbator and rarely if ever came to orgasm any other way. This was partly due to the fear of venereal disease. His father left medical books out on the top of the piano showing men and women ravaged by every form of gonorrhoea and syphilis. And it was partly because of fears of his own inadequacy.

"Naked, comparing myself to school friends, I found that my penis was small, pitiful and soft," he said.

He also read a pornographic novel whose hero "machine-gunned female genitals with ferocious glee, saying that he enjoyed hearing women creak like watermelon". Dalí sadly remarked: "I convinced myself that I would never be able to make a woman creak like a watermelon."

Dalí was not wrong about the size of his penis, according to a friend who saw it in later life. He developed a loathing of large breasts and the female genitals. And although he loved bottoms, the answer, for him, did not lie there either.

"You have to have a very strong erection to penetrate," he said. "My problem is that I have always been a premature ejaculator. So much so, that sometimes it is enough for me just to look in order to have an orgasm."

But the young man could not help being a bit interested in girls. At the age of fifteen, the young Dalí was sending love poems and billets doux to a girl called Estela. Soon his attention turned to Carme Roget Pumerola, a fellow student at the Municipal Drawing School, who was two years older than him. They had amorous encounters in the local cinema. This must have been very disappointing for her.

The relationship was quite innocent, she maintained. He said that he was an insatiable sadist he had tortured her with his cold heart. It ended when he went to Madrid. But once he had lost the woman he said he did not love, he became extremely jealous. When she found herself a new lover, a businessman called Prat, Dalí began following them about and spying on them.

In Madrid, Dalí became close friends with the great gay poet and playwright Federico Garcia Lorca, though he fiercely denied any homosexuality or homosexual leanings himself. That would have been far too normal. Lorca tried to seduce him on many occasions though. According to Dalí, he almost succeeded once. They were naked in bed together but, halfway through, Dalí found sodomy much too painful and begged him to stop.

On a second occasion, Dalí played a cruel practical joke on Lorca. Dalí told him to come his room late at night. But when he slipped into Dalí's bed he discovered, to his horror, that the body he was caressing was that of a naked woman. Dalí had hired a coarse prostitute and was hidden somewhere in the darkened room, laughing.

Dalí's major source of erotic interest, he said was the female anus. But his major source of sexual satisfaction remained his own hands. This he freely admitted. One of his best known paintings is call *The Great Masturbator*.

In Paris, he met Gala, the wife of the surrealist poet Paul Éluard. She had been a virgin when she married Éluard but soon made up for lost time. After her first taste of sex, she became a nymphomaniac. Both took numerous lovers and she would model nude for anyone who asked her. For a time they lived in a *ménage à trois* with a German painter.

Éluard and Gala visited Dalí in Cadaqués, where he would often pass the summer with Lorca, Belgian surrealist painter René Magritte and Spanish surrealist filmmaker Luis Buñuel. Quickly Gala became engrossed in Dalí. When she spotted the scatological elements in his paintings, he asked whether she was coprophagous. The idea of eating shit was, to her, well, distasteful.

SALVADOR DARLING

"I swear I am not coprophagous," Dalí told Gala. "I loathe that kind of aberration as much as you can possibly loathe it. But I consider scatology a terrorizing element, just as I do blood or my phobia for grasshoppers."

To Dalí, Gala was the girl of his dreams. He said that her arrival in Cadaqués was like the serpent slithering into the Garden of Eden. But what good was he, a twenty-four-year-old virgin with a small dick, to a nymphomaniac?

In his autobiography, he claimed that he tried to push her off a cliff and kill her, comparing himself to the king in a Catalonian folk-tale who has three girls brought to his garden every morning. From a secluded balcony, he picks out the most beautiful. That night, she is sent to his bedchamber where the naked king would command her to lie down beside him as still as death. The king would not touch her but, when he awoke in the morning, he would behead the girl with a sword.

The story got around and one girl, who was as clever as she was beautiful, smuggled a dummy with a nose made of sugar in with her. While the king was asleep she put it in the bed beside him and hid. When the kings awoke and beheaded the dummy, the sugar nose flew into his mouth. Tasting its sweetness, the king repented of his ways.

Dalí loved the shorts Gala wore that showed off her rounded buttocks. But, he told her, that what repelled him most about the female anatomy was when a woman had a large gap between the top of her thighs. When they went swimming the next day, he discovered to his embarrassment that she had just this unfortunate attribute.

Gala wanted Dalí and realized that if she made the first move, he would flee to his studio and resume painting excrement. So she began wearing white and playing the virgin.

Finally, on a windy day on the rocky sea shore, she grew agitated and he could hold back no longer.

"What do you want me to do to you?" he asked.

She wept. He asked again and again, insisting that she tell him.

"If you won't do it, promise you will not tell anyone?" she said.

Overcome with desire, he grabbed her hair, pulled her head back and kissed her.

"Now tell me what you want me to do to you," said Dalí. "Tell me slowly, looking me in the eye, in the crudest and the most ferociously erotic words that will make both of us feel the greatest shame."

"I want you to kill me," she said.

"Yes," he cried pulling up her white skirt and there, tearing his knees to shreds on the rocks, he tried to make love to her.

"My limbs no longer belonged to me," he wrote in *The Unspeakable Confessions of Salvador Dalí*, "an unbelievable strength possessed me. I felt myself a man, freed from my terrors and my impotence. By her, I was henceforth gifted with telluric vertical forces such as allow a man to penetrate a woman."

This was probably the first and last time he was to enjoy sexual intercourse.

Éluard, who was away at the time, thought that her affair with Dalí was like all the others and he would get her back.

"Last night, I had the most magnificent masturbation thinking of you," he wrote.

He thought that no amorous affair could shake the bedrock of their marriage. She encouraged him in this view. After all, Éluard was an able and inventive lover. Dalí was pitiful by comparison.

But to Gala, money was all important. Éluard had run through his small inheritance, and Dalí's paintings were selling well.

Dalí made two films with Buñuel – *Un Chien Andalou*, which provoked a riot, and *L'Age d'Or*. Both featured Dalí's obsessions – hatred of the vagina, bottoms, coprophilia, necrophilia, castration and fear of homosexuality. The outrage they provoked made the two men famous and Gala left Éluard and their daughter Cécile and moved in with Dalí. She was a White Russian and ten years older than Dalí. And she was convinced that, with her backing, he would become very rich.

Éluard was devastated.

"I want you so very much," he wrote. "I am going mad... I

want it so that your hand, your mouth, your sex never leaves my sex."

She did not even reply.

He wrote again saying that he had been looking at photographs he had taken of her in the nude.

"You have the most beautiful eyes in the world," he wrote. "I love you. You take my sex in your hand, your legs spread, your body sinks softly, you stroke me furiously, I crush your breast, your hair and suddenly your hand is full of sperm and you are strong and sure of my power over you, of your power over me, over everything."

But Éluard was no slouch. He took on a maid who just happened to be a prostitute, then picked up a waif off the streets. Her name was Nusch and, in return for warmth and shelter, she fell in love with him. And despite his persistent attempts to get Gala back, she remained with him until her death in 1946.

Éluard wrote to Gala regularly, begging for nude photographs of her having sex with two men – one in the vagina, one in the mouth. He invited her to come over so that they could make love in front of Nusch while Nusch played with herself. Gala declined. Grateful for being rescued from life on the streets, Nusch put up with all his excesses.

Gala was very secretive about her sex life with Dalí but it seems that their pleasure took the form of mutual masturbation, which seemed to take up a lot of their time, to start with at least. In 1934, five years after they had met, Dalí and Gala were married. Of their honeymoon, which he took during a major exhibition of his work in Paris, he wrote: "I confess that during our voyage, Gala and I were too occupied by our two bodies that we hardly spend a single moment thinking about my exhibition, which I already thought of as ours."

Although his paintings are full of sexual imagery, his anxiety about sex made him impotent with other women. Friends remarked that his voice would change radically with fear if there was the merest hint of the possibility of sexual intimacy.

Despite his world-wide fame and, in later years, his estrangement from Gala, Dalí never took another lover. A woman friend once took him to a brothel in Barcelona. He liked to watch the girls parading before him but if one tried to touch him he pushed her away, muttering: "The stain, the stain."

Occasionally he would involve a naked woman in one of his surrealist stunts. He used to like to get naked women to crawl through a long red tube he had constructed as if they were being born out of a penis.

He liked having his acolytes pose nude for him, often on a transparent cushion so that he could see their sexual organs in exquisite detail. Or he would get them to stage "erotic masses". He pretended to begin painting them but, instead, was masturbating behind a blank canvas.

In the chapter of his autobiography "How to Pray to God Without Believing in Him", Dalí relates how he directed the buggery of a young Spanish girl by her lover for the benefit of himself and another spectator.

"I have never been able to tell this story without each time having the wonderful feeling that I had violated the secret of perfect beauty," he said.

He would like to hover around the couples he got to copulate for him then, when it was obvious that they were oblivious to anything but their own pleasure, he would make them stop. Then he would throw the humiliated couple out, while he fell to his knees laughing hysterically.

In charge of the entertainment was Captain John Moore, an Irishman and a wartime expert on psychological warfare and former head of the Vatican's propaganda department. If Dalí wanted a boy to be sodomized with a plastic dildo, or if he wanted a girl to put lighted straw in her vagina so that he could watch her expression as it singed her pubic hair, Moore arranged it.

Gala was not invited to these spectacles. It would have spoilt it for him. He merely wanted to watch and masturbate.

Dalí would hire palaces and fill them with dwarves, transvestites, trapeze artists and people of every possible sexual persuasion. He would invite VIPs, including French ministers of state. Mia Farrow was another playmate. And, much to

Gala's chagrin, he was regularly attended by two beautiful acolytes, Nanita Kalachnikov and Amanda Lear. Dalí was Gala's mealticket and she was terrified that she would lose him to a younger woman.

Meanwhile Gala took hordes of young lovers, among them Éluard. Even when she was fifty and they had met after a long separation, she said: "Here, I have a present for you." And she pulled open her blouse so Éluard could caress her breasts. He did not refuse.

"She was a true nymphomaniac," said a friend, "the classic case of a woman who was never satisfied and has to keep on trying with every man she met."

Once she said she hated doctors because one had once "emptied her out completely".

While she and Dalí were having dinner with General Franco's granddaughter, Gala began running her hands all over the poor girl's husband, Alfonso.

Gala then invited him to visit her at the Hotel Meurice in Paris. When Alfonso said he would be delighted to come, Gala snapped: "How can you say yes when you don't even know where the Meurice is?"

Alfonso protested that he did know. He used to visit his grandfather there.

"Did he work in the hotel?" sneered Gala.

"No," said Alfonso, "he was a resident."

And he explained that his grandfather was Alfonso XIII, the king of Spain.

The jealousy that Gala's affairs aroused in Dalí gave him a masochistic delight. He thought it spurred his creativity and he described himself gleefully as "the King of Cuckolds". He would line up beautiful men before her. She would take her pick and fondle them openly in front of Dalí. When a young man tried to refuse her because she was old enough to be her grandfather, she forced him to take a bath in champagne, then kicked him out.

When introduced to a young man, Gala never wasted any time before reaching out and caressing his genitals. However when she discovered that he had had some form of homosexual fling with the English aristocrat Edward James, she packed her bags and Dalí had to bribe her to stay with heaps of jewellery.

Gala and Dalí would hold "sexual experimentation" sessions where they would sit around discussing their sex lives. Gala barred women from these meetings and would regale the assembled throng with graphic details of her amatory exploits, which were always with men. Everyone, except Gala, was repelled by Dalí's scatological fantasies. She encouraged him though to come to terms with his sexual inadequacies. She believed it helped his creativity.

He also used surrealism to protect himself from predatory women. He would invite them back to his apartment, get them to strip off, then put a freshly fried egg on their shoulder. And that was that.

19

Augustus Juan

The poet W. B. Yeats said that Augustus John, was "the most innocent, wicked man I have ever met". John himself put it another way.

"A little restraint would not be a bad thing," he said, "in my friends."

John certainly knew none himself.

In October 1894, a shy young boy from Tenby in Wales enrolled in the Slade school of art in London. It was Augustus John. He was just fifteen years old. There he was to blossom not just as a great artist, but also as a legendary womanizer.

At the Slade, his shyness left him.

"The girls were supreme," he said. They were a "remarkably brilliant group of women students."

His first serious girlfriend was Ursula Tyrwhitt, whom he painted and wrote tentative love letters to. She was six years older than him and he was rather in awe of her. Then something happened that would change his life.

In summer of 1895, John went on camping trip around Pembrokeshire. He stopped at a lot of village fairs and joined in old-fashion games that involved "a good deal of singing and kissing". He also painted his version of *The Rape of the Sabine Women*.

One day towards the end of the holiday, he went swimming.

He stripped off his clothes and dived into the water.

"Instantly I was made aware of my folly," he wrote. "The impact of my skull on a hidden rock was terrific. The universe seemed to explode."

It was said that Augustus John dived into the water an ordinary man and emerged a genius. Certainly, when he returned to the Slade that autumn, he was transformed. Gone was the awkward clean-shaven neatly dressed boy. He now sported a beard. His hair was long and he wore scruffy clothes and a black velvet smoking cap embroidered in gold to conceal the wound.

He threw himself into his work with renewed vigour. The life classes particularly attracted him and he drew "compulsively from the female nude". Ursula Tyrwhitt's father, a clergyman, was so alarmed that he sent his daughter to Paris. John simply replaced her with her best friend, a young Christian named Ida Nettleship, who was engaged to the scion of a wealthy family.

Ida's mother was shocked and horrified by John and his bohemian manner. He did not even pretend to be faithful to Ida. On a trip around Holland, he wrote about all the beautiful women he had met there.

Back in London, John took over a studio in Charlotte Street once used by Constable and began hiring models of his own. His charm was overwhelming, it was said that, on buses, old ladies blushed and gave up their seats for him and young girls fainted when he made his legendary entrances to the Café Royal.

John got to know a prostitute who would always visit him if she could not pick up any trade on the streets. He went "whoring" in Paris and he became involved with a "superb woman of Vienna". Her name was Maria Katerina and she was the parlour maid at boarding house he stayed at in Swanage. When he left, the owner, a Mrs Everett, found a hair pin in his bed and extracted a full confession from the poor girl. John wrote begging Maria to join him in Paris. Mrs Everett wrote back, in Maria's name, accusing him of playing fast and loose with her feelings.

"Woman always suspect me of fickleness," John said. "But will they ever give me a chance of vindicating myself? They are too modest, too cautious, for to do that they would have to give their lives. I am not an exponent of the faithful dog business."

Women had every reason to be cautious. His approach was direct. Some were alarmed, others mesmerized.

In 1900, John got back with Ida, but she refused to live with him unless he married her. He reluctantly consented, provided they did so in secret. So one Saturday morning they eloped to St Pancras.

Once the deed was done, Ida's parents had to accept the situation. Ida herself confessed that she was "a little frightened". John too was frightened by the domesticity of married life. He soon felt like he was in prison.

Then he met John Sampson, a self-taught engraver from Liverpool. Sampson was almost twice John's age. Seven years before they met, he had married a pretty red-haired Scottish girl, much younger than himself. They had two sons and a daughter. But Sampson roamed with gypsies and was casually unfaithful whenever the mood took him with free and easy young gypsy girls.

Under Sampson's tutelage, John learnt how to speak Romany and eat hedgehog. Sampson declared John to be a genius and advised him to "return to your innocence". When John asked how he was to do that, Sampson said: "Sin openly and scandalize the world."

Ida became pregnant and John began having his models in a disused school room. His pastel nudes sold well. It was then that the Café Royal beckoned and he met Wyndham Lewis.

One of his models was the buxom Estella Cerutti whom he took as a lover. Another was the hypnotically beautiful Dorelia McNeill. He did not conceal his growing infatuation with Dorelia from Ida. She realized that a man like John could not be confined by marriage. Besides Ida liked Dorelia and accepted the situation stoically.

"Men must play and women weep," she said.

When John was accused of wanting to have his cake and

eat it, he said: "What's the point in having a cake if you did not eat it?"

The three of them set up a loose *ménage à trois*, until Dorelia went off with John's sister Gwen and her place was taken by Estella Cerutti, who had been waiting in the wings.

Gwen and Dorelia went to Paris where they could support themselves modelling. Gwen modelled for and slept with Rodin. But John grew jealous when he heard that Dorelia was posing nude for other artists. He wanted her back and bombarded her with letters. Eventually he left Ida, who was pregnant again, and went to Paris to get her, but she had gone to Belgium with a young artist called Leonard. Both Gwen and Ida urged Dorelia to return to John. Dorelia refused. Being loved by John and Gwen was too much hard work.

Gwen told Dorelia to give up Leonard who "has had his happiness for a time, what more can he expect?" Leonard wrote to Gwen explaining: "I am no ordinary man as you think." Ida wrote to Dorelia begging her to return so the three of them could live together under John's "wonderful concubinage". John wrote too, but largely about the paintings he had seen.

Eventually Dorelia gave in. She met John in Bruges and travelled back to London with him. Dorelia lived openly with John and Ida and Ida found herself in the strange position of having to defend the situation to uncomprehending friends and family. Some friends cut her completely because of her "immorality".

Everything went swimmingly until John started a double portrait of the two women. But he made a muck of it and found that there was no room on the canvas for Ida. There was an unholy row. First Dorelia said that she would leave. Then Ida said she would go. Then John said, no, he was the one who ought to leave.

Jealousy crept into everything. Due to the tense atmosphere and their immoral behaviour the home help left. Ida insisted that Dorelia take her place. Dorelia said she could not take on any heavy work because she was pregnant. Ida confessed to a friend that she was near to suicide. However, when the baby was born, the two women found that it was a new bond between them, especially as John had begun to turn his attentions elsewhere. Ida, particularly, realized that she needed Dorelia. Together they had more chance of holding on to John than she did alone. Meanwhile, John thought that life in the *ménage* was far too conventional and bought a gypsy caravan with the intention of taking his brood on the road.

After her baby was born, Dorelia began styling herself "Mrs Archibald McNeill", the wife of a naval officer who was away at sea. John was her brother. The child was registered as his son, though.

Ida was envious of Dorelia's position as John's mistress. She wanted to be his mistress too.

"By rights, Dorelia should be the wife and I the mistress," she wrote.

John spent more time away from home, leaving the two women to get on with it. They grew close, managing the house and looking after the children by day and playing long games of chess in the evening. Ida won every game except one. And at night, the two women slept together.

"I do not know whether Ardor [Dorelia] and I love one another," Ida wrote to John. "We seem to be bound together by sterner bonds than those of love."

They hated being apart, even for a day.

During a short stay with her mother, Ida wrote home: "Darling D, Love from Anna to the prettiest bitch in the world. I was bitter cold last night without your burning hot, not to say scalding, body next to me. Yours jealously enviously and adoringly Ida Margaret Anne John."

Ida also felt that she had rather missed out on all the adventure when John had gone chasing after Dorelia all over the Continent. She proposed that the three of them, and all their children, move to Paris. Dorelia was keen. The two women felt that they had a better chance of sustaining their *ménage* there.

When they confronted John with the plan, he agreed. Ida's flirtation with suicide had frightened him and he would do nothing to oppose her. Besides he longed to paint Parisian girls and sculpt. So with Ida pregnant again, they set off to Paris. John never did get the hang of contraception.

John threw in himself into the life of Paris while Dorelia stayed at home to look after Ida. On a trip back to London, John met Alick Schepeler who became his model and mistress for the next few years. She was five foot five with blue eyes and billows of brown hair. And she lived for love – romantic, physical love.

When John was back in Paris, they kept up a long and tedious correspondence. But boredom was the bedrock of their affair. They wrote and asked how bored each other was.

Ida had given birth to another son. Now Dorelia was pregnant again. John planned to move the family, plus their maid Clara, to the Normandy coast and station Alick in Jersey so he could pop over and fuck her whenever he felt like it. The family moved, but Alick headed off to the Cumberland with her friend the pretty young art student Frieda Block instead. John was upset and wrote to her telling her of his fantasies of seeing her naked and longing to make love to her.

He proposed marriage – and more. He proposed to duplicate his situation with Ida and Dorelia, with Alick and Frieda, playing the roles of wife and mistress respectively. They should set up home together in Paris, he suggested.

"I begin to see very plainly that Miss Block will never get on unless she comes to Paris and brings you with her," he said. "I will find her a studio – and will show her things I'm pretty sure she never suspected."

John made no secret of his plans. He was not going to ditch Ida and Dorelia, just add to their number. It was then that Ida and Dorelia realized that even together they could not contain John. Dorelia said that once her baby was born, she would buzz off. Ida said she was going too.

Instead, the whole brood moved back to Paris. John left for London to see Alick and paint her portrait. Dorelia moved out and went back to modelling. Ida was pregnant again. And so was their maid Clara.

"Our marriage," Ida told Gwen John, "was, on the whole, not a success."

AUGUSTUS JUAN

At Christmas, John returned to Paris and the whole clan got together. Wyndham Lewis was buzzing around too. But after the holidays he went back to London and Alick. When Alick's portrait was finished he moved back to Paris. And while Ida was in hospital having her fifth baby, Dorelia moved back in to look after the rest of the kids.

Although the birth went smoothly enough, Ida was found to be suffering from puerperal fever and peritonitis. In a lucid moment, she drank a toast to love in Vichy water, then died.

John found her death an enormous relief and he ran out of the hospital elated.

"I could have embraced any passer-by," he said.

Ida, he concluded, had "rejoined that spiritual lover who was my most serious rival in the old days".

And he set about getting good and drunk.

Dorelia stayed on with John, but soon had a miscarriage. Bloomsbury group painter Henry Lamb and his promiscuous wife Euphemia turned up. She, said the great economist John Maynard Keynes, had more of a sex life than "the rest of us put together".

Lamb became John's pupil while Euphemia posed for him, frequently nude. Dorelia fell for Lamb and John encouraged the liaison so that he could spend more time with the comely Euphemia.

Euphemia liked to dress like a man. She and John were once arrested as homosexuals and she was obliged to strip off in the police station to prove their innocence. In the promiscuity stakes she even out-Johned John. One night, he reported, she had "six men in her room, representing the six European powers, and all as silent as the grave".

Lamb's affair with Dorelia went on for twenty years, but he never succeeded in prising her away from John. Euphemia worked her way through the heterosexuals of the Bloomsbury group and topped it of by becoming the lover of Aleister Crowley.

Meanwhile, back in London, John took Lady Ottoline Morrell, the Bloomsbury-based muse to Aldous Huxley, D.H.

Lawrence and Duncan Grant, as his model and his mistress. He fulfilled her notion of the eccentric genius and she flaunted their affair in polite society, even though her husband, Philip Morrell, was a Member of Parliament.

"Keep Philip happy," John wrote, "and make him blow up the Houses of Parliament."

But Morrell was not happy.

"I think it is evident that your husband does not like me," John wrote six months later. I wonder why?

John protested that he felt that he "cut an offensive figure" when he visited their house. But he said he was "not really surprised that Morrell should have been out of humour". John said that he was sorry to disturb such an admirable person as her husband, for whom he had nothing but respect. But then "I would never question his right to object to me".

He also assured Ottoline that when he was with Dorelia he had not forgotten about her. But "I love no one living more than Dorelia". Bedding her, he explained, was a way to keep up some connection with his poor dead wife.

Ottoline tried to befriend Dorelia, but Dorelia would have none of it. The snooty Ottoline was quite unlike the barmaids, actresses and models he usually fooled around with and she did not know what to make of her. Dorelia was a simple soul. She felt quite out of place among the luminaries of Bloomsbury who populated Ottoline's drawing room.

Dorelia introduced Ottoline to Henry Lamb. Soon Ottoline was posing nude among the beechwoods for him. Quickly Lamb replaced John as her lover.

"I burn to embrace you and cover all of your body with mine," John wrote imploring her to come back to him.

But Ottoline knew, even at the height of their romance, that his heart belonged to Dorelia.

Meanwhile, Dorelia and John were considering marriage in an attempt to wrest John's children from Ida's mother who had taken them when Ida died. She considered Dorelia a thoroughly bad lot. John thought that marriage might give a veneer of respectability to their *ménage* if they were going to pursue the matter through the courts. Dorelia's price was for John to dump Alick, whom she detested. This proved an unnecessary sacrifice as John kidnapped his sons from their grandmother's care on a trip to the zoo, installed them in his gypsy caravan and took them on the road.

At Cambridge, Maynard Keynes said that "John is encamped with two wives and ten naked children". Of all people, Lady Ottoline Morrell had joined them for a taste of the gypsy life. Soon she hurried back to London "chilled and damp and appreciative of my own home and Philip".

John caught up with his old friend John Sampson. He was living in a village in Wales with his wife, a sheep dog called Ashyplet, a dwarf maid called Nellie, their three children and two young girls to look after them.

On his first night there, John felt in need of a little female company. So in his socks, he searched the house for the two girls. In one bedroom, he saw what he took to be the forms of the two slumbering girls, so he lay down beside them and started caressing them. Suddenly one of the slumbering forms awoke and started screaming. For a moment, he thought he had stumbled upon Sampson's boys instead. He told the screamer not to be so silly and went away. But out on the landing he bumped into the two girls. They were holding a candle and looked afraid. He scowled at them and went back to bed.

Next morning, over breakfast, the four-foot maid Nellie asked John what he had been doing in her bedroom last night. He said that he had got lost and it was so dark at night out there in Wales that his only guide was his sense of touch. Nellie said that this did not explain the nature of the caresses he had lavished on her – or on Sampson's young daughter who slept with her. John explained that he had been dreaming about the Henry Fielding novel *Tom Jones*. This feeble excuse fooled no one. Before lunch, John decided to slip away. He was halfway down the street when Sampson caught up with him and told him not to come back.

"Nothing was further from my thoughts," said John.

Anyway, the two men went for a drink together. In the pub,

a gypsy picked a fight with Sampson. Feeling morally indebted, John stepped in and defended his friend in a bloody, bare-knuckled fight in the town square.

He also beat up the Lord Mayor of Liverpool, on canvas at least, whose portrait he was painting at the time. The newspapers called the result "detestable", "an insult", "an artistic practical joke" and "the greatest exhibition of bad and inartistic taste ever seen".

The *Manchester Guardian* said more charitably: "Mr John, one feels somehow, does not spend all his vitality in painting."

John decided that he wanted a break from Dorelia when she fell pregnant once more and did not have the energy to fulfil her duties as a mistress. Lamb, who had now split from Ottoline Morrell, was excited that it might be his child that Dorelia was carrying. But Dorelia miscarried. Even though Dorelia was still unwell, John set off to Italy. Dorelia would be looked after by Lamb's former lover Helen Maitland, while Dorelia's sister Edie would take over as Lamb's model. It seemed the perfect arrangement.

John was enjoying himself with gypsy girls in Italy when he got a letter from Dorelia. Hers had been a false miscarriage. She was still pregnant and she said she would meet him in Provence, with Helen Maitland and a few of the children.

John wrote back: "Splendid news! I hope it is another boy. I wonder what part of the babe will be missing. Its penis perhaps, in which case it may turn out to be a girl after all."

He made his way slowly to Provence, stopping to sample a brothel in Marseilles.

"The ladies were not very beautiful, strictly speaking," he wrote to Ottoline. "But I found them very amiable."

He tried another one in Avignon.

"The ladies of these establishments are absolute slaves," he said. "The patron took all the money and the working girls are not allowed to quit the house without permission."

Still the girls did not complain, provided the owner was kind and did not send them too many clients.

John met up with Dorelia and Helen in Arles. Helen was still in love with Lamb and John was annoyed that she seemed to prefer the pupil to the master. Later she married the Russian artist Boris Arp, who was said to be the only man in London who could stand up to John in a fist fight. After that, she lived with the artist Roger Fry.

John, Dorelia and Helen jumped a train to the coast Martigues, where John had a good time.

"I have seen so many powerful women whose essential nudity no clothing can disguise," he wrote to Ottoline.

Martigues was also handy for Marseilles, where he had more adventures among the whores. Sleeping with prostitutes, especially cheap ones – "*20 sous à la passe*" – he found almost a religious experience.

"It is as if one entered some temple of some strange God where the 'intimacy' really does not exist except to reveal the intraversable gulf that can exist between two souls," he said.

Sex reduced to the single act, without a word spoken, symbolized to him the loneliness of the human condition. And he loved it. Throughout the summer he repeatedly took off to Marseilles, drank whisky and "misbehaved". With whores, he found, the act "never descended into tedium".

Lamb wrote to Ottoline suggesting a *ménage-à-six*. Instead, Ottoline headed off to stay with John at Martigues. She now sought to oust Dorelia, believing that, under her guidance, John could be elevated to the status of a Van Gogh or Michelangelo.

In Nice, John caught up with literary cocksman Frank Harris. John promptly propositioned Harris's wife and was repulsed – though to hear him tell it, she propositioned him and he turned her down, fearful that Harris would put the screws on him for money. Harris mocked him for his failure and, after three nights, John slunk off into the night.

Then Dorelia really did miscarry and nearly died from loss of blood. John was terrified that she might go the way of Ida, but she pulled through. Helen left so John employed "an abominably pretty housemaid" in her place.

Back in London, John began to get on Dorelia's nerves and she took off to Paris for a few days with Henry Lamb, who was still in love with her. When they came back, John had rekindled his interest in Euphemia.

Unable to wrest Dorelia from John, Lamb went to France with Dorelia's sister Edie. The John clan moved to Alderney, where they lived a wonderfully bohemian existence there for the next sixteen years. The biographer and critic Lord David Cecil said he left his hat on the floor one evening and returned six weeks later to find it in the exact same place.

John continued to work in his studio in London and spent most of the week there. This suited him because he could keep up numerous affairs without unduly distressing Dorelia. This arrangement worked well, provided the girls concerned did not turn up at Alderney. When they did, Dorelia retaliated by inviting Henry Lamb to stay.

Sometimes she dealt with his peccadilloes herself. One poor girl turned up with her luggage one afternoon. Dorelia gave her tea, then asked: "What train are you catching?"

She explained that there was a fast train to Waterloo soon and she would have someone drive her to the station.

"But Augustus asked me to stay," the girl said.

"Augustus is not here," said Dorelia, bundling the unfortunate girl and her luggage out of the door.

Contritely, John would tell Dorelia: "You may be sure I want you a great deal more than any other damsels." But want them he did.

And Dorelia put up with it. No worthwhile man is easy, she said. However, if it turned out that he was not a great artist, her sacrifice would have been wasted. When he sired more illegitimate kids, she looked after them. There was only one thing she could not bear about him – he was always late for lunch.

John took lovers from all walks of life and took great joy in his casual affairs.

"The dirty little girl I meet in the street has a secret for me," he wrote to Alick Schepeler. "It is communicable in no language, estimable at no price, momentous beyond knowledge, though it concerns but her and me."

In 1910, while pursuing a fleeing Wyndham Lewis, Frida

Strindberg, second wife of the Swedish playwright August Strindberg, turned up at John's Church Street studio and soon found herself in bed with him. A former nun, she had become a groupie for famous men. She pursued John for two years, even turning up at Alderney one Christmas Eve in her nightie in the snow. Dorelia was not amused.

Frida dogged his every footstep turning up unannounced at parties, at restaurants and on railway platforms whenever he was least expecting her. And if he appeared to be showing too much affection to another woman, she was not above throwing a champagne bottle at him. Sometimes, on seeing her, John simply ran.

Mrs Strindberg had hired a private detective to track his every move. She collected details of all his other love affairs. John was terrified that she would report them all to Dorelia or find some way to bring them out in court or in the newspapers.

She regularly threatened suicide. One evening she sent her maid to tell John that she had swallowed poison. John raced to her bedside, fearing what message she might leave the police. When she went into one of her raving monologues, he grabbed his hat and made for the door, only to be overtaken by Mrs Strindberg before he reached the lift.

On another occasion, it was feared that she might actually die. John's American patron John Quinn advised him to get out of the country. They planned a trip to Paris with Euphemia and the stunning model Lillian Shelley. When they arrived at Charing Cross station, the two girls were not there, but Mrs Strindberg was. And she was carrying a gun.

John asked the guards to handle the situation as discreetly as they could. They took the gun, but allowed Mrs Strindberg to follow John on to the boat at Dover. John locked himself in a cabin, while Quinn tried to put her off the scent by agreeing to meet her the next day.

He did not turn up. Instead Quinn and John went out on the town. John met a gorgeous young black girl who "exhaled the delicious odour of musk and sandalwood". Back at their hotel, Quinn noted disapprovingly, "John went with the girl". Then

Mrs Strindberg turned up and feigned suicide once more. Quinn borrowed a seventy-five-horsepower Mercedes and "the best chauffeur in Europe" from a millionaire friend and headed out of Paris. From a brothel in Marseilles, John tried to resurrect the plan of getting Euphemia and Lillian over. But Dorelia got wind of it and put a stop to it.

When John arrived gingerly back in London, he discovered that Mrs Strindberg was there, so he went to Wales and hid out.

While Dorelia gave birth to another child, a girl, their eldest son Pyramus died of meningitis. John headed off to comfort himself in Marseilles. When she was well enough, Dorelia would follow. He wrote asking her to bring with her a model with a good figure. Dorelia arrived alone. August was spent in Paris, carousing with Modigliani.

Dorelia retreated to Alderney, but John was always on the move. He wrote love letters to her, telling her how much he wished she was there so he could sleep with her. But as she would not accompany him on his jaunts, he took the precaution of taking with him a model – Lillian or Nelly or Nora or Kate who he had met in a dockside bar in Galway City.

He travelled to Ireland a lot, but in Galway the house he rented belonged to Bishop O'Dea who stipulated that there was to be no painting of nudes done there. John obeyed the bishop's injunction to the letter, but not the spirit. The two girls he picked up on the street and painted were undressed, but not entirely nude.

In 1914, John "conceived a wild passion" for one of his models, a music student called Nora Brownsword twenty years his junior, and "put her in the family way". He promised to give her £50 to set her up in a cottage, and £2 a week to live on. Of course, he could not find the £50. But that did not bother him much.

"Her father is wealthy man," he wrote to Quinn. "He has just tumbled to the situation and I suppose he'll be howling for my blood."

Nora, who was always referred to as Brownsword among the Johns, visited Alderney a number of times during the pregnancy. Dorelia greeted her calmly. She bought Nora a ring and offered to bring the child up, provided Nora never saw it again. The girl refused.

John did try to help the girl too.

"I'd marry her if necessary – Dodo [Dorelia] wouldn't mind," he told a friend.

John Hope-Johnstone, tutor to John's boys, also offered to marry her, though he seems to have done this in the hope of getting some money out of John. Although most of his sexual practices involved lithe young men, prepubescent girls were the real object of his lust and Nora thought it best not to have him around while she was bringing up a daughter. But she did take his surname, Johnstone, for her child.

Whether John offered her money and she refused it or she demanded it and he did not pay up is a matter of dispute. But with her music degree she managed to support herself and her child without his assistance.

John refused to learn any lesson from Nora's pregnancy. The list of girls went on – Sybil Hart-Davis, Iris Tree, Lady Tredegar, a famous Russian ballerina whom John was said to have "borrowed" from her husband. He was cited as co-respondent in Sylvia Gough's divorce case. At a party in John's Chelsea home, Dorelia overheard him in the hallway kissing his female guests goodbye. Each one was told how much she meant to him. He told them that he was always thinking of them, implored them to see him again soon and threatened to drown himself if they denied him. Dorelia got the impression that he actually thought he meant what he was saying.

His womanizing – along with that of the American poet Ezra Pound – became so legendary that a poem was made up about it. Called "The Virgin's Prayer", it goes:

Ezra Pound
And Augustus John
Bless the bed
That I lie on.

John began to complain that the world "does not even wait

until I am dead before weaving its legends about my name". And if Dorelia would only come to live with him in London – "I promise to be good," he wrote to her, "I am discharging all my mistresses at the rate of about three a week."

But Dorelia preferred to stay in Alderney with her garden which, now that the First World War was on, she turned over to vegetables. And John could not leave town and live in the country. He was king of the bohemia of Soho and Fitzrovia. His generosity was so famous it was presumed upon. One night in the Eiffel Tower Restaurant in Percy Street with Nancy Cunard, John found that his bill for dinner also included the cost of a bed for the night and breakfast for fellow delinquent Welshman, the poet Dylan Thomas.

This generosity caused money troubles. His creditors went unpaid. One day, he was grumbling about his financial problems to a friend who volunteered to search John's Chelsea home. He found hundreds of pounds in cash and uncashed cheques.

He gave lavish parties in Chelsea, inviting young female students from the Slade whom he attempted to seduce. Dora Carrington remembered one given in honour of John's favourite barmaid, a girl with prominent breasts.

"It was wonderful to see John kissing this fat pussycat, and diving his hand down her bodice," she told Lytton Strachey. John had also, Dora said, "made many serious attempts to wrest my virginity from me". But she found him "too mangy".

"Twenty years ago it would have been a very different matter," she told him.

After the war, John got himself more organized by hiring a secretary, twenty-two-year-old Kathleen Hale. She lived in the spare bedroom of his Chelsea house and Dorelia was suspicious of their relationship. She was right to be.

"I felt a frisson whenever he came into the room," Kathleen said. "Sometimes there would be mock battles between us, when he would try and 'rape' me."

The scuffles would usually end in laughter.

"I have always found laughter as good as a chastity belt," she said. "Once, though, out of curiosity, I allowed him to seduce me."

Once the sex barrier was down, Kathleen admitted, it added a certain warmth to their friendship.

Lloyd George commissioned John to paint the Paris Peace Conference that marked the end of the First World War. This brought him, for the first time, into aristocratic circles. He met the Marchesa Casati. The daughter of a Milanese industrialist, she had married into one of the noblest Roman families. Inspired by Sarah Bernhardt, she used their money to turn her life into a theatrical extravaganza. She became the mistress of the Italian writer and proto-Fascist Gabriele d'Annunzio, self-styled "Prince of Decadence". She was painted by the Futurists, often nude. Marinetti even dedicated the *Futurist Dance Manifesto* to her.

John painted her too and they became lovers. And, in the 1930s, when the last of her several fortunes had been spent, she depended on his kindness to eke out her declining years in a dingy flat in a house once owned by Byron.

In 1921, John Hope-Johnstone turned up at John's Chelsea home with a cheeky sixteen-year-old girl called Chiquita. She was an admirer of John and he asked her to sit for him. She agreed, provided there was somewhere private to undress. But she only posed for a few minutes before he pounced. She became pregnant and turned for help to Dorelia who arranged an abortion. But when the time came, she could not go through with it.

She had the baby and fostered it with a family in Islington while she earned her living as a photographic model. But a row broke out when the foster family wanted to adopt the child. John was away in Spain at the time so Chiquita turned for help to Seymour Leslie, a patron of the Eiffel Tower. He said that he would get the baby back, provided Chiquita became his mistress. They spent four days in Paris closing the deal. The relationship lasted for six months, until Leslie went on a trip to Russia. He returned to find that Chiquita had married Michael Birkbeck, another friend of John's, and was living with him and her daughter in the country.

There were other models too but John's chief mistress, apart from Dorelia, was Eileen Hawthorne. Later crowned "Miss 1933", she did all sorts of modelling work and was constantly in the newspapers. He had grown wary in his old age and begged her not to go near journalists. Nor was she to telephone him in Alderney, for fear of upsetting Dorelia.

Although he shared her favours with the composer E.J. Moeran, it was John who paid for her abortions. He grumbled about it, but he paid up out of fear of scandal.

A more devoted admirer was the widowed Mrs Valentine Fleming, mother of James Bond creator Ian Fleming, who lived in the house in Chelsea where Turner had once lived.

She would drive down to Alderney, picked up John and spirit him off. A determined woman, she wanted to wrest John away from Dorelia and have his baby. She told him that she would give up her fortune if he would marry her. John told Dorelia that, for a quiet life, he was thinking of marrying Mrs Fleming, giving her a child, then a quickie divorce, before returning to Alderney. Dorelia said that, if he did that, she would not be there when he returned. She would have eloped with Henry Lamb, who was then still on the scene.

But in 1928, Lamb married Pansy Pakenham, daughter of the Earl of Longford, informing Dorelia only days before the wedding, and that was the end of that.

Mrs Fleming was heartbroken when she heard about Chiquita. But anything a slip of a girl could do, she could do better. She accompanied John when he went to Berlin to paint the former German Chancellor Gustav Stresemann. A few months later, she closed up her Chelsea home and announced that she was going on a long cruise. A postcard from Switzerland informed John that he was a father again.

On returning to London, Mrs Fleming pretended that she had adopted a daughter. But John openly acknowledged that the child was his, and Mrs Fleming's daughter, Amaryllis, along with Chiquita's, Zöe, were regular visitors to Alderney. Amaryllis became a cellist, one of the first female cellists to hold the instrument between her legs like a man, rather than ride it side-saddle. Zöe went on the stage. Both were beautiful and sat for him. He said: "I wish I could paint you on your back".

John painted the promiscuous Hollywood goddess Tallulah Bankhead. One critic declared it to be the greatest portrait since Gainsborough's scandalous *Perdita*.

John took the family back to Martigues where he grew angry when his daughters donned make-up to go to a dance. He himself passed the time in the local brothel, where he could be found playing draughts.

Travelling frequently to the US, John avoided the "tarty-looking damsels" on New York's Fifth Avenue, who gave him the glad eye, for fear of scandal in William Randolph Hearst's yellow press. But he went up to Harlem where he painted a number of black girls semi-nude. He also made advances to John Quinn's lady friend Jeanne Foster.

Commissioned to paint the portraits of the children of Governor Fuller of Massachusetts, John found that Mrs Fuller had "designs on my virtue".

"I can't tell you all," he wrote to Dorelia.

And his affair with the actress Harriet Calloway, star of the Broadway show *Blackbirds* and singer of the hit song "*Diga Diga Do*" made the gossip columns.

In 1931, Mrs Vera Fearing, niece of the American artist Whistler, pursued him back across the Atlantic and sat for him. In 1935, as Mrs Montgomery, she turned up with her husband and two children. John, generously, offered to give her another one – but confessed her portrait was still not finished. It was not completed until 1960. When he sent it to her, her new husband, a Mr Stubbs, did not like it and it was hung in a disused shed.

John travelled to Venice and then to Jamaica with his daughter Vivien and Dorelia in tow to keep him out of trouble. But she inhibited his fun so much that he sent them home.

Back home, the fifty-six-year-old John acquired a new mistress, twenty-four-year-old Mavis Wright. At the age of sixteen, during the General Strike, she had hitchhiked to London, where she became a waitress at Veeraswamy's, the famous Indian restaurant in Swallow Street. She won a number of beauty contests and found that she liked sex very much. In 1931, she met fifty-year-old Old Etonian Horace de Vere Cole, cousin of Neville Chamberlain who became prime minister in 1937.

Cole left his wife and moved in with Mavis. Two years later, when he obtained a divorce, they married. The marriage was a turbulent one. He lost all his first wife's money in a disastrous venture in Canada and fled to France.

John, a friend of Cole's, stepped in to give Mavis a hand. She was sexy and made him feel young again. At the drop of a hat, she would fling off her clothes. He wrote her poems about orgasms.

"She is really a good wench," he told Dorelia, but she suspected different. Mavis, she thought, was a threat.

In 1935, Mavis presented him with another son, Tristan Hilarius John de Vere Cole. John acknowledged the child as his, though the father could have been Wyndham Lewis. Cole had stung Lewis for £20 before he left for France which he never repaid and Lewis "felt no compunction in taking it out in kind".

John suspected Mavis was seeing other men – and, indeed, other women.

"She seemed so amiable and gay, I was rather taken with her," said Dora Carrington. So was Dora's lover Beacus Penrose.

But these affairs were a ruse to get him to leave Dorelia. When he would not rise to the bait, Mavis put Tristan in a children's home and announced that she was going to marry a man who was six foot seven and she called "the tapeworm". John's only reaction was to adopt Tristan.

With John, Mavis met the archaeologist Mortimer Wheeler. She decided to marry him, but told John that she would keep him as her lover on the side. John became uncharacteristically jealous.

"It would be like an amputation to let you go," he said, telling Wheeler: "You must wait, I haven't finished with her yet."

When he caught Wheeler climbing into Mavis's room at John's new home, Fryern Court, near Fordingbridge, he challenged him to a duel. Wheeler, having been a field gunner, chose field guns. John considered this "very ungentlemanly conduct".

Eventually John gave way. Wheeler and Mavis married in 1939. Soon after there was a battle for custody of Tristan. This caused a slight hiatus in the affair between Mavis and John, but it resumed quickly enough after things had settled down again. In 1940, at the age of sixty-two, John was still writing to Mavis saying he was "stiff and strong" and pining over "that last marvellous embrace".

Mavis's position as model and mistress was taken over by Caitlin and Brigit Macnamara. They were the daughters of his old friend Francis Macnamara, who had inherited several of John's mistresses, including Euphemia Lamb and Frieda Block. In return John had bedded Macnamara's wife Yvonne and her sister Grace, who were, he told Dorelia, "beyond praise". Another of Macnamara's lovers was Erica Cotterill who had bedded both Rupert Brooke and Bernard Shaw.

John's affair with Brigit lasted spasmodically for many years. It was complicated by the fact that she was engaged to his son Caspar. Dorelia wanted to know why the wedding was constantly being postponed. Caspar found it difficult to accept that his bride-to-be was sleeping with his father. A date was eventually set, but two days before, Brigit and Caspar were in bed together when he told her that he could not go through with it.

Caitlin also fancied Caspar. At the age of fifteen, "all dolled up and ready" in a special negligée she presented herself in his bed. But he refused her, saying she was too young. She was not too young for daddy though. She was already posing nude for him and started flirting with him. He could not resist. Years later, she said he raped her.

"Not the best introduction to the carnal delights of the marriage bed," she wrote.

Nevertheless, the affair continued, on and off, for several years.

In later life, she dismissed John as "a disgusting old man who fucked everyone". But it was John who introduced her to her husband Dylan Thomas. They met at the Wheatsheaf pub in Fitzrovia. Within ten minutes they were in bed together and spent the next few days in the Eiffel Tower charging everything to John's account.

When they had had their fill, Caitlin went back to John at Fryern Court, while Thomas went to Cornwall. John took Caitlin to stay at novelist Richard Hughes castle in Laugharne, when Thomas, who by then had caught the clap, turned up. Caitlin and Thomas pretended not to know one another, but John was not taken in.

Thomas stayed the night. Next morning, John took the matter in hand. He took Thomas to the pub and staggered back alone. Asked where Thomas was, John slurred: "In the gutter. He was drunk and I couldn't bring a drunk man into a house like this."

In fact, there had been a fight.

John took the spoils of the victor that night. But the following day, Thomas turned up. There followed a French farce as they chased each other round and round the castle.

Thomas and Caitlin were married the following year and John and Hughes were godfathers to their first child. John would even stay with the Thomases at their house, Sea View, at Laugharne. He bought them furniture, including a wonderful bed, and would stuff his pockets with ten-shilling notes and hang his coat over a chair at night so they could steal the money from him. They were too proud to ask.

John was in demand to paint portraits of the great men of the day. Field Marshall Montgomery sat for him.

"Who is this chap?" Monty enquired. "He drinks. He is dirty. And I know there are women in the background."

He also complained that John had not got his ear in the right place.

Slamming the stable door after the horse had bolted, John joined the Voluntary Contraception League and took up other good causes. During the second World War, he took in five evacuees. He would go about the streets of Chelsea patting children on the head "just in case it was mine". And numerous people claimed, usually falsely, to be his illegitimate offspring.

Well into his seventies, John was still making lunges at women, but gave up gracefully if they resisted.

"A little of Augustus went a long way," said Diana Mosley.

One night a young woman with fair hair beat on his door shouting that she loved him and demanding to be let in. Robert and Cynthia Kee, who lived next door, heard him descend the stairs and open the door. There followed a rumpus. Next day, some of the banister was missing and there was blood on the floor. Apparently, he had tried to shag her on the stairs and there had been a terrible accident when the banister had given way under the pressure.

John visited the poor girl in hospital.

"She said she still loves me," he said, somewhat puzzled.

John still painted young women in the nude including, on one occasion, his daughter-in-law. Even his own daughters were not safe from his attentions. In 1961, when Zöe came to stay, he blundered into her bedroom in the middle of the night.

"I though you might be cold," he said, ripping off her bed-clothes.

He lay down beside her. Soon he grew calm.

"I can't seem to do it now," he said ruefully.

After a little while, she took him back to his room and tucked him into bed. A few months later he was dead.

In lieu of an epitaph, he justified his bohemian lifestyle to art critic D.S. MacColl.

"I drink but I am not a 'boozer'," he said. "I have affairs of the heart but I do not 'womanize'." Yeah.

20

Wyndham Lewdness

One of Augustus John's greatest rivals in sex and in art was his
friend Wyndham Lewis. When Lewis arrived at the Slade, John
was already a legend for his drinking and womanizing. Lewis
followed John to Paris where John was already installed with
his wife, mistresses and numerous babies. John mocked
Lewis's "uncontrollable erections" and his feeble attempts to
get laid.

Lewis was critical of John's unremitting lechery and drunkenness. He was particularly critical when Ida died and John
went on a binge.

"John has been drunk for the last three days, so I can't tell if
he's glad or sorry," he wrote. "Dorelia McNeill has taken up her
position in the vacant chair, in the vacant bed: the queen is
dead, long live the queen."

Later, when John visited Lewis's rented country cottage and
crudely molested the vicar's young daughter who had come by
on an errand, Lewis was furious. But his own behaviour was not
much better.

By 1905, he had his own Ida, a heavy German girl who
posed for him. He cruelly satirized the affair in his first novel
Tarr.

"I am engaged in a very extraordinary love affair," he wrote
to his mother. "The German lady, to my unquenchable amaze-

ment, asked me to kiss her, and threw herself in my arms and kissed me with unabated vigour for three hours."

When Ida had his child three years later, he disowned it and returned to England. His mother sent Ida five guineas.

Lewis's friend Sturge Moore warned against women who used the "slop of sex" to trap him.

"If a man puts his genius between her legs, she will cover it with any petticoat that takes her fancy and no one will see it again," he said.

In Spain, a tall, lithe servant girl called Flora gave Lewis his first dose of the clap. He wrote to John about his condition. John replied: "I am a distressed to hear of your persistent illness... Fly and linger not."

Back in England, Lewis got involved with Vorticism and two "art tarts", Helen Sanders and Jessica Dismorr. They vied for his affections. At the Slade, Helen had a schoolgirl "pash" on him. When he went to fight in the First World War, she wrote to him. But in 1920, he had to call on her brother to free himself from his entanglement. The poor girl had got quite the wrong impression it seems. Lewis had been happily two timing her with Jessica Dismorr, who he eventually fell out with over money.

But the backbone of Vorticism was his affair with Kate Lechemere. They set up the Rebel Art Centre and published *Blast*. The whole thing foundered when Lewis brought the philosopher and critic T.E. Hulme to the centre. He immediately took a fancy to Kate. Lewis was wildly jealous and when the two of them split the centre and *Blast* folded.

Lewis had a series of new mistresses. He indulged in casual sex and loved to tell anecdotes about his adventures. One of his favourites at the time was about a casual encounter with his landlady's daughter. He was screwing her in the hallway when the postman made his delivery and showered his bare behind with letters. Such tales fill his correspondence.

"Leaving cunts on one side," he wrote to a friend, "you're the only person in London I really care to see or talk to – just now I'm sick to death of clap and poverty and inactivity."

His gonorrhoea was so bad he was forced to spend long periods immobilized in bed. He wrote to a friend, the painter Walter Sickert, about his condition.

"Treat it like a common cold," Sickert wrote back. "I've had it dozens of times."

Not all his friends were so sanguine.

"Not long after I was married to Hilda Doolittle [in 1913] he came one afternoon and asked me to lend him my shaving things," wrote Richard Aldington. "As he completed, he remarked that he had been copulating for three days! (I hated his attitude toward women.) Now mark. Some time later I ran into him in a little restaurant in Church St. (W8) and halfway through dinner he announced that he had the clap! Nice for me with a young wife to think he had used my shaving brush a short time before."

Hilda left the fastidious Aldington to live with a woman.

Lewis liked to boast of his gonorrhoea, as if it were a badge of virility. He probably passed it on to Beatrice Hastings, when she co-edited *The New Age*, a short-lived arts journal that published Lewis's short stories, with her lover Alfred Orage. Lewis took her from Orage. From Lewis, she moved on to Modigliani.

Lewis then took up with the American heiress and novelist Mary Borden Turner, who was then married to her second husband and father of her three children, the Scottish Missionary George Douglas Turner. She became Lewis's patron, and soon, when Turner was out of town on religious business, his mistress. She was very beautiful, except for her teeth which were blackened by chain smoking. They, too, fell out over money. She divorced Turner in 1918 and married a general.

Next came Augustus John's mistress and model Alick Schepeler, who was then a secretary at the *Illustrated London News*. In June 1915, Lewis wrote to her: "You caused me this morning to alter all my arrangements: for the pink night-gown on Sunday (though I don't believe you've got one) captured my senses. I regret to say that I shall be away on Sundays... and could not, save by extreme dislocation of arrangements, get back in time for the pink night-dress. Perhaps I may yet hope to have a glimpse of that garment?"

He had two children with Olive Johnson, a woman who he had met by chance in a restaurant in 1909 and continued to see until 1918. The children were raised by his mother and her companion.

During the First World War, John introduced Lewis to Sybil Hart-Davis, the wife of a stockbroker. She was also the elder sister of Alfred Duff Cooper, Minister of War in 1935, and mother of the publisher Rupert Hart-Davis. Lewis compared her classical beauty to a female Rupert Brooke. He had developed a taste for affairs with married women, which gave him the thrill of intrigue without fear of entanglement.

From 1918 to 1921, Lewis lived with the poetess Iris Barry, née Crump. They had two children, a boy and a girl, whom neither of them wanted. When Lewis left Iris, she gave the children away.

"Was there more than one?" she said when asked about them later.

The boy went to her mother, then to an orphanage in Essex. The daughter was adopted by a prosperous businessman from Lancashire.

Lewis denied them altogether, as he did all his children.

"I have no children," he once said, "though some, I believe, are attributed to me."

His daughter by Iris reciprocated. She once bought on of Lewis' oil paintings and threw it in the dustbin.

The relationship between Lewis and Iris was far from idyllic. He kept the affair secret and forced her to sit in the kitchen when friends visited. When she returned from hospital with her new-born baby daughter, he was having sex with Nancy Cunard in his studio and Iris had to wait out on the step with the baby until he had finished.

But Iris, who was thirteen years younger than Lewis, was besotted. Lewis, she said, was the only man who never bored her. She went on to a distinguished career in literature and movie criticism in London and New York, married a Wall Street financier and lived the last twenty years of her life with an olive oil smuggler, twenty years her junior, whom she had met at the Cannes film festival. Lewis felt bitter towards her though. Nine years after they split she sent him one of her novels in the hope that he would pen a kind word the publisher could use for publicity.

"Our relationship was an unfortunate disaster," Lewis wrote back. "I don't want to have anything more to do with you."

The American heiress Nancy Cunard was much more his style. She had already been the lover of the avant-garde French poets Louis Aragon and Tristan Tzara. She had been photographed by Cecil Beaton and Man Ray, sculpted by Brancusi and painted by Kokoschka. Lewis drew her five times.

She was still in her early twenties and invited Lewis out to stay in her house in France. They travelled on to her palazzo in Venice. But they rowed on the way back to Paris. Uncharacteristically, Nancy wrote patching it up.

They were back together again in Venice when Aldous Huxley fell in love with her. But Huxley was not really her type. Being in bed with him was like being crawled over by slugs, Nancy said. On the other hand, Lewis was "half a shit. But a great painter. And a splendid letter writer."

The love triangle was satirized by Huxley in his 1923 novel *Antic Hay*, portraying Lewis as a "moonstruck and sickly giraffe".

During the 1920s, Lewis's mistress was the concert pianist Agnes Bedford, who had been introduced to him by Ezra Pound. With a very large hooked nose, she was no beauty. When his friend and patron Sir Nicholas Waterhouse encouraged Lewis to marry her, he said: "I can't look at that face every day at breakfast."

Instead, for a wife, he turned to the beauteous Anne Hoskyns, a model at the Royal Academy. They had met in 1918, when she was just eighteen. He was thirty-six and still in uniform. He seduced her immediately.

During the Iris and Nancy years, he did not neglect her. He had always managed to keep several affairs going at the same time. When he split from Iris, they moved in together in a flat in Paddington. As well as being beautiful and young, Anne had the added advantage of being tolerant of his constant infidelity. But he was discreet. He kept on the studio where he had lived with Iris and used it to conduct his affairs with Nancy, Agnes and numerous other mistresses and models.

And they were legion. John Beevers, who sat for him in the 1930s, said that Lewis would invite him over and "introduce me to Mrs Lewis: an unsettling experience because she was always a different girl and, once introduced, these girls always vanished to leave us alone".

Anne knew about his other women and accepted his affairs without jealousy. But he was excruciatingly jealous of her. He introduced her to none of his friends and never allowed her to see a soul.

Friends of thirty years standing never even knew of her existence. Some knew but never saw her. Those few invited home would usually only see her hands as she pushed food through the serving hatch.

After ten years cohabitation, in 1930, they married, secretly in a registry office. But that was as far as he would go. He never allowed her to have any children.

With marriage, his womanizing did not stop. He still attempted to sleep with every woman he met. He even tried to seduce Edith Sitwell when she sat for him, though he found her repulsive. The result was an unusually flattering portrait.

21

Dirty Diego

Diego Rivera was Mexico's greatest muralist, a pioneer Cubist, a Communist agitator and a prodigious lover.

He claimed to have lost his virginity at the age of nine. Doing the honours was a young American teacher at the Protestant school. She was eighteen and "as beautiful and sensitive creature as any I have known".

Already virile, she awoke in him a deep masochism, reciting stories of the Christian martyrs. Rivera was profoundly grateful when she gave him her voluptuous body, so that he became fully a man without going through that awkward solitary, yearning, masturbatory phase.

With this training under his belt, he moved right on to a black girl, the wife of a railroad engineer. When he was away fixing the line, the twelve-year-old Rivera would lay her in a nearly field.

At the age of eighteen, Rivera ate a woman for the first time. This was not the usual youthful experimentation with oral sex, but full-blown cannibalism. While attending anatomy classes at the Medical in Mexico City, he heard of a French fur dealer who improved the pelts and general health of his cats by feeding them other cats and wondered whether it worked for humans too.

DIRTY DIEGO

A number of students pooled their money and bought bodies from the city morgue. They chose the fresh corpses of murder victims, rather than the bodies of those who had died from disease or old age.

The group fed on human flesh for two months and everyone's health improved. Rivera discovered that he liked to eat the legs and breasts of women best. They were great delicacies. But he also enjoyed the ribs of young women breaded and women's brains vinaigrette.

In 1907, Rivera won a scholarship to study and travel abroad. He went first to Spain, then Paris. In Brussels, in 1909, he caught up with María Gutiérrez Blanchard, a painter he had first met in Spain. She was a hunchback, but Rivera was much taken with the beauty of her head and hands.

María had in tow a slender young blonde Russian painter, named Angeline Belloff. She was a kind, sensitive, almost unbelievably decent person.

"Much to her misfortune," wrote Rivera, "Angeline would become my common-law wife two years later."

He travelled with Angeline to London, where he was very impressed with the impeccable manners of the English. He noted that, when English beggars rummaged through the garbage, the men never dipped their hands in the waste until all the women had had their turn.

In 1910, Rivera returned to Mexico alone. The following year, he returned to Paris where he was passionately reunited with Angeline. They lived together for the next ten years.

"During that time, she gave me everything a good woman can give a man," he said. "In return, I gave her all the heartache and misery that a man can inflict upon a woman."

She even gave him a son, his only son, though the child died from meningitis before he was two.

In 1914, Rivera and Angeline travelled to Majorca. Among the party was the beautiful dancer Varmanova, to whom he was instantly attracted. When war was declared, they saw an English destroyer firing on a German submarine just off the coast.

When they got back to Barcelona, their money ran out. Rivera's grant from the Veracruz government had ended with the downfall of Madero. Then his cousin turned up with an interesting money-making ruse. For a small charge, Rivera could reclaim his family's title in the Spanish courts, then he could renounce it again for a larger sum. This gave them the money to travel to Madrid, then back to Paris.

In Montparnasse, he met the gifted young Russian painter Marevna Vorobiev. She seemed to have no friends in Paris, so Angeline and Rivera began to invite her home.

She had a wild beauty and a passionate nature. Marevna and Rivera soon became lovers. In 1917, Rivera left Angeline and moved in with Marevna. The union was tempestuous and, after six months, he decided to go back to Angeline. Marevna demanded one last tryst. They met in hotel room, but the meeting proved frustrating as Marevna was menstruating.

Rivera was just leaving to go back to Angeline when Marevna gave him one last embrace. She had a knife hidden in her sleeve. When he kissed her, she slashed him across the back of the neck. He collapsed and, as he lay there unconscious, she cut her own throat.

Neither of them died. And as the First World War had just ended, the heavily bandaged Marevna became a popular mascot among the returning troops.

Six months after Rivera had returned to Angeline, Marevna began standing outside their front door day and night. She was heavily pregnant and accused him of leaving her with a child.

When the child was born, Marevna exhibited the girl as living proof of his infamy. She succeeded in turning friends and benefactors against him. Even art collectors said they would boycott his work, unless he recognized the child. Rivera took no notice. When the child grew up, she bombarded Rivera with letters. He never replied.

"Even if, by the barest chance, I was really her father," Rivera said, "neither she nor Marevna ever actually needed me."

Indeed, Marevna went on to have affairs with both the great

writer Maxim Gorky and his son. Their rivalry for her favours left them permanently estranged.

Rivera painted Angeline suckling their son. But he had done no work during his time with Marevna and now could sell none. They were down and out and he could not even afford medicine for the sick child. After the boy died, Rivera left for Italy, then went home to Mexico.

Back in Mexico City, he was visited by the beautiful singer Concha Michel. She called him a bastard – he was in love with her, she said, and yet he refused to tell her so and constantly went out with other women.

Sooner or later, she said, she was going to leave the brave, stupid, honest man she lived with for a worthless womanizer like him. Rivera said she might as well make it sooner. Concha said that she had already taken steps to stop that happening.

"I realize that the only thing that can keep us apart is another woman who is prettier, freer and braver than I am," she said. "So I have sought her out and I have brought her to you."

She went to the door and cried out: "Lupe!"

In walked, a six-foot-tall black-haired bombshell. She had green eyes, full lips and long legs that reminded Rivera of a wild filly.

Concha introduced her friend Lupe Martin from Guadalajara to "the great Diego Rivera". Then she ran out of the door.

Rivera was painting some fruit at the time. Lupe asked whether he would not prefer to paint her. She had not eaten for two days. In return for the fruit, she would sit for him. He agreed. She took her clothes off and, soon, they became lovers. He was to paint her over and over again, usually nude.

From that first day, they found it hard to be apart. Lupe even attended his Communist Party meetings. One day, she made a speech. Mustering political, social, economic and personal arguments, she demonstrated that, if Rivera was not entirely a fool, he would marry her. He seconded the motion.

Soon after, Rivera was completing a mural for the auditorium when a twelve-year-old schoolgirl came up and asked whether she could watch. Rivera noted the fire in her eyes and her fully developed breasts, and said of course she could. This inspired the jealousy of Lupe who was posing nude for the mural. She tried to see the girl off with insults but the girl took no notice. This earnt Lupe's grudging respect. The schoolgirl's name was Frida Kahlo and, seven years later, she would become Rivera's wife.

Rivera's life with Lupe had a hectic intensity. He loved painting her nude. She was a beautiful, spirited animal but also intensely jealous. And she had a lot to be jealous about. Rivera was not a faithful lover and was always meeting women too desirable to resist. She even caught him making love to her sister and left him. He went to Guadalajara to fetch her back but the reconciliation was not a happy one.

He began an affair with the painter and photographer Tina Modotti, who later became the mistress of the exiled Cuban revolutionary leader Julio Mella. When he was killed, Tina was accused of murdering him. Rivera managed to establish that Mella had been assassinated on the orders of the Cuban government and had Tina freed.

Rivera accepted an invitation to go to the Soviet Union to get away from Lupe. Shortly before he left, the poet Jorge Cuesta told him that he was in love with Lupe. Rivera gave him his blessing to woo her, but warned him that she was dangerous if a man was not very tough with her.

As Rivera's train pulled out of the station on the first leg of his journey to Russia, Lupe shouted after him: "Go and play with your big-breasted girls." That was what she called Russian women.

While Rivera was away, Lupe and Cuesta were married. She bore him a son. Then Cuesta came apart at the seams. He castrated himself and the boy. The following year, he hanged himself.

Rivera was working on the frescos of the Ministry of Education, when a beautiful eighteen-year-old girl begged him to come down from the scaffolding. She was an artist, she explained, and wanted to show him her paintings. He was impressed. But when he praised them, she chided him. She had been told by his friends that he was always complimentary about the work of a pretty woman. She said she was a simple girl who must work for her living and she wanted criticism not praise.

He persisted in saying her work was good and that she must continue to paint. In that case, she said, he must see more of her work. He did not paint on Sundays, so he must come over to her place the following weekend. She gave her address in Coyoacán and her name. It was Frida Kahlo, the well developed schoolgirl who, seven years before, had admired his mural.

He went to see her the following Sunday. When he knocked on the door, she stuck her head out of an upstairs window and whistled the Internationale. A few days later, he kissed her. And when he finished at the Ministry of Education he began courting her in earnest.

Rivera felt awkward wooing the eighteen-year-old Frida as he was more than twice her age. But her family approved and they became engaged. Rivera and Frida noticed that, when they kissed under the newly installed electric street lights of Coyoacán, the lights mysteriously went out. They tried it six times. This they decided was a propitious omen. They were married by the Mayor of Coyoacán in the town's ancient city hall. The Mayor proclaimed the marriage to be a historic event. But Lupe turned up at the reception and caused a scene. Frida and Rivera honeymooned in San Francisco. Rivera could still not get the hang of fidelity but they were together, on and off, until Frida died, twenty-seven years later.

They travelled back to the United States together in 1931. Rivera was commissioned to paint a mural on the walls of the Arts Institute in Detroit, which was condemned as pornography by Father Coughlin, an outspoken priest who had his own radio programme.

While in Detroit, Frida was involved in a traffic accident. The bus she was riding in collided with a trolley car and she was badly injured. Since she had been twelve-years-old, she had wanted Rivera's baby. Her injuries meant that a pregnancy would threaten her life. Nevertheless, she tried to have a baby three times. Each pregnancy ended in miscarriage.

After Rivera painted a highly uncomplimentary portrait of Hitler, there was an assassination attempt. Fortunately, Frida's sister was sitting in her chair when a gunman shot through the studio window. The sister was three inches shorter than Frida and the bullets passed harmlessly over her head.

This did not stop Mussolini inviting him to come and paint a mural in Italy. In Paris, Rivera had known Angelica Balabanova, a lover of Lenin who had gone on to become Mussolini's mistress. He had also been acquainted with Margherita Sarfatti, who had been close to Modigliani and went on to replace Angelica as Mussolini's mistress.

Margherita contacted him personally to pass on Il Duce's invitation, but Rivera turned it down. He had already had enough trouble, after Nelson Rockefeller sacked him in 1933 halfway through completing a mural on the RCA building in New York which depicted Lenin as the unifier of the world. If he pulled a similar stunt with Mussolini, he could expect more than the sack.

Even Mexico was not safe. Frida and Rivera were having lunch together one day in the Acapulco Restaurant in Mexico City when four armed assassins came in. Frida leapt in front of Rivera and taunted the gunmen to kill her first if they dared. Her screams and curses were so loud that she attracted a huge crowd. The gunmen turned and fled. A few days later, while trying to escape across the Rio Grande, all four were gunned down.

The incident left Frida emotionally drained. Rivera packed her off to stay with Clare Boothe Luce, the wife of the magazine tycoon. From there she went to Paris where she was proclaimed an artistic genius in her own right. Kandinsky, Marcel Ducamp and Picasso all sang her praises. The haute couturier Elsa Schiaparelli even designed *La Robe Madame Rivera*, a Mexican-style evening gown, in her honour.

But when Frida returned to Mexico, she found that Rivera was having an affair with her best friend. Normally, she took such things in her stride, but she was ill again with injuries she had suffered in her accident. To spare her any further torment, Rivera left her. They had been married for thirteen years.

Although Frida said that she did not mind him having other lovers, she said that she could not understand why he chose women who were beneath him. She found it humiliating. But Rivera objected to her limiting his freedom in any way and asked her for a divorce.

They were apart for two years. What got them back together again was the assassination of Russian Revolutionary Leon Trotsky in Mexico City. After a gun attack on the exiled Trotsky at his house in Mexico, Rivera was suspected. Tipped off by Charlie Chaplin's young wife Paulette Goddard, who was sitting for him, Rivera went into hiding and Frida helped organize his escape to the United States.

After a visit with the Chaplins in Los Angeles, he moved to San Francisco. When Trotsky was finally bumped off, this time with an ice pick, it turned out that Frida had met the assassin in Paris and had twice invited him to her house to dine. Rough handling by the police left her ill again. Rivera brought her to San Francisco to recuperate.

Their medical adviser said that their separation had taken a heavy toll on her and urged them to marry again. The doctor warned her that Rivera was an incorrigible philanderer and that she could never expect sexual fidelity from him, but he did truly love her. Eventually she consented, on the proviso that there would be no sexual intercourse between them. The images of all the other women he had loved made an insuperable mental barrier for her. On that basis, they remarried on 8 December 1940, Rivera's forty-fifth birthday.

In 1948, Rivera fell in love with the movie actress María Félix. He planned to divorce Frida and use a life-size portrait of María as the centre piece for his latest exhibition. Neither plan came off. María refused to marry him, making the divorce unnecessary, and she refused to lend him her portrait for his exhibition. He replaced it with a provocative life-size nude of the poetess Pita Amor.

Frida died in July 1954. Nine months later Rivera was diagnosed with cancer of the penis. The doctors wanted to amputate, but he did not want to live without it. Besides he wanted to marry again, this time to Emma Hurtado who, ten years before, had opened a gallery devoted solely to his work.

Despite his condition, they married secretly a year after Frida's death. Soon after, he went to Moscow for cobalt treatment on the affected organ and, seven months later, was released from hospital with everything in working order.

Although he was now in his seventies, he still could not be faithful. But Emma realized for a man like Diego philandering was necessary. In order to paint as he did, he had to feel all sorts of emotions. And, she said, it was other women chasing after him, rather than the other way around. Angeline Belloff put it quite simply that he gave to art the fidelity he could never find it within himself to give to a woman.

22

Erection in Cookham

Stanley Spencer was born in Cookham, Berkshire, in 1891 about thirty miles from London, near Henley-on-Thames, where he set a series of paintings depicting resurrection scenes, including, most famously, *Resurrection in Cookham Churchyard*. He also shocked the village with his bizarre sex life.

Spencer spent an enchanted childhood in Cookham. He would sit for hours with a worm or a newt on his thigh, relishing the sensation. A warm glow filled him at the sight of girls' bare legs. He touched their legs to see how soft they were and fantasized about girls squatting before him. At seventeen, he felt another boy's penis and was surprised how small it was. He longed for the boy to do the same thing to him.

His first love was his cousin Dorothy Wooster, whom he drew as a fairy being loved by a prince. The prince was a life model at the Slade where he was studying.

Working with nudes at the Slade, Spencer got the idea that it was prudery that separated us from God. The way back to God was through sex. And if humankind was made in the image of God, how come there were men and women? Surely to make God manifest, the sexes had to fuse. But he was a gawky and shy young man, so these ideas remained intellectual, expressed through his painting. Only later did he get an opportunity to put his theory of sexual fusion into practice. Nevertheless, his pictures were full of flowers flaunting their sexual beauty and seed which he longed to provide.

Through the Slade he got to know the Bloomsbury group of writers and intellectuals. Then came the First World War. He joined up and was posted to Palestine where he met up with Augustus John's pupil Henry Lamb. Still a virgin – he had not even kissed a girl – Stanley was shocked when Lady Ottoline Morrell sent him a picture of a girl diving into a stream.

Back in England, he met Hilda Carline, a painter and another graduate of the Slade. His brother Gilbert brought her down to Cookham one day but, of the two brothers, she indicated that she preferred Stanley. Together they would often go and visit Augustus John at Alderney.

Although his paintings were already full of sexual imagery, he still had no experience. Casual sex was unthinkable to him and, when Hilda came to visit, the proprieties were scrupulously observed.

On a Carline family holiday to Yugoslavia, Stanley got to sleep alongside Hilda – fully clothed from head to toe. It was only when they reached Sarajevo that Hilda took his arm. Overwhelmed, Spencer proposed marriage.

Back in London, Stanley lodged with the Carlines and things really heated up.

"I used to love passing the open door of her bedroom and see her changing some stockings and just for a moment her pearly leg," he said. "She loved to show as much leg as possible."

They got engaged. But almost as soon as the announcement was made, he broke it off. Then it was on again. He did this six or seven times. The Carlines were bemused, but Spencer, having had no sexual experience, was worried whether he was up to the task.

Stanley went to stay with Henry Lamb in Poole. Another of Lamb's guests was T.E. Lawrence (of Arabia) and a friend of Augustus John's. Lawrence, Stanley wrote to Hilda, "hates the thought of women", while he, Stanley, "hated the thought of sex". Must have been a fun house party.

ERECTION IN COOKHAM

Then it happened. Whatever it was that happened occurred at 2.45 pm on a Tuesday in May probably in 1923. It seems to have been sexual and its epicentre was Hilda. Suddenly the creative barrier between his religious work and his sexual nature dissolved and he began work on *Resurrection in Cookham Churchyard.*

Stanley and Hilda were married in 1925. They honeymooned in a cottage in Wangford, Suffolk. The bedroom there became a place of pilgrimage for Spencer in years to come.

Stanley had found his sexual fusion and it made him want to shout for joy. He and Hilda were spiritually joined now, never to be parted. He had seen the face of God between her thighs.

"Eat me, darling," he scribbled on one drawing. "Let me become you. In the midst of your belly I cry out my love for you."

His joy in this new well of pleasure flooded into *Resurrection* and other paintings.

In 1932, Stanley, Hilda, their two children, their maid Elsie and Miss Herren, a humourless Christian Science friend of Hilda's moved into semi-detached villa in the centre of Cookham.

His happiness should have been complete but he wrote: "Dear Darling Hilda, You are so precious to me, why cannot I love you completely?"

By this he meant that they must stop using any form of contraception that would take the edge off his pleasure in sex. On the other hand, he did not like babies. And he did not like having other people around the whole time so that they could not make love whenever he wanted. But then again, he rather liked other women around.

"My admiration for the different women you rather despise me for, all this is admirable," he told Hilda. "It is the same thing I admire in Elsie and this Preece girl. It is when I feel that their joyfulness and readiness to have a good time is clearly the result of a forthright instinct and desire for real life that I know then that they are on the threshold of experience, that hunger and thirst are going to be filled."

SEX LIVES OF THE GREAT ARTISTS

This Preece girl was Patricia Preece, another graduate of the Slade who turned up in the tea shop in Cookham one day. They got talking. She lived in a house in the village with Dorothy Hepworth, her long-term companion who liked to dress in men's clothes. Spencer soon became a regular visitor.

Although Stanley reassured Hilda that he still felt the joy in lovemaking with her, just as much as before, his interests were now broadening.

"I feel this spiritual marriage, this oneness and consequent feeling of rejoicing, with several women," he said.

What he was feeling was good old fashioned lust. But lust, for Spencer, was the way to contact God.

"I believe that fear of lust and the thought of such a thing existing does a terrible lot of harm," he said. "It may be a nuisance that with me a strong sex impulse plays a big part."

Patricia began joining them on picnics and Stanley began finding her alluring in ways that Hilda was not.

"It gave the feeling that everything I went to touch would blow up and burst into smithereens before I could get at it," he wrote.

Hilda was also getting disquieted at the burgeoning relationship between Patricia and Stanley. While he was content to see Hilda in the same old jumper, he longed to buy Patricia flimsy underwear and high-heeled shoes. He spent lavishly on her. It was part of his spiritual quest.

"God speaks eloquently through the flesh," he said. "That's why he made it."

This was no ordinary married man with the seven-year itch, it was a great artist wrestling with the very nature of things.

"The artist wished to absorb everything into himself," he said, "to commit a kind of spiritual rape on everything."

His ambitions, or course, were much more earthly. Spencer saw the contrast between the two women starkly.

"In spite of my excitement at Hilda's inelegance, I have a passion for feminine daintiness and elegance," he said. "It fits more with my sexual needs."

Stanley had to go to Switzerland on business. After a couple of days, he telegraphed Patricia and invited her to come out. They spent a few days alone together in the remote village of Saas Fé. When they returned to Cookham, Hilda left. She stayed away for a month before timidly returning to the fold.

On Stanley's long walks around Cookham with Patricia, he began to hatch a scheme. Why didn't Patricia move in with them? That would leave Hilda more time to indulge her growing interest in Christian Science. Augustus John managed a *ménage à trois*. Why shouldn't he?

He told Hilda that he did not want Patricia sexually, it was just that she personified the youthful longing for the girls of Cookham he had felt years ago. And also, of course, the two women were complementary.

"Patricia supplies what I miss in you," he told Hilda. "You supply what I miss in Patricia. You each make the other supportable and enjoyable."

What he wanted was free sexual access to both women. In this area, Patricia particularly intrigued him. She and Dorothy flaunted the lesbian love affairs that they had in Paris during the 1920s and painted each other nude. But sex with her was limited to love games that got him "all tightened up and tense like a violin string".

For Patricia, love making was a down-to-earth activity. For Stanley though, it was still a sacrament. This meant, in his mind, that he could never "fuse" with Patricia in the way he did with Hilda. But such high-flown twaddle meant nothing to Patricia. She told her friends that Stanley's urges were distinctly working class.

Patricia was happy to move in with the Spencers, provided Hilda was agreeable. Her own painting was far from lucrative, but she felt if she could get Stanley to drop this sexual/religious rubbish and stick to landscapes he could make a lot of money. As she was basically a dyke, it did not matter to her if he kept on screwing his wife.

To Stanley, his new sexual arrangements had a political dimension.

"During the war," he wrote, "when I contemplated the horror of my life and the lives of those with me, I felt that the only way to end the ghastly experience would be if everyone suddenly decided to indulge in every degree and form of sexual love, carnal love, bestiality, anything you like to call it." Right on!

Hilda was pleased that Stanley had found a new interest in life and thought he should get on with it – alone. While Hilda filed for divorce, Stanley began a series of studies of Patricia in the nude and, cheekily, incorporated himself, though she stopped him exhibiting them.

Four days after Hilda's divorce from Stanley was finalized, he married Patricia. But it was to be a legal formality only. Stanley wanted Hilda back and Patricia would go on living with Dorothy until Hilda consented to the *ménage*.

The happy couple were to honeymoon in Cornwall. Dorothy would go with them. Stanley even invited Hilda. He phoned her on the night of the wedding. While Patricia and Dorothy went ahead to St Ives, Stanley remained behind in Cookham. Hilda was coming over to pick up a few personal items, including her letters to Stanley which he had kept tied in bundles and numbered. When she arrived, he explained the whole plan. Patricia would handle the business side of his life while she, Hilda, fulfilled the sexual side. Patricia wanted it that way, he said. So they went to bed together.

"That perfect day seemed to wipe away all the last few years and to have put things right between Stanley and me," she said.

However, when he reached St Ives, Patricia was less than pleased with his progress. When he told his bride that he had just slept with his ex-wife, there was an unholy row.

"He said that he intended to sleep with Hilda whenever he wished," Patricia recalled, "and that he required two wives, his work needed absolute sexual freedom. I was dumbfounded."

While he was away, Hilda moved back in. Patricia got cold feet about cohabiting with the two of them and continued to live with Dorothy. Sex between them grew more difficult and Patricia found refuge in Dorothy's room.

But Stanley was determined. He got Patricia to write a long

letter confirming that she wanted the three of them to live together. Hilda wrote back an equally long letter, refusing the arrangement. She also objected to being Stanley's mistress when once she had been his wife and began to ration her sexual favours. Instead of having sexual access to both women, Stanley soon found he had neither. He still lived in hope though.

He invited Hilda to go to Wangford with him and stay in the cottage where they had had their idyllic honeymoon. Hilda said he should being doing that sort of thing with his new wife and if there was any problem with that side of their marriage he should take her to a gynaecologist.

Throughout this toing and froing, Patricia, now in charge of business, whipped Stanley into action. He was scheduled to produce one landscape every ten days. But things were going so badly he had to sell his erotic studies of her.

Painting began to give him an erection and he wrote to Hilda complaining about it. He even expressed a desire to go gay.

"You know, ducky, I wish I had the experience of being a bugger," he wrote to Hilda. "I am sure I would show more real understanding of it... I want the female but I also want the male, because the evocation of sexual desire comes from a sense of worth and worthiness of a living thing regardless of sex."

Frustrated, he put more of his erotic feelings into his paintings and his "sex-pictures", as he called them, began to cause disquiet in the England of the 1930s.

The only sexual satisfaction Spencer was getting at the time was voyeuristic.

"I like the sexual business to be the result of a conscious joy and pleasure we find in each other, and I love to sit and stare and watch you," he told Patricia.

But if she knew he was watching her, she felt inhibited and would stop and insist that he watch her surreptitiously.

In 1938, Patricia accused Stanley of spreading gossip around the village that she was a lesbian and threatened him with legal action. Bankruptcy also loomed and Spencer was struck with impotence. This was doubly bad news as his artistic output was linked to his desire for sex. So both his physical and financial prospects drooped.

The only way out of his financial fix was to sell the house in Cookham. That meant abandoning all hope of setting up his long-hoped-for *ménage à trois*. He travelled to North Wales, where Hilda was holidaying with her mother, in a last ditch effort to persuade her. But Hilda was ill and "it puts her in the wrong mood for discussion".

Patricia now dismissed his *ménage* plan as caprice. He said that if it was a meaningless whim, it was a whim that had inspired many of his greatest paintings. He was fed up with painting landscapes, so he put the furniture into storage, rented the house out and moved into a small room.

As he was in such a bad way, George and Daphne Charlton, whom he knew from the Slade, invited him on a painting holiday in the village of Leonard Stanley in Gloucestershire. George frequently left Stanley alone with his wife and, in her care, Stanley was reborn.

"Our bedroom love was taken up Gypsy Lane and over the stiles and across the meadows and along the roads back up to our room," he wrote. "Then, after more love in the bedroom, we went out among the elm trees and cattle and chickens, and were conscious and did as we had just done in bed, so that our private life was public."

The villagers were amused at these strange goings on – and bemused at George's tolerance. There was no secret about the affair. Stanley, naturally, celebrated his new love in paint.

The three of them spent a second summer at Leonard Stanley, but Spencer began to find Daphne possessive and began to hanker after Hilda again. He loved Daphne no more than he loved Patricia, he concluded. Hilda was the one he really wanted.

Halfway though a third summer at Leonard Stanley, Spencer left, despite Daphne's protestations. He took a room in Epsom, where his children had been evacuated at the beginning of the war, and on Saturday mornings taught at Epsom Art College.

The girls there were, he said, "such pets, such darlings" and he longed to kiss them all.

Daphne and Patricia visited him at Epsom, so his creativity kept on flowing. But Hilda stayed away.

In 1942, Spencer moved back to Cookham, working in the house with Patricia and Dorothy but lodging with his cousins where Daphne could visit him.

While Stanley reminisced about his courting of Hilda on the canvas, being without him began to tell on her. She had a breakdown and was taken to a mental asylum in Banstead, Surrey. Stanley would save up his wartime sweet ration to take her chocolates when he made the tedious journey down there to visit her.

Hilda's illness manifested itself in many different ways. She gave Stanley impossibly generous cheques which he went through the motions of cashing. Once she gave him a letter addressed to Buckingham Palace, which Stanley and Daphne went to some lengths to try and deliver. And she was suffering from a religious mania not dissimilar to Stanley's. She believed that she was married to God "without the physical side of it". He grew jealous of her. She was seeing God while he, regularly deprived of sex, was not.

So Stanley found himself a new muse. In Glasgow to paint the shipyards as a war artist, Stanley met Graham and Charlotte Murray. Charlotte was a German refugee who had studied philosophy at Heidelberg with Goebbels and psychiatry under Jung.

She was bowled over by Spencer, but Graham was not at all happy with the arrangement. Stanley wanted her to have his baby.

"I would love it and it shall not be a burden to you," he said, "even if Graham should behave unreasonably."

They needed to be discreet as Charlotte was trying to get her German psychiatric qualifications recognized by the British Medical Association. Any whiff of scandal would snooker that. However, she had to make frequent trips south to lobby the BMA. She visited him at Cookham, where she examined

Patricia who was also suffering some nervous tension.

Charlotte opened the pathway for another burst of creativity. Under her stimulation, Stanley became obsessed with sex and death and began painting fleshy resurrections again. In *The Temptation of St Anthony*, he depicts the said in his coffin surround by nude women. One of them is plainly Hilda.

Hilda then became physically ill. She was rushed to hospital to have a breast removed. Slowly her mental condition improved.

More than ever, Stanley wanted Hilda back. He suggested divorce to Patricia who was surprisingly complaint. She would grant him a divorce, she said, provided nothing reflected badly on her or Dorothy. The grounds, she insisted, were to be his adultery with Hilda when he should have been on his honeymoon.

When Stanley told Hilda this, she went crazy. Divorce was not good enough – because it acknowledged that he had been married to Patricia. So Stanley borrowed some money and sent Patricia and Dorothy on holiday in the South of France. When they got back, they were greeted by a petition for the annulment of the marriage on the grounds of non-consummation. This was an inspired move. If Patricia contested the annulment, her relationship with Dorothy would be brought out in court. And Hilda would be satisfied. If the marriage was annulled, it meant it had never taken place. Patricia took her revenge by circulating some drawings Stanley had left with her. The newspapers reported that he faced prosecution for obscenity.

While the annulment dragged on, Hilda died with Stanley at her bedside. Eventually he was persuaded to drop the court proceedings which were unlikely to succeed and now pointless anyway. However, Stanley felt he had repossessed Hilda and she continued to be the inspiration for his odd fusion of erotic and religious art for the remaining ten years until his death.

23

Bumhol

Andy Warhol famously said: "In the future everyone will be famous for fifteen minutes." Sorry, Andy, you seemed to be around a lot longer than that.

Warhol was a reptilian fag in a fright wig who changed art for ever. He was the great artist of consumerism. He made some terrible films in which nothing ever seemed to happen. And, sadly, they all lasted a lot longer than fifteen minutes.

Born Andrew Warhola to Czech immigrant parents in Pittsburgh 1928, there was never any doubt that Andy was going to grow up gay. He liked dolls and, when he was confided to bed with a nervous disorder when he was six, he entertained himself drawing copies of Maybelline ads. Due to his illness, he stayed at home with mama until he was twelve.

He had a picture of Dick Tracy on his bedroom door and fantasized about Dick's dick. He thought of it as a lollipop going in and out of his mouth.

Popeye was his other sex idol. His mother once caught him masturbating during a Popeye cartoon. He liked to dream about making love with the stars and even allowed his Charlie McCarthy doll seduce him once.

When he finally went to school he was called "Spotty" because he was already losing the pigment from his skin. Puny and bespectacled, he was never picked for the team.

"I certainly was not a butch kind of guy by nature," he said, "but I must admit, I went out of my way to play up the other extreme."

His elder brothers protected him from the worst bullying.

"But I never had a friend," he recalled.

At school, he painted in a Van Gogh style. His only fun was working at the five and dime. Isolated because of his sexuality, like all gays in those repressed times, he sought consolation in the cinema, though he remembered watching mesmerized when the kids in school sucked off a boy.

At college he had a girlfriend, whose name was Ellie. But the most intimate she got was writing his essays for him. She amused herself sexually elsewhere. But she was a bohemian and liked his gay friends who were principally dance students. He was twenty-three before he lost his virginity.

When Warhol and his gay friends graduated, they regrouped in Greenwich Village. Andy moved into an apartment off St Mark's Place with his classmate Philip Pearlstein. Soon he was moving effortlessly through the gay subculture of the art, theatre and fashion worlds.

Andy tried to stay in the closet. Indeed, despite surrounding himself with transvestites and other sex freaks, he never officially came out. But throughout the 1950s, he became increasingly obsessed with drawing the male nude and he came on strong to any man he found attractive. It was said that he was swimming alone in unknown waters, but he always kept his eye cocked for a handsome lifeguard.

Andy and Philip moved to a loft on West 21nd Street in Chelsea. It had been used as a dance therapy studio for disturbed children and featured a proscenium arch at one end. It was in this weird theatre that Andrew Warhola metamorphosed into Andy Warhol.

He began to hang out with Larry Rivers, a painter and jazz saxophonist. Ostensibly straight, Rivers was friends with the macho action artists like Jackson Pollock. But he indulged in homosexuality for fun. Andy had no other choice. He was made that way.

BUMHOL

Rivers was married but he had sex with men when he got drunk. He genuinely fancied women, which Andy never did. Andy was a homosexual all the way, though other gays could not make him out. He always seemed cold and detached, and he envied Rivers' thirst for life.

Andy had begun writing creepy fan letters to the novelist Truman Capote in Pittsburgh. In New York, he began stalking him. When Capote complained to his mother, she went down and invited Andy to go for a drink with her. Although Andy would occasionally bump into Capote with the photographer Cecil Beaton, they were never friendly – though they exchanged pictures of each other naked and screwing. This was partly because, when Capote got fed up with his mother and checked into the Plaza Hotel, Andy would sit in the lobby pretending to be him. At that time, Capote was as thin as Warhol. But he was pretty. Warhol was not. When this finally sank in, Andy began cultivating what he called his "counter-image".

Warhol claimed that he was secretly engaged to Capote for ten years. They were catty about each other. It amused Warhol greatly that *capote* was French for condom. When he noticed that Capote favoured older men, Warhol remarked: "They're not very attractive and so dull."

Andy himself fancied gorgeous young hunks.

Truman gave as good as he got. In his biography of socialite Edie Sedgwick, Capote wrote: "Andy Warhol would like to have been Edie Sedgwick. He would like to have been a charming, well-born debutante from Boston. He would like to have been anybody except Andy Warhol."

Andy was seeing a number of men. He used to go out on dates with a fashion photographer, who was married. But no one could figure out whether they were having sex. He was fascinated by the details of other people's sex lives, but never volunteered any information about his own. He was positively tight lipped. However, it is known that he was a voyeur and was called on by men who liked to be watched.

Although he hung out in gay bars, Andy was usually too painfully shy to chat up attractive men. He knew that good looks and a ready wit were the passports to success in the gay world. He had neither. Usually, he would just sit quietly and watch.

When Philip Pearlstein left to get married, Andy went into panic. He had never lived alone. Ellie moved in briefly. Then his mother came to stay, saying she would not leave until Andy was married, which gave all his friends a good laugh. Although this had the advantage that he was not alone, it meant that he could not bring men home and he was extremely sexually frustrated until he rented studio a few blocks away where he could take them.

Andy dabbled with Abstract Expressionism, but found it too macho. He compensated by doing a serious of drawings of men, in some cases kissing each other. These were far too daring to be exhibited in the 1950s. Nevertheless, Andy moved on from his "Boy" drawings to "Famous Cocks".

This was the idea of Ted Carey, who hung out in the "tea rooms" – that is, the lavatories – of Grand Central station and frequently asked Warhol to watch him having sex with his latest conquest.

The first "famous cock" was to be that of the designer Dick Banks. He wore special bright red, see-though underwear that he thought would get Andy going for the occasion. In the event, the sitting turned into a little dinner party and Andy got engrossed in celebrity gossip.

After dinner, Carey said: "Now it's time to draw Dick's cock."

Andy said that he had forgotten to bring his equipment. But Banks was a designer and had everything he needed. He sat down, spread his legs and said: "Okay, Andy, here it is. Take it out, if you want to."

Warhol unzipped Banks' pants. When he saw Banks' red underwear he said: "Oh, gosh! Gee!"

Banks said: "Well, take it out."

Warhol did.

"Oh my God," thought Banks. "I am being touched by Andy Warhol."

BUMHOL

Carey had a mannequin's hand. Warhol arranged this so it held Banks's cock and added a rose to the composition. By this time, Banks had a hard on.

"In those days, it got hard if you just looked at me," Banks said.

Andy drew while Carey raved. Then Banks got Carey's boyfriend, John Mann, to hold his cock for him and Andy made another drawing. The thing quickly degenerated into a serious sex session. Mann gave Banks a blow-job while Andy sketched. Carey art directed the scene and Banks gave a running commentary.

After that, at social gatherings, Andy would approach men and ask whether he could sketch their cocks. His manner was so inoffensive that he got away with it. Many of them would take him up and dropped around to his studio. Warhol like to draw his cocks while they were hard if possible and did everything in his power to facilitate this.

At the time, Warhol was obsessed with cocks. Giving head was his favourite pastime. Even Capote would entertain him there. In 1964, he made a film called *Blow Job*. And in 1968, he contributed a piece to the literary quarterly *Intransit* about admiring another man's penis and teasingly holding out the promise of "swooping down on it".

Warhol made a collection of Polaroids of men's penises and other sexual parts. He liked to photograph men giving each other blow-jobs or screwing each other. How much of this was for "art" and how much for his own voyeuristic pleasure it is hard to tell.

Warhol loved nudity in others, especially those who surrounded him in The Factory, his studio variously at East 47th Street and Lexington Avenue, 33 Union Square and 860 Broadway and any boy who walked in would be asked to strip off. Andy would take close ups of their genitals and asked them to bend over so he could photograph their ass. If he felt like a little relaxation, he would take a little break, suck a little dick, then get back to work.

In 1956, Andy, then the highest paid fashion illustrator in

SEX LIVES OF THE GREAT ARTISTS

New York, had an intense affair with a polished young Kentuckian called Charles Lisanby, who designed sets for *The Gary Moore Show*. They went to Honolulu together, but fell out when Lisanby brought a man he had picked up on the beach back to their room.

With Lisanby, Warhol began to get a following of handsome young men, which he held on to after the relationship foundered.

"It was when I became a loner, I started to get a following," Warhol said.

Warhol indulged in long periods of celibacy. One particularly long dry patch ended in 1961, when he was seduced by a leading figure in the art world.

The man said that Andy was very good in bed, so light-fingered that Andy brought him to new peaks of pleasure. He particularly liked to engineer Warhol into a quickie while other people were going about their business unknowingly close at hand. The affair lasted until 1963.

At that time, the gay world was strictly divided into butch and femme. Andy was definitely femme. Although Warhol never made any public pronouncement about his sexuality, he was seen as a pioneer in the struggle for gay rights.

"Andy made a point of his gayness by the way he walked, talked and gestured as a kind of statement, but it was very qualified," said one young hustler who knew him.

He kept himself out of his work and never put the make on anyone he was involved with professionally. Generally, his taste ran to perverse, delinquent boys who were at least ten years younger than himself.

In 1962, Andy began going out several nights a week with John Giorno, a twenty-two-year-old stockbroker who went on to become a poet and was involved at various times with the artists Jasper Johns and Bob Rauschenberg, and the writer William Burroughs.

The relationship was frustrating for Warhol because Giorno would not let Andy go down on him. He thought it would be "gross and disgusting as he wasn't beautiful and he was older than me". They made out in other ways a lot though and Giorno also remarked on how light-fingered Andy was. But Warhol would still occasionally stick his face in Giorno's crotch in an undignified fashion. On one occasion, Giorno did let Andy suck him off and was rather disconcerted to see five or six different coloured stripes of hair poking out from under his silver wig.

One day, Giorno discovered a new side to Warhol's sexuality, when Andy started licking and kissing his shoes.

"I had always heard he was a shoe fetishist," said Giorno. Indeed, Warhol's first big break in New York was designing ads for the shoe store I. Miller.

"It was hot," said Giorno. "I jerked off while he licked my shoes with his little pink tongue. When I wanted to finish him off he said: 'I'll take care of that.'"

Warhol also flirted with S&M. When invited to a torture chamber in a flat on the Upper East Side, Andy was on the rack with his fly open in a flash. He also visited the Hell Fire Club on 14th Street, where they specialized in golden showers, brown showers and fist fucking.

Giorno was chronically unfaithful, having sex with up to three other people a day. Warhol retaliated by playing him off against his aide-de-camp Gerard Malanga. But by the time Giorno mended his ways, Warhol already had another boy in tow.

Strangely enough, a number of women found Warhol sexually attractive. And he liked to be seen around sexy women. The beautiful Venezuelan sculptor Marisol said that she wanted to go to bed with him, but nothing came of it. The Elizabeth Taylor-lookalike Ruth Kligman, an art groupie who had lived with the artists Franz Kline, Willem de Kooning and Jackson Pollock, wanted to add Warhol to her score sheet. He told her that he was celibate.

"You're better off putting all your energy into your work," he told her. "Sex takes up too much time."

And she was quite offended when he then asked her to take her clothes off – only so he could photograph her.

Underground movie star Naomi Levine pursued Warhol

with the express purpose of seducing him. Sorry Naomi.

Warhol exploited the situation. He got Naomi to strip off while he filmed her. She was the first nude in a Warhol movie. She thought she was making progress with him and stripped off another few times – poor deluded girl.

In fact, Warhol was sexually timid. When he went to Hollywood an art dealer gave him the number of the best hustler service in tinsel town. But did he have boys sent up like so many steaks from room service? No. The number went unused by Warhol or any of his entourage and was eventually thrown out with a used Kleenex.

With the boys in the band things were different though. One night the poet Taylor Mead was nervously preparing for a reading when Warhol asked Mead to give him a blow-job – it would calm him down. Another acolyte Wynn Chamberlain did the same.

"Blow us," he said. "It'll calm you down. Give us a blow-job."

"It was a totally evil thing to do," said Mead, "cold-blooded and ruthless shit."

Andy could be jealous. One afternoon, Gerard Malanga pulled and Warhol was furious when he came back to find the door of their hotel suite locked. He was even more furious when Gerard opened the door and Andy found he was with a naked girl.

When Gerard and Andy went out, everyone assumed they were lovers. The truth was very different.

"It was almost as if he was sexless," Malanga said. "He cringed from physical contact. It was that celibacy that gave him enormous manipulative power over the magnificently beautiful people he brought together."

He grew so squeamish that he could not bear to be touched by anyone and he turned to phone sex. And he fantasized about having extensions so that he could carry on three-way, even seven-way, sex conversations.

In 1965, Warhol staged an extravagant orgy on the Amusement Pier in Santa Monica and filmed people making love on the carousel horses. Filming people screwing ultimately became his thing because, whether it was on the silver screen on in the backroom of a gay club, Andy was just as happy watching. He was even thrown out of an orgy one time for not joining in.

"Sex is an illusion," Warhol said. "The most exciting thing is not making it."

"Sex is so nothing," Warhol said. Even with celebrities.

"The last time Truman put his cock in my mouth, I felt nothing," he told factory-ette Ultra Violet.

But that thought is not going to be famous for even fifteen seconds.

24

Action Man

Jackson Pollock painted with his bollocks, or so he liked to think. Abstract Expressionism was the most macho of art movements. Its master, action painter Jackson Pollock, just threw paint at the canvas like he didn't give a damn. He saw himself as the Ernest Hemingway of the art world. And like Hemingway he was insecure about sex and covered up his insecurity with drink – to the point that he became "inaction man".

Brought up in rural Iowa, sex was all around him from an early age.

"We didn't need to be told the facts of life," he said. "We learned that from the animals. We grew up with roosters and hens, dogs and bitches, boars and sows, studs and mares. Sexual activity was everywhere."

Getting some for himself was harder though. A sensitive boy, he was seventeen before he had his first girlfriend, a dark-haired serious-looking girl called Berthe Pacifico. Even then the situation was far from satisfactory.

"All he was interested in was smooching," she complained.

But only once, when they were sitting on a bench, did she allow him to kiss her. The only good thing about the relationship was that she let him draw her, over and over again.

At eighteen, Pollock was considered too young for life classes. Instead, he asked Berthe to marry him. She said yes, but refused to go and live in New York with him.

When he reached the Big Apple, the first thing he did was enrol in a life class.

The model was a young girl with "the pleasing fruity contours and surface textures of a warm peach," he recalled. "She sat on a stool and was distinguishable from the rest because she was nude and without a drawing board."

Returning home, Pollock found that Berthe had started dating someone else. When she visited him, she came with her sister Pauline. They found Pollock painting a crude mural on the garage door. He was plainly drunk and he made a grab at Pauline and tried to kiss her.

Pollock lost his virginity back in New York to Rita Benton, the wife of an artist friend. She was a very flirtatious woman and had already bedded Jackson's older brother Frank.

"She had winning ways that were pretty damned hard to resist," Frank recalled.

When he met her, she had been reading *The Well of Loneliness*, Radcliffe Hall's celebrated novel about lesbianism. But it was just her way of bringing up the topic of sex. She took him to a club in Harlem and, while a male stripper called Snake Hips bumped and ground on stage, she put her hand on his knee. With Jackson, she simply initiated him into the world of sex as a favour.

Things were pretty relaxed in New York. The sexy young models liked to hang out with the students and "you were rarely turned down if you propositioned them". And there were wild student parties.

"It wasn't uncommon for girls to come to these binges without any clothes on," recalled one student. "I danced with one and all she had on was charcoal dust. When I walked away, I realized that half her costume had come off on me."

Despite his macho posturing, Pollock was a bit afraid of sex. There was a rumour that he was having an affair with the wife of his art teacher, though he probably started it himself.

"He bragged about a lot of conquests," a classmate said. "But it was pretty evident that they didn't culminate to the extent that he claimed they did."

In fact, women were bit afraid of Pollock – with good reason. His brother Frank turned up one day at the studio-apartment they shared with his girlfriend Marie and her friend Rose Miller who took a shine to Jackson.

They drank a bottle of whiskey. Jackson got drunk and started pawing Rose in a very menacing fashion. When Marie tried to pull him away, Jackson grabbed an axe.

"You're a nice girl, Marie," he said. "I would hate to have to chop your head off."

Then he turned and buried the axe in a painting, splitting the canvas in two and lodging the axe deep in the wall behind it.

This did not put Rose off though. Frank returned home late one night, drunk, and found her in bed with Jackson.

"There is no question in my mind that she seduced him," said Frank.

It was preplanned. Marie had even bought a dozen red roses and put them in a milk bottle beside Jackson's bed for the big event.

But the affair was doomed. Even though Rose had money, they never went out on dates together. After sex, Jackson would not even walk her to the subway. Within months, the relationship was over.

"Rose didn't know what happened," Marie said. "The interest just wasn't there – on his part, that is, not hers."

In life classes, Pollock began to take more of an interest in the male nudes than the female ones and he used to poke and pinch the models to show other students where the muscles were. At the same time, he would get roaring drunk and pursue frightened young women around the corridors of the art school like a satyr pursuing nymphs. And his work was full of sexual ambiguity.

Concerned about Jackson's conspicuous lack of sexual success, his two older brothers took him to New Orleans. In Storyville, the women sat in the doorways inviting them in. One said: "Any way you like for a quarter."

Pollock paid his twenty-five cents.

ACTION MAN

Hitchhiking to Los Angeles, he stopped off to do a bit of whoring in a mining town in Indiana and got himself arrested. Back in New York, he would ride the subway up to Harlem to pick up whores. But this still did not help him develop any finesse about sex.

"He had no idea how to strike up a conversation with the opposite sex," said a friend, "or how to maintain a conversation once it began."

At a Christmas party in 1936, while dancing clumsily with a woman, he whispered drunkenly in her ear: "Do you want to fuck?"

She felt his erection rubbing against her, pushed him away and slapped him.

"It was like when a dog gets on your leg," she said. "He was trying to have an orgasm."

Another friend recalled: "He approached a woman almost like a dog, bending down and smelling them. He could tell by the smell if a woman was having her period, and if she did, he would tell her so."

He would aggressively accost women, randomly grabbing at them and kissing them. One day his brother and sister heard scuffling and found Jackson trying to physically manhandle a young woman into his bedroom. And he began seeing a very plain woman called Sylvia, who obviously had trouble finding a man. The added advantage was that she was willing to pose for him.

Drinking heavily, Pollock entered Jungian analysis.

"Jackson didn't really want to be helped," said his sister-in-law, "he wanted to be taken care of."

At a party in his Eighth Street apartment, he went gaga over a lovely young woman from Tennessee called Becky Tarwater. He watched her enraptured while she sang hillbilly ballads, accompanying herself on the banjo. When she left, he followed.

Normally, there would have been a crude assault and a fight, but somehow he restrained himself. He walked her to the subway, where she told him that she could not come home with him. She was living in a hotel and was afraid of scandal. Besides, she

229

had a fiancé. But she would see him again, largely because she had left her banjo behind in his apartment. When she called to collect it, she found him picking on it. He had even bought a book on how to play.

They met for dinner and kissed occasionally. He even managed to stay sober around her.

"He was very much in love with her," said a friend.

When it came time for her to return to Tennessee, he turned up with a single white gardenia and asked her to marry him. She refused on the grounds that their backgrounds were too different. Then she took the gardenia and walked away. They never saw each other again.

In drunken desperation, he began to chase after women in the street. Full of drink, he poured out his feelings to Rita Benton. For the seven years since she had popped his cherry, he had had the torment of watching her with her husband, other men and sunbathing nude. Now he asked her to marry him. She said no.

Under analysis, Pollock began to explore his homosexual urges. He work was soon full of nude men and homosexual situations.

At that time beautiful young Jewish painter Lee Krasner was living on Ninth Street with the White Russian Igor Pantuhoff. Explaining their stormy relationship, an acquaintance said: "The only thing his family knew about Jews was how to kill them."

"I am not anti-Semitic," he would bellow during domestic rows, "I am anti-Jewish."

The cause of the rows was that he was a portrait painter and had discovered that his fees went up if he slept with his sitter. Shortly after Pantuhoff had left her for one of his society clientele, Lee was invited to exhibit in a show, alongside Willem de Kooning, whom she had already tried to seduce. She knew all the other artists whose work was going to be included except one – Jackson Pollock.

When she asked around she discovered that he lived on the next street, she went to visit him. It was not just painting that she had on her mind. She wanted a man. She had just turned thirty-three and was afraid of dying "a fucking old maid".

Friends reminded her that she had once seen Pollock at a party. He had trampled over her feet. Nevertheless, she had pencilled him in as a potential lover.

When she turned up at his studio, he had an enormous hangover. But she was bowled over. Though she did not find much merit in his work, she found him "the most beautiful thing that ever walked on two feet".

"He was indescribable, he was magnificent, he was tremendous," she told a friend.

Soon she became convinced of his genius too.

To a New Yorker whose family came from Odessa, Pollock, whose family had been, America for five generations, was much more exotic than a White Russian. The exhibition organizer was referring to Pollock as "the greatest painter in America". This really turned Lee on. She threw herself at him and he caught her.

"They took to each other because no one else would have them," said an uncharitable observer.

Her friends looked down on him. They did not like his drunken antics and hated his work.

"This guy is going to be a great artist," she insisted.

She used all her contacts to promote Pollock's career. This irritated him. He did not like talking about art, just doing it. The VIPs she brought to his studio found themselves intimidated by the squalor. One picked up a brush and the entire palette came with it.

"You could kill a man with that," he said.

"That's the point," said Pollock.

As Lee began to immerse herself completely in his career, Pollock began to depend on Lee for the intellectual input into his painting. She also gave him, for the first time, sexual fulfilment.

Her figure began to appear in his work nude and his paintings began to drip sex. And that attracted more women – notable Peggy Guggenheim. It was said that Peggy had made had sex with practically every man she had ever met and that she could do it anywhere, anytime, even with the window cleaner watching. Queen of the one-night stand, she pursued men, women and, according to malicious gossip, dogs with equal vigour. She had a particular thing about seducing homosexual men. She enjoyed being able to turn them on against all the odds.

When Lee was out of town and Pollock was too drunk to resist, Peggy dragged him into the bedroom and demanded that he show her how grateful he was for her patronage. But he was unable to live up to her lubricious demands. Peggy said that the event was "very unsuccessful". That was an understatement. Pollock threw up in her bed, pissed himself and threw his underwear out of the window. In his own defence, Pollock said: "To fuck Peggy, you would have to put a towel over her head."

When America entered the Second World War, Pollock was rated 4F for psychological reasons. But it was generally assumed that when an apparently fit young man like Pollock was not it uniform, it was because he was a homosexual. Indeed, Pollock admitted that he had had some homosexual experiences when he was young. Most of Peggy's crowd were gay and Pollock hung out with them during the war. One of them claimed to have "screwed him in the ass" when he was drunk and defenceless at Tennessee Williams's house. His forays into the gay demimonde became more frequent and Lee became suspicious. Nobody had any doubt that he was having homosexual affairs. In his drunken state he would have to have been the passive partner. Except on canvas, inaction was his thing.

After Pollock took a homosexual holiday in Provincetown, Lee insisted that they get married. Pollock wanted a church wedding, but they found it hard to find a minister that would wed a non-practising Jew and an unbaptized Presbyterian. Peggy Guggenheim was decidedly frosty about the whole thing.

Marriage, temporarily, put Pollock on a more even keel and he began to put more of his sexuality into his paintings. Soon he began his drip paintings, laying the canvas flat on the floor and dripping paint on it. He said the idea came to him when he suddenly remembered as a child watching his father urinating on a flat rock and making patterns on the stone with his pee.

For Pollock, urinating standing up in the open like this was a symbol of masculinity. Privately, Pollock himself preferred peeing sitting down, but when he got drunk he loved to piss in public. He loved to pee by the side of the road in broad daylight and yearned to go to France where, he had been told, that it was common for a man to get his penis out and have a piss while his date looked on.

He pissed in Peggy Guggenheim's fireplace and he was an unpopular houseguest as he often wet the bed.

Rumours that "Jack the Dripper" actually urinated on the canvas spread. It was part of the controversy that surrounded his paint splattering technique, which some critics dismissed as the work of a poorly potty-trained child. Pollock himself saw them as altogether much more grown up. When a woman asked him how he knew when he had finished one of his action works, he replied: "How do you know when you have finished making love?"

It seems that in Pollock's mind, creativity and sexual potency had been reduced to a peeing competition. He was a *real* piss artist.

Things were not going well between Pollock and Lee in bed. He openly encouraged the attentions of other women and Lee, who was losing her looks, suspected he was having affairs.

When the husband of a neighbour was away, he would stand outside her house making menacing sexual suggestions and he would often lunge at men friends and wrestle with them in an almost sexual way.

With his growing fame, Pollock began to pick up women while out on benders and liked to flaunt them in front of Lee. The beautiful groupies of the art world began circling him, but he was usually too drunk or too scared to take advantage.

Fed up with his bedwetting, Lee replaced their double bed with twin beds and began talking about divorce. But it was clear to everyone that, as a hopeless alcoholic, he could not survive without her.

Pollock and Lee had not made love for three years. However, in his cups, Pollock would rave about women's bodies. He would end up making a gross pass at the nearest women. A young woman from Idaho was greeted with the inevitable: "Let's go to my place and fuck."

She replied calmly: "Not right now, I haven't got the time."

"Neither have I," he said, leaving in a huff.

Friends got so sick of this behaviour that they chipped in to hire a hooker. They stationed her nearby him in a bar where he was getting slaughtered.

He said: "Wanna fuck?"

She said: "Okay, let's go."

He collapsed.

The relationship between Lee and Pollock was on its last legs when twenty-five-year-old art student Ruth Kligman turned up. She was young and beautiful. He was the most famous painter of his generation.

She found seducing him hard work. He was usually either too drunk to do it or did not remember who she was. But eventually she got him back to her apartment on Sixteenth Street and, although, he could not recall any of the details, they had sex.

Pollock was so proud of his sexual conquest that he liked to show her off. He was now as famous as any movie star. She was glamorous and he took her to all the right clubs and restaurants. They flaunted their love openly in public, but in private there was little sex. When he was not dead drunk, he wept a lot.

Lee tried to ignore the affair. She suggested a trip to the Venice Biennale. Pollock refused, saying that he would miss his analysis.

Pollock liked the idea of having both Lee and Ruth. But Ruth was determined to force him to choose. She moved to Sag Harbor to be nearer to his house in Springs so he could visit her every day. Then she fell pregnant.

He was delighted. He had proven his masculinity at last. But now he was in a dilemma. He thought of buying a big house where he could live with Lee, Ruth and the baby. He said Ruth should come over and the three of them could talk it through. Ruth accused him of being too cowardly to confront Lee on his own. He then asked Ruth to marry him. What was he going to do with the current Mrs Pollock? she asked.

The situation came to a head when, in a fit of drunken hubris, Pollock and Ruth slept together in his studio while Lee was in the house. In the morning, they found Lee in a dressing gown at the door of the studio.

"Get this woman out of my house," she said, "or I will call the police."

Lee gave him an ultimatum. Either he stopped seeing Ruth or she would leave him. He said go ahead and leave.

For what she thought of as a "trial separation", Lee took a trip to Europe. Pollock soon found he missed her and he sent her flowers. Ruth moved in but was soon the victim of the same drunken abuse Lee had suffered. Although they admired her beauty, his friends looked down on Ruth and Pollock derided her efforts to paint.

One night in a drunken rage at a party, he shouted at Ruth: "Fuck you."

The room fell silent.

"Don't brag," she said.

Later, during a row, she began smashing the crockery. He beat her up. She left. They had lived together less than three weeks.

In an attempt at reconciliation, Ruth returned one weekend with a pretty twenty-five-year-old, Edith Metzger. Drunk, Pollock crashed the car into a tree killing both himself and Edith Metzger. Ruth Kligman was flung clear and survived unharmed.

25

A Rasher of Bacon

For the first time in one of my *Sex Lives* books, we come across someone I actually knew, albeit only slightly. The painter Francis Bacon used to drink in the French Pub in London's Soho where I too am a regular. I also saw him at the Colony Rooms, a bohemian drinking club he used to frequent. And his biographer, Dan Farson, once made a drunken pass at me. Sadly, I am not a homosexual so Farson did not have his wicked way with me. I say sadly because had I been gay I should almost certainly have known Bacon a great deal better.

Francis referred to himself as "completely homosexual", never contemplating any other option. He used to recount only one youthful flirtation with heterosexuality with a prostitute who use to eat chips while her clients went about their business. There is also a rumour that he once had attempted sex with his friend and model Isabel Rawsthorne. It was unsatisfactory.

When as a boy, Francis began showing signs of effeminacy, his father, an Irish landowner, had him horsewhipped regularly by grooms. This was a source of erotic pleasure for Francis and he responded by having sex with the grooms. His father also sent him away to boarding school to "make a man of him". What was he thinking of? It was the very place the adolescent Francis would have free rein to explore his burgeoning homosexuality.

A RASHER OF BACON

After a fling with a Persian boy who had "developed early", he was expelled from school. And when his father caught him trying on his mother's underwear, he was kicked out of home too.

This did not discourage young Francis who, for the rest of his life, indulged his passion for wearing female underwear.

Francis headed for London and gravitated to its homosexual underworld. It was the only place he could feel at home.

"Being homosexual is a defect," he often said. "It's like having a limp."

Being with other limpers, he could stay in step. And although his parents had told him he was ugly he found that lots of gay men were attracted to him.

He did whatever was necessary to get by. One day, he was picked up by a wealthy Greek in Mayfair. They went to his apartment. After they had had sex, the man went to the bathroom. Francis seized the opportunity to go through the man's pockets – and got caught.

"What are you doing?" said the Greek.

"You know what I am doing," said Francis.

"You don't have to do that," said the Greek who pulled out a hundred pounds and gave it to him.

Francis's father made one last misguided attempt to save Francis from himself. There was an uncle on his wife's side of the family called Harcourt-Smith, who was a byword for masculinity in the family. He was going on a trip to Berlin. Why not take young Francis with him?

But during the declining years of the Weimar Republic, Berlin was the European capital of decadence. Every type of sexual pleasure was on offer openly. There were a hundred and seventy homosexual brothels licensed by the police. Young men in full make-up sashayed down the Kurfürstendamm, many of them schoolboys earning a little extra pocket money. And there were clubs where you could watch nude wrestling and dancing, or government ministers chatting up sailors. Berlin was, as the poet W.H. Auden put it, "the bugger's daydream". Francis was like a kiddie in a sweetshop. His uncle got fed up and went off in pursuit of women, leaving Francis to get on with it.

"Berlin showed me how to follow my instincts," he said.

He moved on to Paris where he hung out with a homosexual prostitute and the men he picked up. His homosexuality was his entrée into the artistic world. And he began to paint.

Returning to London began living with Jessie Lightfoot, his childhood nanny. He supported the two of them and his painting by a little casual prostitution. He would advertise himself in *The Times* as "gentleman's companion". The replies poured in.

"My old nanny used to go through them all and pick out the best ones," he recalled. "I must say she was always right."

One wealthy old man even took him back to Paris, but Francis did not stay with him long. He always liked to have someone new. It bolstered his ego.

Even though homosexuality was against the law Francis flaunted it. He used to dye his hair with boot polish and wear make-up. One old queen said of Francis: "When I knew her, she was more famous for the paint she put on her face than the paint she put on canvas."

He indulged his passion of sado-masochism freely. Painting also excited him as he tried to recreate the extreme sexual sensations he enjoyed on the canvas. He was famed for his ability to withstand pain. At the doctor's, he would refuse an anaesthetic. Only once did his courage fail him. Fearing that a particularly violent lover was going to kill him, Francis fled into the street wearing only a pair of fishnet stockings.

In 1935, he gave up painting and threw himself with renewed vigour into a life of brutal sex, excessive drinking and reckless gambling. He wanted to see how far you could go before you fell off the edge. This life of total abandonment was support by running a series of illegal gambling clubs.

When he got into financial difficulties, civil servant Eric Hall helped him out. Hall became his lover and encouraged him to paint. They stayed together for fifteen years.

The war years and the London blackout were a non-stop orgy for Francis. The prospect of imminent death sharpened everyone's sexual hunger. London's urinals heaved with bodies.

A RASHER OF BACON

"It was often quite impossible of anyone who genuinely wanted to relieve himself to get in," Francis reported. "In the darkness exposed cocks were gripped by unknown hands, and hard erections thrust into others. Deep inside, trousers were forcibly – or rather tender-forcibly – loosened and the impatient erections plunged into unknown bodies, or invisible lips."

Francis loved all this. It cut out all of the unnecessary preambles and moved straight to the main event.

Curiously, Francis did not like having sex with other homosexuals. He preferred seducing straight men, who for money or on a sudden whim might succumb. With the dislocation caused by the war, many ordinarily heterosexual men found themselves overwhelmed by the mesmerizing personality of Francis.

But Francis continued in the role of "official" lover of Eric Hall, who was married with two children. One afternoon, the two of them visited Hall's son at Eton and took the boy out to tea, despite the outraged stares of the other diners.

Hall's wife sent threatening letters to Bacon and Hall's father came to his flat to remonstrate with him. Hall's son became mentally ill and blamed Bacon for his condition. Nevertheless, Hall left his wife and moved in with Francis and his nanny.

Despite his louche lifestyle, Francis was aware of the death and destruction going on all around him. Volunteering for the ARP (Air Raid Precautions) he was sometimes involved in pulling mangled bodies out of bombed houses. This gave him the idea for *Three Studies for Figures at the Base of a Crucifixion* and, in 1944, with Hall's help, he started to paint again.

Sexual activity between Hall and Bacon waned early on in their relationship, but Francis enjoyed his encouragement and patronage. However, in Bacon's life, all father figures had to be rejected in the end.

When Bacon no longer needed Hall's money, he replaced him with Peter Lacy, who satisfied his masochistic needs. He did this without compunction. He had made up his mind early on that he was going to live, go everywhere, see everything.

And if that meant using people along the way, so be it.

Francis met Lacy in the newly opened Colony Room and, for the first time, fell in love.

"Of course it was a disaster from the start," Francis said. "Being in love in that extreme way – being totally, physically obsessed by someone – is like having a dreadful disease. I wouldn't wish it on my worst enemy."

Lacy was very beautiful. The problem was he was into little boys. Francis was over forty by then and did not fit the bill.

He asked Francis to move in with him in his cottage in Berkshire.

"You could live in the corner of my cottage on straw," Lacy said. "You could sleep and shit there."

"He wanted to have me chained to the wall," said Bacon. "He liked to have people watching us as we had sex. And then he liked to have someone bugger me, then bugger me himself right after."

Francis was tempted by the offer, but turned it down. Being chained to the wall and sleeping on straw would make it rather difficult to paint, and he was not prepared to give that up. His need to paint was stronger than his need for love.

Francis's relationship with the kinky and neurotic Lacy opened a new well of creativity. In jealous rows Lacy would beat Bacon up, which he loved, but he also slashed his canvases.

When Lacy went to Tangier to indulge his paedophilia, Bacon pursued him there and hung out with the likes of Tennessee Williams, Truman Capote, Nöel Coward, Paul Bowles, Ian Fleming, Allen Ginsberg and William Burroughs. He visited the brothels, watched others being whipped. His main hangout was a bar called Dean's. Ian Fleming, the creator of the fiercely heterosexual James Bond, described it as "a cross between "Wiltons and the porter's lodge at White's".

"There's nothing but pansies," Fleming wrote to his wife Ann, "and I have been fresh meat for them."

Francis tried to continue his work in Tangier, sometimes dashing out pornographic paints for celebrity sitters. But, again, Lacy destroyed many of his canvases.

However, he did not return to London empty-handed. The poet Allen Ginsberg had given him some pornographic photographs of himself and his latest lover in various hotel bedrooms. Francis used them as the basis of a series of nudes.

In Tangier, Lacy drank increasingly heavily and fell in love with an Arab boy. He phoned Francis to tell him it was all over between them. Then, much later, he telegrammed him, begging him to come over. When Francis arrived at Lacy's villa in Tangier, Lacy was not there. There was only Lacy's Arab boy up a tree, picking figs. Lacy came home to find Bacon and the boy in bed together and smashed everything in the place. Eventually he drank himself to death.

In the 1960s, homosexuality was legalized. Francis did not approve.

"Being queer was really so much more interesting when it was illegal," he said.

Francis loved what he called his "gilded gutter life" in low dives, preferring it to the increasingly dizzying circles he was now moving in. One night at a party given for Cecil Beaton and choreographer Frederick Ashton, Francis was eager to get off to meet his date, Ted, in Piccadilly Circus. The hostess Ann Fleming persuaded Francis to go and pick up Ted and bring him back.

Beaton was terrified. Knowing Francis's tastes, he feared that Ted would be carrying bicycle chains and razor blades. But Francis returned instead with a mild mannered teddy boy who blushed when anyone spoke to him.

Francis began another serious relationship with George Dyer, another denizen of the Colony Room and small-time crook whom Francis used as a model. He embarked on a series of portraits of Soho bohos, whom he felt uniquely qualified to paint.

"Homosexuals are obsessed with the physique," he said. "They simply never stop looking at the body. That's why if I want to know what someone really looks like, I've always asked a queer."

One of his models was legendary Soho-ite Henrietta

Moraes, whom he portrayed flayed. He sent photographer John Deakin around to do preliminary studies. Deakin photographed her naked on a bed with her legs spread. Later she found Deakin selling pictures of her to sailors at ten shillings a time. She was furious.

Through Dyer and the actor Stanley Baker, Francis met the homosexual gangster Ronnie Kray, who fascinated him. He would frequently come around to Francis's studio, but his men started pinching Francis's painting and he had to pay large sums of money to get them back.

Francis's life of heavy drinking and sexual excess continued through his sixties and seventies. But Dyer could not keep up the pace. Eight years after meeting Francis, at the age of thirty-eight, he killed himself. Francis's new companion was pub manager John Edwards. But he still went out on drinking sprees which often ended in injuries inflicted by sadistic lovers he had picked up along the way.

In Paris he would visit the bath houses and cruise the Club des Set on the Rue Sainte-Anne, famous for its huge black transvestites known as the *Brésiliennes*.

In 1989, when Francis was eighty, he receive several fan letters from a young Spaniard. They met. He was handsome and well educated, very different from the rough trade that Francis usually preferred. They became passionate lovers, despite the age difference which was nearly fifty years.

His new young lover flattered his vanity and gave him a new lease of life. He nursed Francis after he had a kidney removed. Ill again in 1992, Francis flew to Madrid, against doctor's advice, to see his young lover. When he arrived, he was so ill he had to be helped from the plane. He was admitted to hospital where he was nursed by nuns. After the demolition job he did on the Catholic Church in his *Popes* series, this was his worst nightmare. Five days after arriving in Spain, he died.

So, Francis, rest in peace – though I know that it is the last thing you would ever have wanted.

Select Bibliography

Augustus John by Michael Holroyd, Chatto & Windus, London, 1996
Augustus John: Papers at the National Library of Wales by Ceridwen
  Lloyd-Morgan, The National Library of Wales, Aberystwyth, 1996
The Autobiography of Benvenuto Cellini, Phaidon, Oxford, 1983
Blasting and Bombardiering by Wyndham Lewis, Calder & Boyars,
  London, 1967
Caravaggio by Howard Hibbard, Thames and Hudson, London, 1983
Caravaggio and His Two Cardinals by Creighton E. Gilbert,
  Pennsylvania State University Press, University Park, Pennsylvania,
  1995
Caravaggio Studies by Walter Friedlaender, Princeton University
  Press, Princeton, New Jersey, 1955
Cellini by John Pope-Hennessy, Macmillan, London, 1985
Cézanne: The First Modern Painter by Michael Hogg, Thames and
  Hudson, 1989
Claude Monet: Impressions of France by John Russell Taylor, Collins
  & Brown, London, 1995
Dalí: A Biography by Meredith Etherinton-Smith, Sinclair-Stevenson,
  London, 1992
Degas by Ian Dunlop, Galley Press, New York, 1979
Degas: His Life, Times and Work by Roy McMullen, Secker &
  Warburg, London, 1985
Delacroix: A Life by Timothy Wilson-Smith, Constable, London,
  1992

SEX LIVES OF THE GREAT ARTISTS

Diary of a Genius by Salvador Dalí, Pan Books, London, 1976

Diego Rivera: Paradise Lost at Rockfeller Center by Irene Hernier de Larrea, Edicupes, Mexico City, 1987

Edouard Manet: Rebel in a Frock Coat by Beth Archer Brombert, Little, Brown and Company, Boston, 1996

The Enemy: A Biography of Wyndham Lewis by Jeffery Meyers, Routledge & Kegan Paul, Boston, 1980

Eric Gill by Fiona MacCarthy, Faber and Faber, London, 1989

Eugène Delacroix: Further Correspondence, Clarendon Press, Oxford, 1991

Famous for 15 Minutes: My Years with Andy Warhol by Ultra Violet, Methuen, London, 1988

Francis Bacon: Anatomy of an Enigma, Michael Peppiatt, Weidenfeld & Nicolson, London, 1996

Gainsborough by Stephen Butler, Studio Editions, London, 1992

Gauguin by Belinda Thomson, Thames and Hudson, London, 1987

Gauguin by David Sweetman, Hodder and Stoughton, London, 1995

Gauguin by Gauguin, Bracken Books, London, 1990

Gaugin's Letters from the South Seas by Paul Gauguin, Dover Publications, New York, 1992

Gaugin's Skirt by Stephen F. Eisenman, Thames and Hudson, London, 1997

Gauguin: The Search for Paradise by Bernard Denvir, Collins & Brown, London, 1992

Gauguin: The Quest for Paradise, Françoise Cachin, Thames and Hudson, London, 1992

The Gilded Gutter Life of Francis Bacon by Daniel Farson, Pantheon Books, New York, 1993

Goya by Alfonso E. Perez Sanchez, Barrie & Jenkins, London, 1990

Goya: The Missing Years by Wilhelm Weiner, WA Publishing, Douglas, Isle of Man, 1993

Goya: A Witness of His Times by Pierre Gassier, Alpine Fine Arts Collection, Fribourg, 1983

H. de Toulouse-Lautrec by Lesley Stevenson, Weidenfeld & Nicolson, London, 1991

Hogarth: A Life and a World by Jenny Uglow, Faber and Faber, London, 1997

The Ingenious Mr Hogarth by Derek Jarrett, Michael Joseph, London, 1976

The Intimate Journals of Paul Gauguin by Paul Gauguin, KPI, London, 1985

SELECT BIBLIOGRAPHY

Inventing Leonardo: The Anatomy of a Legend by A. Richard Turner, Papermac, London, 1995

Jackson Pollock: An American Saga by Steven Naifeh and Gregory White Smith, Barrie& Jenkins, London, 1989

Jackson Pollock: A Biography by Deborah Soloman, Simon and Schuster, New York, 1987

Jan Vermeer: Veiled Emotions by Norbert Schneider, Benedikt Taschen, Cologne, 1994

John Constable: The Man and His Mistress by John Lloyd Fraser, Hutchinson, London, 1976

The Journal of Eugéne Delacroix, edited by Hubert Wellington, Phaidon, Oxford, 1951

Leonardo by Robert Payne, Robert Hale Ltd, London, 1978

Leonardo: The Artist and the Man by Serge Bramly, Michael Joseph, London, 1988

Leonardo da Vinci: A Memory of his Childhood by Sigmund Freud, Arc, London, 1957

The Letters of Vincent van Gogh edited by Ronald de Leeuw, Allen Lane, London, 1996

A Life of Picasso by John Richardson, Jonathan Cape, London, 1991

The Life of Rembrandt by Charles Fowkes, Hamlyn, London, 1978

The Life and Times of Raphael by Liana Bortolon, Paul Hamlyn, London, 1968

The Life and Times of Titian by Liana Bortolon, Paul Hamlyn, London, 1968

Life with Picasso by Françoise Gilot and Carlton Lake, Virago, London, 1964

Loner at the Ball: The Life of Andy Warhol by Fred Lawrence Guiles, Bantam Press, New York, 1989

Lost Earth: A Life of Cézanne by Philip Callow, Allison & Busby, London, 1995

The Love of Many Things: A Life of Vincent van Gogh by David Sweetman, Hodder and Stoughton, London, 1990

Man and his Mountains: The Life of Cézanne by Hugh McLeave, W.H.Allen, London, 1977

Manet by Himself: Correspondence and Conversation, Macdonald, London, 1991

Memoirs of the Life of John Constable by C.R. Leslie, Phaidon, Oxford, 1980

Michelangelo by Howard Hibbard, Penguin Books, London, 1975

SEX LIVES OF THE GREAT ARTISTS

Michelangelo: A Biography by George Bull, Viking, London, 1995

Michelangelo: A Psychoanalytic Study of his Life and Images by Robert S. Liebert, Yale University Press, New Haven, Connecticut, 1983

Mistress of Montmartre: A Life of Suzanne Valadon by June Rose, Richard Cohen Books, London, 1998

Modigliani by Carol Mann, Thames and Hudson, London, 1980

Modigliani: The Biography by William Fifield, W.H. Allen, London, 1978

Modigliani: The Pure Bohemian by June Rose, Constable, London, 1990

The Murals of Diego Rivera by Desmond Rochfort, Journeyman Press, London, 1987

My Art, My Life by Diego Rivera with Gladys March, Dover Publications Inc, New York, 1991

Paul Gauguin: Life and Work by Michel Hogg, Thames and Hudson, London, 1987

Picasso by Patrick O'Brian, Collins, London, 1976

Picasso: Creator and Destroyer by Arianna Stassinopoulos Huffington, Weidenfeld and Nicolson, London, 1988

Picasso and Dora by James Lord, Weidenfeld and Nicolson, London, 1993

Picasso: The Man and His Image by Richard B. Lytte, Atheneum, New York, 1989

Picasso: Portrait of Picasso as a Young Man by Norman Mailer, Abacus, London, 1995

Portrait of Delacroix by Elspeth Davis, The Pentland Press, Edinburgh, 1994

The Pre-Raphaelites by Jan Marsh, Collins and Brown, London, 1996

Raphael by Roger Jones and Nicholas Penny, Yale University Press, New Haven, Connecticutt, 1983

Raphael Santi: His Life and Works by Alfred Baron von Wolzogen, Smith, Elder & Co, London, 1866

Rembrandt by Christopher White, Thames and Hudson, London, 1984

Rembrandt: His Life, His Paintings by Gary Schwartz, Viking, 1985

Rembrandt: Life and Work by Jakob Rosenberg, Phaidon, Oxford, 1964

Renoir: My Father by Jean Renoir, Columbus Books, London, 1962

Rodin: A Biography by Frederic V. Grunfeld, Hutchinson, London, 1987

SELECT BIBLIOGRAPHY

Rodin: The Shape of Genius by Ruth Butler, Yale University Press, New Haven, Connecticutt, 1993

Peter Paul Rubens: Man and Artist, Yale University Press, New Haven, Connecticutt, 1987

Rubens: A Double Life by Marie-Anne Lescourret, Alison & Busby, London, 1993

Sandro Botticelli: Life and Work by Ronald Lightbown, Paul Elek, London, 1978

The Search for Thomas Gainsborough by Adrienne Corri, Jonathan Cape, London, 1984

Seurat by John Rewald, Thames and Hudson, London, 1990

Seurat by Pierre Courthion, Thames and Hudson, London, 1989

The Shameful Life of Salvador Dalí by Ian Gibson, Faber and Faber, London, 1997

Sir Joshua Reynolds: The Painter in Society by Richard Wendorf, National Portrait Gallery, London, 1996

Sisley by Richard Shone, Phaidon Press, London, 1992

Standing in the Sun: A Life of J.M.W.Turner by Anthony Bailey, Sinclair-Stevenson, London, 1997

Stranger on the Earth: The Life of Vincent van Gogh by Albert J. Lubin, Paladin, London, 1972

Stanley Spencer: A Biography by Kenneth Pople, Collins, London, 1991

Stanley Spencer by his brother Gilbert by Gilbert Spencer, Redcliffe, Bristol, 1991

Thomas Gainsborough by John Hayes, The Tate Gallery, London, 1980

Thomas Gainsborough: A Biography by Isabelle Worman, Terence Dalton Ltd, Lavenham, Suffolk, 1976

Thomas Gainsborough: His Life and Art by Jack Linday, Granada, London, 1981

Titian by Dario Cecchi, John Calder, London, 1957

Titian's Venus of Urbino, edited by Rona Goffen, Cambridge University Press, Cambridge, 1997

Titian's Woman by Rona Goffen, Yale University Press, New Haven, Connecticutt, 1997

Toulouse-Lautrec by Bernard Denvir, Thames and Hudson, London, 1991

Toulouse-Lautrec: A Life by Julia Frey, Weidenfeld and Nicolson, London, 1994

SEX LIVES OF THE GREAT ARTISTS

Toulouse-Lautrec: A Retrospective, edited by Gale B. Murray, Hugh Lauter Levin Associates, New York, 1992

Turner in His Time by Andrew Wilton, Thames and Hudson, 1987

Turner: The Man and His Art by Jack Lindsay, Granada, London, 1985

The Unspeakable Confessions of Salador Dalí as told to André Parinaud, Quartet Books, London, 1977

Van Dyck by Alfred Moir, Thames and Hudson, London, 1994

Van Gogh: A Documentary Biography by A.M. and Renilde Hammacher, Thames and Hudson, London, 1982

Vermeer and His Milieu by John Michael Montias, Princeton University Press, Princeton, New Jersey, 1989

Vincent van Gogh: A Life by Philip Callow, Allison and Busby, London, 1990

Warhol by Victor Brockris, Frederick Muller, London, 1989

Wicked Lady: Salvador Dalí's Muse by Tim McGirk, Hutchinson, London, 1989